FROM RISK TO RENEWAL

Charting a Course for Reform

FROM RISK TO RENEWAL

Charting a Course for Reform

By the editors of
EDUCATION WEEK newspaper

Editorial Projects in Education
4301 Connecticut Ave., N.W.
Suite 250
Washington, D.C. 20008

Library of Congress Catalog Card Number 93-71681

ISBN 0-9636804-0-4

Printed in the United States of America

To order additional copies of this book, call (202) 364-4114 or write to:
Education Week
From Risk To Renewal
4301 Connecticut Ave., N.W.
Suite 250
Washington, D.C. 20008

Price: $12.95 per copy; $8.95 per copy for orders of 20 or more.
(Price includes shipping and handling.)

CONTENTS

ACKNOWLEDGMENTS

Education is a big beat, affecting every community in the United States and cutting across virtually every area of human endeavor. Covering that beat week in and week out is a full-time job for *Education Week*'s editorial staff. That makes producing a special report like "From Risk to Renewal" an add-on. And an effort as ambitious and extensive as this one, stretching as it did over more than six months, sorely taxes an organization as small and lean as ours.

If ever a book was a collaborative effort, therefore, this is it. Every member of *Education Week*'s staff contributed directly or indirectly to the project— from the research assistants who helped gather data and proofread pages to the editors who conceived the project and helped pull it all together.

The staff writers, whose bylines appear in the following pages, were the front-line workers who spent weeks reporting and writing their articles even as they continued to turn out stories in their regular beats. The staff writers who did not write specifically for this special report worked overtime writing in their own beats and covering for their colleagues on special assignment.

Krista Nicholson Platt, our art director, deserves special plaudits for both designing and directing the production of the weekly installments of the series and for designing and producing this book. Photo Editor Benjamin Tice Smith deserves a special mention, too, for coordinating the photography that illustrated both the series and the book as well as shooting several of the assignments himself.

Behind the scenes, the business staff—marketing, promotion, circulation, and advertising—attended to all the details so crucial to the success of a project like this.

As every reporter knows, a story is only as good as its sources. We are deeply grateful to all of those thoughtful, articulate, and committed people whose insights and wisdom inform our pages—not only in this report, but throughout the year in the columns of *Education Week*.

Eleven of the nation's leading school reformers helped us wrap up our special coverage by participating in a roundtable discussion on next steps for the reform movement, and we are particularly grateful to them for their contributions. David W. Hornbeck, the co-director of the National Alliance for Restructuring Education and a senior adviser to the Business Roundtable, moderated the roundtable. Joining us on that cold, rainy day in March were:

Samuel R. Billups, Delaware's coordinator for Re:Learning; Christopher T.

Cross, the executive director of the education initiative for the Business Roundtable; Michelle Fine, a senior consultant to the Philadelphia Schools Collaborative; Susan H. Fuhrman, the director of the Consortium for Policy Research in Education; Patricia Albjerg Graham, the president of the Spencer Foundation; Kati Haycock, the director of the school/college trust at the American Association for Higher Education; Richard P. Mills, the commissioner of education in Vermont; Robert S. Peterkin, the director of the Urban Superintendents' Program at Harvard University's graduate school of education; Gov. Roy Romer of Colorado, the chairman of the National Governors' Association; and Robert F. Sexton, the executive director of the Prichard Committee for Academic Excellence in Kentucky.

We want to express special gratitude to the John D. and Catherine T. MacArthur Foundation and particularly to Peter Gerber, its education program director, for providing a grant to underwrite the editorial and production costs of producing this special report in *Education Week.*

We are also grateful to the Pew Charitable Trusts and Robert B. Schwartz, its education program director, and to the Rockefeller Foundation and Hugh Price, its vice president, for grants to underwrite the cost of producing and distributing this book.

Ronald A. Wolk   Virginia B. Edwards
Editor   Executive Editor

May 1993

EDUCATION WEEK

EDITOR Ronald A. Wolk

EXECUTIVE EDITOR Virginia B. Edwards

MANAGING EDITOR Gregory Chronister

NEWS EDITOR Tom Mirga

SENIOR EDITORS Harrison Donnelly,
Lynn Olson, M. Sandra Reeves

ASSOCIATE EDITORS Gregory Byrne,
Robert Rothman

WASHINGTON EDITOR Julie A. Miller

ASSISTANT EDITORS Ann Bradley,
Deborah L. Cohen, Lonnie Harp, Debra Viadero

STAFF WRITERS Karen Diegmueller,
Millicent Lawton, Mark Pitsch, Jessica Portner,
Joanna Richardson, Peter Schmidt,
Meg Sommerfeld, Mark Walsh, Peter West

COMMENTARY EDITOR M. Sandra Reeves

COMMENTARY ASSISTANT Sally K. Gifford

EDITORIAL/RESEARCH ASSISTANTS
Laura D. Miller, Sara Sklaroff

EDITORIAL INTERN Robin Jones

ART DIRECTOR Krista Nicholson Platt

ASSISTANT ART DIRECTOR
Elizabeth A. Richards

PRODUCTION ASSISTANT Kari L. Burr

PHOTO EDITOR Benjamin Tice Smith

SYSTEMS MANAGER Michael J. Aubin

ASSISTANT SYSTEMS MANAGER
Catherine M. Hess

ASSOCIATE PUBLISHER Carolyn Kaye

CONTROLLER Eric W. Arnold

STAFF ACCOUNTANT Janice Brunson

CIRCULATION MANAGER
Peter D. LeMaster

CIRCULATION ASSISTANT
Christina S. Jessie

MARKETING MANAGER Karen Creedon

SPECIAL PROJECTS MANAGER
Sharon Williams Brandt

MARKETPLACE ADVERTISING
Michael Horkan

ADMINISTRATIVE ASSISTANTS
Megan Drennan, Karen Koostra, Christy J. Zink

DISPLAY ADVERTISING DIRECTOR
Michael McKenna

ACCOUNT REPRESENTATIVES
Irving Carpenter, Terri Pilkerton, Richard Sieber,
Jimmie Williams Jr.

ADVERTISING TRAFFIC MANAGER
Carol Kocian

ADVERTISING ASSISTANT Moana Daley

PUBLISHING CONSULTANT
Lawrence A. Durocher Jr.

MAIN EDITORIAL OFFICES:
Suite 250, 4301 Connecticut Ave., N.W., Washington, D.C. 20008
(202) 364-4114 FAX (202) 364-1039

MAIN BUSINESS OFFICES:
Suite 432, 4301 Connecticut Ave., N.W., Washington, D.C. 20008
(202) 686-0800 FAX (202) 686-0797

ABOUT THE PUBLISHER

Since its inception in 1958, Editorial Projects in Education has had one clear mission: To help raise the level of awareness and understanding of important issues in American education.

E.P.E. began informally when a group of university alumni editors collaborated to produce a special report ("American Higher Education: 1958") that they then bound into their magazines. That first "Moonshooter Report" was so successful that E.P.E. incorporated as a nonprofit, tax-exempt organization and continued to publish special reports for alumni magazines for the next 22 years, reaching as many as three million alumni a year through some 350 college magazines.

In 1966, E.P.E. launched *The Chronicle of Higher Education*, which it sold to the editors in 1978. In September 1981, *Education Week* was established as American education's newspaper of record. And in 1989, E.P.E. created *Teacher Magazine*. Both *Education Week* and *Teacher Magazine* are also available on-line through G.T.E. Educational Network Services.

More than 30 foundations have made grants to E.P.E. in support of these ventures.

INTRODUCTION

The Editors

Education Week and the current school-reform movement were conceived at virtually the same time. We have covered its ideas and developments continuously and in depth since September 1981. The summary of events, chronicled in Appendix A, demonstrates just how extraordinary the scope of the reform activities has been.

On April 27, 1983, *Education Week* published the full text of *A Nation at Risk,* a report that shocked the nation with its grim assessment of student achievement, its martial metaphors, and its dire warning of a "rising tide of mediocrity." It summoned policymakers, citizens, parents, teachers, and students to action, proclaiming that learning is "the indispensable investment" for success in an information age.

That message rang true to Americans. We have always viewed education as the gateway to a brighter tomorrow, both for the individual and for the society as a whole. And our belief has deepened rather than receded over the past decade, as evidenced by our willingness to invest in the promise of schooling.

Since the National Commission on Excellence in Education issued its report in 1983, spending for K-12 education has gone up 40 percent in inflation-adjusted dollars. And we have witnessed one of the longest and most sustained periods of school reform in the nation's history.

By the end of the 1980's, virtually every state had acted to impose the higher standards called for by the commission. Forty-two states had raised high school graduation requirements. Nearly every state had instituted a student-testing program. Three-fourths of high schools reported stricter attendance standards. And 70 percent set academic standards for athletics and extracurricular activities.

But all of these efforts, however well intentioned, have scarcely touched the classroom. As a new century nears, our schools seem firmly anchored in the old. And so, as we mark the 10th-year anniversary of that fiery call to arms, the challenge we face and the urgency of our task are even greater.

It seems only fitting, then, as a new decade of school reform begins, that we should pause and take our bearings: What have we learned from the past decade? What course should we set for the future? With this book, *Education Week* tackles those questions.

Part I looks at the need to agree on a mission for our schools, the lessons that we have learned from a decade of reform, and the growing consensus about what "good schools" should look like. In Part II, we examine the key areas where change must occur if reform is to succeed. And in Part III, we conclude with an *Education Week* roundtable on how we get from where we are to where we want to be.

The assessment properly begins with a question: Has the "indispensable investment" in public education paid off for the nation and for its children? The answer, for anyone who believes in the public schools, is humbling and disturbing.

"We were doing a lousy job 20 years ago, and we're not doing a better job now," Patricia Albjerg Graham, the president of the Spencer Foundation, lamented at a news conference called in 1992 to release nationwide trends in student achievement since 1970. "Twenty years ago," she added, "it didn't matter as much."

True, there have been some notable gains. Earlier this year, for instance, the National Assessment of Educational Progress reported significant improvements in students' mathematics achievement over the past two years. Black and Hispanic youngsters have made some real strides in reading performance. And the high school graduation rate is rising, particularly among minorities.

But most gains for poor and minority students have been in the area of basic skills, not in higher-order thinking. And the proportion of American youngsters performing at high levels remains infinitesimally small. Only 7 percent of high school seniors in 1990 could solve multi-step mathematics problems, about the same level as in 1982, according to the National Assessment of Educational Progress. And our students still lag behind those of other countries in international comparisons of science and math achievement.

Moreover, nearly half of all public school teachers reported in 1992 that at least 25 percent of their students were unprepared for grade-level work. And a report by the American College Testing Program found that 25 percent of high school seniors who took the college-entrance exam will need remedial math in college.

Clearly, the gains we have made have not been enough. Few would contend that the schools are anywhere near what they must be to meet the demands of the future.

What has changed markedly is our understanding of the task at hand—our conception of what it will take to get from educational risk to educational renewal.

At the beginning of the 1980's, most of us were incrementalists. We believed that if we simply ratcheted up the existing system and cracked down on the idlers, things would improve.

"Somehow, [we thought that] if we just shook people up, let people know students didn't know enough, shook up policies at the top, we could do more," Ann W. Lieberman, the co-director of the National Center for Restructuring Education, Schools, and Teaching at Teachers College, Columbia University, recalls of that time. Now, she adds: "It's a much more complicated agenda."

Indeed it is. In the intervening years, as we have blunted our reform swords against the shields of inertia, we have come to realize just how much effort it will take to change an institution as intricate and durable as the school.

In public education, everything is connected to everything else. We can't have a challenging new curriculum unless teachers are willing and able to teach it; or a shift to higher-order thinking skills without assessments that provoke students to go beyond drill-and-skill and that truly measure their progress.

New research on cognition and learning has also served to emphasize just how backward and counterproductive many of our current instructional strategies are. More than a century after Frederick W. Taylor's ideas about scientific management of the nation's industries first swept the United States, educators continue to churn out workers for obsolete factory-floor assembly lines: Students who sit in rows, do as they are told, and ask few questions.

As the education professor Theodore R. Sizer notes in his book *Horace's School*, "We too rarely realize that today we know far more about the stunningly complex processes of learning than we did 90 years ago, but that the template of American secondary education that was struck then is very much in place."

Meanwhile, our long-held belief in universal access to public education—previously honored more in the breach than in practice—is being tested as never before. In recent years, we have opened the schoolhouse door even wider to the poor, the handicapped, the minorities, the children of migrant workers, the non-English-speaking. And they have poured through that door in growing numbers, bringing with them the heavy baggage of society's failures.

Neither schools nor teachers are equipped to solve the social and economic problems that afflict their students. But neither can they turn their backs on the brutal conditions under which many American children and their families labor. Such conditions, reflected in what the social commentator Jonathan Kozol calls "savage inequalities," separate schoolhouses in one community from another. They make a mockery of America's commitment to education as a route out of poverty and despair. And they undercut a vital function of the public school in a democracy—to serve as a meeting place where people from all walks of life and all social backgrounds can come together to learn and grow through a common intellectual and cultural experience.

In the early 1980's, we thought that we could mandate excellence. Jolt the country out of its complacency with bold references to war and global competition. Force the schools to improve through the sheer effort of our will.

In the 1990's, we know better; we have begun to accept that every school must become its own center of excellence. We now recognize that government policies can provide the incentives, the framework, and the environment needed to support good schools, but they can't create them.

Creating the kind of "learning society" called for in *A Nation at Risk* will take more than a refinement of the educational system.

Indeed, if there is one overriding lesson to be learned from a decade of reform effort, it is that a massive and systemic overhaul of public education is required—root and branch—at every level of the enterprise. A cultural change is needed in the ways that we think about schools, not just in how they operate.

A first step in that direction, as the first chapter suggests, is to rethink what it is we should expect from our schools. From a cacophony of demands, we must forge clear and realistic goals and a coherent strategy to fulfill them.

The unprecedented effort now under way to spell out what American students should know and be able to do could be the centerpiece of such a strategy. To realize its promise, however, we must figure out how to balance clear and high expectations for our schools with the freedom that they need to respond to the needs of individual students and communities.

Indeed, there is no blueprint for building the school of tomorrow, no one-size-fits-all. A school that could thrive in East Harlem would be unlikely to meet the needs of rural North Dakotans.

But there is a widening consensus about what a "good school" should look like. As the third chapter illustrates, a good school is a child-centered school where students take more responsibility for their own learning, where teachers lecture less and coach more, where critical thinking, not rote memorization, is the objective, and where the task is to prepare the young for what President Clinton calls "lifetime learning."

A good school is a place where decisions are made as close to the heart of the educational enterprise as possible: in the classroom.

Howard Gardner, the noted Harvard psychologist, believes that designing schools that truly reflect such an "education for understanding" would produce the "biggest revolution in education."

But Mr. Gardner knows how difficult a task that is and implores public school advocates not to underestimate it. "Most people who don't know much about education either feel a good kick in the butt would turn things around, or a good weekend workshop," he laments. "The motto has got to be, 'It's as hard as changing people.'"

That's another important lesson the past 10 years have taught: Complex social institutions resist change. Part of their reason for being, after all, is to provide continuity and stability to a society in flux. This may be particularly true of educational institutions, charged as they are with preserving and transmitting civilization's cultural and intellectual heritage.

To a great extent, politicians and educators underrated the barriers to reform at the beginning of the 1980's. In retrospect, the limited results produced by the straightforward recommendations in *A Nation at Risk* might have been anticipated.

The lesson to be learned here is that one should never underestimate the status quo's power to prevail. The second chapter examines the formidable obstacles that have stymied even the most intensive reform efforts and reflects on what researchers have learned from the failures.

If systemic reform is to succeed, ways must be found to surmount these barriers. Part II of this book focuses on the critical areas that must be addressed if real renewal is to occur.

In 1983, the members of the National Commission on Excellence in Education declared, "If the tasks we set forth are initiated now and our recommendations are fully realized over the next several years, we can expect reform of our nation's schools, colleges, and universities." Ten years later, we are still looking for an action plan sufficiently robust and powerful to get us from here to there.

Gov. Roy Romer of Colorado, the current chairman of the National Governors' Association, describes the need best when he calls for an educational "war room" that would pull together the various local, state, and national initiatives into a coherent strategy that spells out what needs to be done when.

"Governors and the President can't do this alone," Mr. Romer cautioned in an interview in 1992. "We've got to get all institutions in America, including the family, engaged or else we're not going to get the job done."

In Part III of this book, we highlight the opinions of some of the nation's leading educators and policymakers on the various reform strategies now under way and on the need for a more comprehensive approach to school change. And we take a close look at the state of Kentucky, which has done more than any other state to pull together all the pieces of a coherent reform agenda.

Although Americans cannot rejoice at having made great progress over the past decade, we can find cause for hope and optimism. Never before has the nation carried on such a sustained and serious dialogue about educational renewal.

The country's governors continue to press the cause, not only in their own states, but at the national level as well. Hundreds of state and local initiatives have taken root, tenuously, but with promise.

Several large and ambitious educational enterprises are well under way that attempt to address major components of the educational system, ranging from the New Standards Project to the Coalition of Essential Schools, from the Accelerated Schools Project to the Collaboratives for Humanities and Arts Teaching, and from James P. Comer's School Development Program to the New American Schools Development Corporation.

The media, notoriously derelict in their coverage of education over the years, have given more attention to the reform issue than most dared hope for a decade ago.

A Nation at Risk asserted that, "if the people of our country, together with those who have public responsibility in the matter, care enough and are courageous enough to do what is required," the problems of our educational system can be both understood and corrected.

That is still true. The requirements have changed, and the vision has broadened. But, as the second decade of struggle begins, the challenge remains the same: To move from risk to renewal.

PART ONE

MISSION IMPOSSIBLE?

By Ann Bradley

On the eve of her 80th birthday, Julia Child, the eminent chef whose television shows have brought French cooking to the American masses, sat down in her kitchen for an interview with a reporter from *The Washington Post.*

Despite her best efforts over a long career, Ms. Child complained, too many people in today's health-obsessed society are afraid to eat too many things. Many don't even know how to cook, she lamented.

For a solution, Ms. Child turned to a familiar cure-all: the schools. Why couldn't they tackle the problem of culinary ignorance? "You could do it with a hot plate, a portable oven, and a table," she advised. "If we teach the little kiddies how to cook and eat, they can teach their parents."

However well-intentioned her remarks, Ms. Child's suggestion is symptomatic of the attitude that has historically beset American elementary and secondary education.

Virtually no one in our diverse and fractious society hesitates to offer an opinion about what the schools should be doing—from fielding football teams to raising students' self-esteem. Because we have all been to school, we are all instant experts on the subject.

As Lawrence C. Cremin, the noted educational historian, wrote in 1989, Americans have a "longstanding ... tendency to try to solve social, political, and economic problems through educational means, and in so doing, invest education with all kinds of millennial hopes and expectations."

Balancing these conflicting and often unrealistic demands, Mr. Cremin argued, is the "real and abiding crisis of popular schooling in the United States."

Now, many at the forefront of the reform movement have become convinced that this confusion about the aims of public schools could permanently hamper efforts to improve them. After all, they reason, organizations that don't have a clear and common understanding of what's expected of them aren't likely to succeed.

In an era of rapid social change, controversies swirl around all aspects of schooling, including the most fundamental questions of what to teach, whom to teach, and what services to provide.

To address this lack of focus, reformers have embarked on an unprecedented push to establish a coherent set of goals and expectations for schools. Their vision takes the form of a national system of standards and assessments—a remarkable development for a country distinguished by a long history of local control of schooling.

Diane S. Ravitch, the former U.S. assistant secretary for educational research and improvement, describes the attempt to establish national standards as "the most fundamental shift in education in decades."

"Standards identify what your goal is, what the outcome measure is, and say, 'This is what we're trying to accomplish,' " she says.

That push began with the education summit in Charlottesville, Va., in 1989, and, soon afterward, with the agreement between the nation's governors and then-President Bush to set six national education goals.

"Not only are we going to set national performance goals, which are ambitious," then-Gov. Bill Clinton of Arkansas said at the summit. "Not only are we going to develop strategies to achieve them, but we stand here before you and tell you we expect to be held personally accountable for the progress we make in moving this country to a brighter future."

Three and a half years later, we are still standing on the edge of that brighter tomorrow, realizing just how hard it will be to achieve.

Nonetheless, many credit the summit agreement and the subsequent goals-setting effort with focusing educators' attention on the need to develop a clear and common understanding around the two most often-cited missions for public schooling in the United States: preparing an educated citizenry and supplying a productive workforce.

But even as the national education goals themselves make clear, our ability as a nation to meet these twin challenges may be more difficult than ever.

For one thing, our definition of what it takes to be a good worker and what it takes to be a good citizen has expanded dramatically since the turn of the century—from that of an obedient factory hand to an individual who is able to think for a living, analyze problems and their solutions, and work cooperatively in a team.

Second, despite our long-professed belief in universal education, Americans have never really taken the steps needed to insure that every student has the chance to meet the same, high standards. If our mission for public schooling is to be an all-inclusive one, we must do a better job of following through on our stated beliefs.

Finally, we are renewing our commitment to universal education at a time when the diversity of students entering the public schools has never been greater. At the same time, the support that schools and educators have traditionally received from other social institutions is waning.

How to get beyond vague polemics to a workable mission for our nation's schools, how to act on it on behalf of all children in all communities, and how to get individual schools and school districts to elaborate on and embrace that vision may indeed be the abiding challenge for the 21st century.

50 Years of Change Underscore Need for Redefined Mission

Beginning in the late 1970's, the alarming realization that our public schools were failing to accomplish their central academic mission triggered the longest and most intensive school-reform effort in American history. But the federal commission that helped sound the alarm and most of the policy documents that followed made one fundamental mistake: They largely assumed that the mere act of raising standards would solve the problem of poor academic achievement.

In so doing, they neglected to recognize that the sweeping social, economic, and technological changes of the past 50 years had permanently compromised the ability of the public schools to fulfill their traditional aims.

Schools, laboring with outdated methods and assumptions, and striving to be all things to all people, had become anachronistic, precisely at the time that the expectations for them had reached new heights.

For most of their history, the public schools—sharing responsibility for educating and socializing the next generation with the family, the church, and the community—were able to achieve some degree of balance among their many and conflicting demands.

Since World War II, however, profound demographic and social transformations have eroded the traditional family, diluted the influence of religious institutions, and strained community relationships.

As a result, children increasingly arrive at school ill-prepared for learning and with unmet medical and emotional needs. An increasing number are from one-parent or even no-parent homes. Violence, drugs, and poverty distort their lives.

Even the luckier ones—those from middle- and working-class families in relatively stable neighborhoods—are shaped as much by the influences of television and the other mass media as they are by school, church, or parents. In the competition for their time and attention, school often comes in second place at best.

As these traditional institutions have faltered, schools have felt called upon to cope with the intractable problems of the larger society and to pay more attention to students' nonacademic needs.

David W. Hornbeck, a prominent education consultant and the former Maryland superintendent of education, is among the many reformers who repeatedly point out that children can't learn if they are hungry, abused, or sick. "If you don't get into that," he says, "you can't accomplish the educational mission."

To address such shortcomings, the Central Kitsap school district in Silverdale, Wash., has two full-time staff members who work with handicapped preschoolers and two employees who teach young people how to be better parents.

The school, says Eugene R. Hertzke, the district's superintendent, "has become as much a social agency as an education agency."

"Whether that's proper or not, I don't know," he adds. "It's putting a lot more pressure on us. There is a feeling of futility, almost."

Given this new role, schools are being asked to assume responsibility for addressing some of society's most volatile social dilemmas: ranging from teaching children about homosexuality and AIDS to preparing pregnant teenagers for motherhood. The results can be explosive.

Just in the past year, for example, the New York City school board became embroiled in a bitter debate over sex education, the distribution of condoms in schools, and the use of a multicultural curriculum that teaches youngsters tolerance for homosexuality. The controversy, which grew more and more heated, resulted in the dismissal of the chancellor.

The complex relationship between schools and society shows that schools alone can't redefine their missions.

As Howard Gardner, a professor of psychology at Harvard University, notes, "Schools in the future aren't going to be different unless society is different. I don't believe for a minute that you can change the schools without changing society."

At a minimum, if public schools are ever to achieve the lofty aims that their constituencies have set for them, schools and the community institutions that surround them must work out a new understanding about their mutual obligations to each other and to the children they serve.

For Tomorrow's Students: More Brains Than Brawn

Even if schools could focus more clearly on their central academic mission, the very definition of what it takes to be a good citizen and a productive worker has expanded dramatically as the world has become more complex.

Productivity in the workplace today is more a matter of brains than brawn. And responsible citizenship entails understanding and reacting to a host of problems so complex that 19th-century Americans couldn't have even imagined them.

Once, preparing educated workers meant teaching children the basics— reading, writing, and arithmetic—and instilling the habits of punctuality and respect for authority. Higher levels of learning were reserved for the privileged few.

In 1918, for example, the Commission on the Reorganization of Secondary Education argued that the main objectives of education were "1. Health. 2. Command of fundamental processes. 3. Worthy home-membership. 4. Vocational education. 5. Citizenship. 6. Worthy use of leisure. [and] 7. Ethical character."

As Ms. Ravitch notes in her book *The Schools We Deserve: Reflections on the Educational Crisis of Our Time*, "The academic curriculum, no longer considered appropriate for all students, became a special program for those who intended to go to college. Others, who were heading for the workplace, were directed to more practical pursuits better fitted to their later destination."

In contrast, today's students graduate into a rapidly changing, high-technology world in which those with only a high school diploma are at a permanent economic disadvantage. Everyone is expected to think for a living.

"All students, not just some, now need the knowledge and skills required for middle- and high-skill jobs," Sue E. Berryman and Thomas R. Bailey argue in *The Double Helix of Education and the Economy*.

"[M]ore than in the past," they note, "individuals will need to be able to acquire, organize, and interpret information. Workers will also have more direct interaction with their co-workers, and therefore will need more experience in general social skills such as group problem-solving and negotiation. These changes clearly involve more than an accumulation of the type of knowledge traditionally learned in schools."

In the not-too-distant past, most Americans could also expect to spend a lifetime in one job, earning a decent wage by providing low-level skills that didn't require more than an 8th-grade education.

Children born in today's era of exploding knowledge and swiftly changing circumstances can expect to change jobs a number of times during their working lives. If they are to succeed, they will need an education that allows them to adapt to changing circumstances, to think and respond to challenges they can't foresee.

By the late 1970's, the civil-rights movement and federal legislation that required the education of handicapped children and those whose native language isn't English had also greatly expanded this nation's longstanding pledge to provide universal access to public schooling.

Today, that promise has taken on an even greater urgency, as the nation realizes that it doesn't have a citizen to waste.

"Historically, from the economic point of view—not the moral point of view—we have not needed all the children," Mr. Hornbeck observes. "We had the economic luxury of 'throwaway kids.' Now, with our workforce needs and the demography of the country, we no longer have that luxury."

Previously, Ms. Ravitch notes, the concept of educating all children was linked with the phrase, "to the best of their ability." Students with small cups got a little bit of water; those with gallon containers got more. "Now, we're saying that not everybody will come out at the same point," Ms. Ravitch argues, "but that we will set higher expectations across the board."

Needed: 'A National Vision of Good Schools'

Helping all students reach these new, higher standards will require a shift in thinking and approach. The teacher as dispenser of information becomes the teacher as coach and guide; drill and practice and the rote memorization of material are replaced by authentic problem-solving and higher-order thinking; and the emphasis on educational inputs, like the number of books in the library, is supplanted by one on the outcomes of public schooling.

To meet these new challenges, we must rethink our traditional assumptions about education and how it is organized.

"I think it's time to have a national vision of what good schools would be like," says George H. Wood, the principal of Federal Hocking High School in Stewart, Ohio. "I'm hopeful that the new Administration can put forth a vision of schools as places where there is active work going on, where kids are engaged, and staffs are turned loose to find the best ways to meet the needs of students."

The movement to set national standards has heartened many who support just such a vision.

A. Graham Down, the president of the Council for Basic Education, says the standards debate has had a "palpably intellectual effect on the schools." If there were an interdisciplinary, core curriculum for all students, he reasons,

"We wouldn't be fighting so much about the edges or the center. We would just agree that English, history, the arts, and sciences are an integral birthright of all Americans and get on with it."

But the process of developing national standards and assessments is itself fraught with peril.

Since the national education goals were devised, for instance, advocates have protested that some subjects—the arts is most frequently mentioned—were slighted. Even those subjects included in the original goals statement are plagued by deep divisions over what is most important to teach.

Furthermore, as Mr. Cremin so aptly noted, America's educational malaise is rooted in deeper societal conditions that won't disappear simply because the country adopts a set of national standards and assessments.

In particular, the United States has always been a nation with a strong anti-intellectual bent, and that isn't likely to change overnight.

Albert Shanker, the president of the American Federation of Teachers, complains that there are no meaningful incentives to prompt the great majority of students to buckle down and work hard in school. The problem, he says, is that nearly everyone can get into college somewhere and that most employers ignore transcripts when hiring workers.

The presence of clear national standards—and authentic assessments that measure how well students are able to meet them—could help create new incentives for students. But only if those standards were widely accepted and acted on by the rest of society.

David Berliner, a professor of education at the University of Arizona, also notes that Americans have a different notion of childhood than do, say, the Asian nations whose school systems have been so widely praised. Children in America, Mr. Berliner says, are expected to work, date, participate in sports, and socialize with friends. American parents, he asserts, want to raise a well-rounded child, not a "Japanese nerdy kid."

"Our conception of childhood is not designed to produce high levels of math and science and language achievement before the college years," Mr. Berliner says. "People don't want to face that."

The Mission of Schools Can't Come From Above

Even if Americans sharpen and redefine the mission of public schooling in the United States—through the creation of national standards and assessments—that rethinking will only provide a destination, not a road map.

More than a decade of research on effective schooling has amply demonstrated that good schools must devise their own goals and character. "It is more important that the school has a mission and tries to realize it than what the mission is," Mr. Gardner of Harvard argues.

One thing is certain: If such missions are to be meaningful, they can't be handed down from above. "I don't think the federal government can tell the ... schools in this country what their mission is," Ms. Ravitch says. "It can't be mandated."

Indeed, one of the central dilemmas of the reform movement over the next few years will be how to marry the development of national standards with the ability of individual schools and school districts to set their own paths.

Throughout the nation, the shelves of superintendents' offices and board members' chambers are stacked with well-intentioned "mission statements" that have gathered dust since earlier efforts to redefine the vision of schooling. Many consist of little more than empty slogans and catch phrases that were disregarded soon after they were committed to paper.

In contrast, districts and schools that have taken the time to develop powerful and articulate mission statements of their own soon realize that their goals can't be accomplished by educators alone.

To take root, missions must be developed with the help and advice of entire communities. Only then does it become clear that educating children is everyone's responsibility.

In Houston, for example, the district has worked closely with the business community to set goals for the schools. The next step, Superintendent Frank R. Petruzielo says, is to spell out how the community institutions can help.

Otherwise, he fears, schools will be expected to work by themselves to solve such entrenched urban problems as gang activity. "What we are trying to build here," he says, "is a culture that suggests there are lots of agencies and groups that are going to have to take some responsibility for, and ownership of, these problems and challenges."

In Fort Worth, educators, businesspeople, and civic leaders took a hard look at their schools and decided to emphasize putting knowledge into practice. Starting with detailed analyses of the skills needed in real-world jobs, the district and its partners discovered that the skills required for work and college aren't so different: the ability to think, solve problems, and work with others.

"You don't take one track to college and another to vocational education," Superintendent Don R. Roberts argues. "Everyone is going to work— Ph.D.'s and M.D.'s work. The key is, you have to have knowledge and know-how to apply that knowledge."

As a result, the district has enrolled many more students in higher-level mathematics courses. And, in an effort to motivate students to work hard throughout high school, it has launched an extensive program that offers 7th graders the chance to spend time working with local businesses.

Without a unifying local vision, teachers and principals can easily lose their way.

In the book *The World We Created at Hamilton High*, Gerald Grant, a professor of the cultural foundations of education at Syracuse University, tells the story of a high school buffeted by social change.

"Teachers began to feel like functionaries in a world that was created elsewhere," he says, "and they lost the essence of efficacy and of responsibility for making a world here."

Such feelings of defeat can be overcome with the right combination of leadership, time for teachers and others to meet, solid information that can be used to chart a new course, and the willingness to face hard facts, diagnose problems, and devise solutions.

First and foremost, though, it requires faith that a school will be allowed to shape its destiny.

When teachers and principals do carve out the time, says Mr. Wood, the Ohio principal, they should start by thinking about what they want their students to look like after they leave school. That moves the discussion from test scores and demerit points to what kinds of neighbors, citizens, and co-workers the students will make. Schools should then work backward to set policies that will help students achieve those goals.

These aren't easy questions, Mr. Wood notes. But when teachers tackle them, he says, "I can't get meetings to end. It gets them back to why they went into teaching—because they believe they can make a difference in the world. And we ought to be talking about what that world should look like."

OBSTACLE COURSE

By Robert Rothman

When historians look back on the 1980's, they will likely see it as "the education-reform decade," as the Educational Testing Service characterized it in a 1990 report.

They will write that 42 states raised high school standards. That the number of states with student-testing programs rose to 47, while the number with teacher-testing systems grew to 39. That three-fourths of high schools reported stricter attendance standards, and that 70 percent set academic standards for athletics and extracurricular activities.

But historians must also point out that, despite all that activity, "schools pretty much look today like they did 30 years ago," as Linda Darling-Hammond, the co-director of the National Center for Restructuring Education, Schools, and Teaching at Teachers College, Columbia University, puts it.

As educators and researchers are now discovering, reformers at any level face daunting barriers that thwart or limit even the best-intentioned efforts. The reforms of the 1980's didn't achieve their goals because reformers either failed to recognize the barriers or couldn't surmount them.

But the barriers remain, and any serious strategy to transform schools must confront them, or reform will again be doomed to fail.

The largest barrier to spurring true and lasting reform, of course, is the sheer size of the reform task, which has proved to be much greater than the authors of *A Nation at Risk* ever dreamed. While that report generally urged more of the same—more academic coursework, more homework—reformers now talk of a radical transformation in teaching and learning in a vast educational complex consisting of 80,000 public schools, each of which is itself complex.

As the preceding chapter notes, the job of educating students is made even more difficult by the growing social problems faced by children and their families.

Moreover, the reformers often face skepticism and outright resistance from

Schools have long modeled themselves after workplaces, reflecting their mission of preparing young people for jobs. Traditional schools, which were organized to provide basic skills for most students, looked like factories.

schoolpeople and the public.

But even if they had such support, those attempting to change schools would still have to cope with layer upon layer of a governance structure that obstructs and thwarts what they are trying to accomplish.

And unlike other large enterprises that have managed to reform themselves over the past few decades, schools often lack the capacity to bring about large-scale change.

In many cases, change demands money, which is in short supply or isn't used to institute reform. Change requires inspired leadership, the lack of which can stop a reform from getting in the schoolhouse door. And lasting change needs an "infrastructure" in place to insure that good ideas can be replicated.

But perhaps the most significant barrier to change is that state policy, on which we so heavily rely, is ill-suited to the reform task. Despite the best intentions of governors and legislators, the policy levers they have at their disposal aren't powerful enough to move classroom practice. A new type of policymaking is needed—one that fosters change within schools and classrooms, rather than one that tries to mandate them to act.

"There is widespread agreement," says Edward Pauly, a senior research associate at the Manpower Demonstration Research Corporation, "that, sooner or later, you're going to have to deal with folks in the classroom."

Some, like Mr. Pauly, search for "pressure points" within the system that allow changes to take hold. Others talk of redefining the role of state and local policymakers so that they "enable" change, rather than dictate it.

Whatever the strategy, the trick, according to Lauren B. Resnick, the director of the Learning Research and Development Center at the University of Pittsburgh, is to insure that the successes outnumber the inevitable failures.

"What we're trying to do," she says, "is to get changes to come in at a rate that will be faster than the rate at which they are knocked out, yet deep enough that they are worth it."

The Magnitude of Reforms Poses a Formidable Barrier

Change in education has always been stymied by one set of barriers or another, and the problem of setting lasting change in motion is certainly not limited to education.

Change in any institution is troublesome, notes Henry M. Levin, the director of the Center for Educational Research at Stanford University. "Do families change their cultures because they are dysfunctional?" he asks. "Do religious groups change their cultures? That's almost an oxymoron."

But achieving change in education is likely to be even more difficult because the system is so large and complex. Moreover, the greater the changes being advocated, the greater the barriers to attaining them. Education reformers, after all, are calling for a major overhaul of the educational system, down to the teaching and learning that goes on in every classroom every day.

"The theory of knowledge that is in place won't do for the future," Ms. Resnick says. "It says that knowledge is lots of accumulated bits that students can acquire by some form of listening, hearing, and memorizing; application [of knowledge] is separate. The education system we inherit is, by and large, built around that theory."

In contrast, Ms. Resnick has argued for a "thinking curriculum" built around students' abilities to use and apply their knowledge, not simply regurgitate facts. And, indeed, some schools have enthusiastically embraced such strategies and are revamping their curricula and instruction to spark student engagement.

Magdalene Lampert, an associate professor of teacher education at Michigan State University, describes the new form of student learning as a "cultural revolution" in which understanding and intellect are more highly valued than they typically have been.

"Children ought to be learning to reason, whether in science, writing, or mathematics," she says. "Those things are very different from what schools now expect."

Implementing that new vision is a complex task. Simply reforming a single school is a major undertaking, observes Theodore R. Sizer, a professor of education at Brown University and the chairman of the Coalition of Essential Schools, a network of reform-minded high schools.

"Everything important inside schools affects everything else inside schools," he says. "You can't do things one at a time—say, do a math or science curriculum. If you do it properly, and standards are raised, you have to change time, scheduling, and everything else."

"It's difficult to persuade people to look at things whole," Mr. Sizer says. "We have a long tradition of piecemeal reforms. They don't work."

As an example, many cite the blizzard of curriculum-reform projects funded by the National Science Foundation in the 1960's. Although the projects produced highly regarded materials and textbooks, they didn't transform schools, and, by 1976, a study by the N.S.F. found, they had vanished from classrooms.

But as difficult as implementing the changes in one school may be, replicating them in other schools is even more difficult.

Ms. Darling-Hammond of Teachers College points out that the relative handful of successful reform efforts has failed to spread widely. "You can do it in a magnet school," she says, "because you're spending $20,000 a kid, you've sucked in a disproportionate number of the scarce supply of highly knowledgeable teachers, and you have waivers" from regulations.

Beyond that, putting the reforms in place in 80,000 public schools represents a formidable barrier.

"Most folks really don't understand how much there is [for teachers] to learn," says David K. Cohen, a professor of education and social policy at Michigan State University. "They don't appreciate how arduous and long the learning will be. And it has to be done by people with full-time jobs."

In a widely read article in *American Educator*, entitled "Revolution in One Classroom (or, then again, was it?)," Mr. Cohen illustrates the magnitude of the hurdles reformers face. It cites the case of Mrs. Oublier, a 2nd-grade teacher in California who was eager to change her math instruction and who sought out new materials and workshops to learn how to revise her teaching methods. By Mrs. Oublier's way of thinking, she considered her classroom transformed. In reality, though, her teaching "did not realize these ambitions," Mr. Cohen writes. Even as she tried the new methods, she couldn't quite abandon the old ones.

"If the recent reforms are to succeed, students and teachers must not simply absorb a new 'body' of knowledge," he writes. "Rather, they must acquire a new way of thinking about knowledge and a new practice of acquiring it. ... Additionally, and in order to do all of the above, they must un-learn much of what they know, whether they are 2nd graders or veteran teachers."

Instead of confronting the hurdle of revamping instruction for the nation's 2.4 million-strong teaching force, though, the policymakers who govern education frequently duck it.

In fact, because politicians like to win elections, they often focus on creating new policies and programs, rather than building on and improving existing programs. As Joe Nathan, the director of the Center for School Change at the University of Minnesota puts it, politicians suffer from "edifice complexes."

Moreover, writes Susan H. Fuhrman, the director of the Consortium for Policy Research in Education at Rutgers University, "politicians are attracted to the type of policies that are most easily used as campaign issues:

simple, easily explained policies that can be featured in a 'sound bite.' "

"Policies with immediate effects and clear benefits are simpler to explain than longer-term efforts with more diverse or remote benefits," Ms. Fuhrman writes in a new book. "Subtlety can lose out to flashiness; careful developmental efforts can lose out to quick pushes that have less chance of success because the developmental groundwork was lacking."

Ms. Darling-Hammond points to the widespread interest in the 1980's in alternative certification for teachers as an example of one problem and its quick-fix solution. Although such policies were generally aimed at increasing the supply of teachers, they did nothing to address the question of revamping instruction.

In fact, at a time when all teachers need to be educated in a new way, Ms. Darling-Hammond argues, alternative certification not only did not solve the problem, but it also made it worse by creating a new cadre of teachers unschooled in the new methods.

"Rather than try to reform and take on the teacher-certification system and improve it," she says, "[advocates of alternative certification] said, 'Let's induce states to avoid it altogether.' "

"That's one of the ways we've created and exacerbated a barrier to change," she adds.

Layers of Governance Lead to Reform 'Overload'

In addition to all the other barriers, reform itself has become a hindrance to change by setting off in too many directions at once and by being so scattered and uncoordinated.

"It is probably closer to the truth to argue that the main problem in North American education today is not the absence of or resistance to change," Michael Fullan, the dean of the faculty of education at the University of Toronto, suggests, "but rather the presence of too many ad hoc, fragmented, uncoordinated changes."

Ms. Fuhrman notes that the problem of fragmentation grew worse in the 1980's, when states took a more active role in school reform. Although states expanded their activities, she points out, local districts didn't reduce theirs; in fact, they "made more policy as well."

"More policy led to more policy," Ms. Fuhrman says.

On top of those policies, social problems—such as disintegrating families, drug abuse, and violence—also made teachers' jobs more difficult, Mr. Fullan notes.

In addition to their instructional duties, teachers have become responsible for dealing with students who are hungry or homeless. In some urban schools, they fear for their lives as schools can no longer keep the world at bay.

Such social problems have deepened at a time when other institutions— like churches and families—have become less able to cope with them, putting an even greater burden on the schools.

The combination of swelling mandates from above and mounting social pressures from the outside has loaded up schools with yet more responsibilities.

"It's an old American thing," Mr. Sizer of the Coalition of Essential Schools says. "If you have a new problem, add it to the curriculum. The shopping mall gets bigger and bigger, with more and more stores. ... And the trivialization continues."

Moreover, the policies often contradict one another. As one example, Mr. Sizer points out that, at the same time states authorized more autonomy for local schools, they were reluctant to cede power over some aspects of schooling—such as assessment—that would make the schools' power meaningful.

"On the one hand," he says states said to schools, "you say you need school-site management. On the other hand, that doesn't mean you can pick your own people, set your own budget, or decide the shape of the schedule or the curriculum, much less how to assess results."

"Higher levels of government aren't prepared to let go," Mr. Sizer says.

In other cases, the contradictions may be more benign, but equally problematic. While educators are developing new standards for teaching, based on knowledge about effective practice, Ms. Darling-Hammond notes, they are left with the legacy of previous state teacher-evaluation policies that are "absolutely countervailing" to the new standards.

Florida, she points out, "marks teachers down if they relate a lesson they are working on to a student's personal experience—which we know is a foundation of good teaching."

"The state policy structure in most states is loaded with a geological dig of regulations, laid on top of each other, that are self-contradictory and accumulated over decades by intrusive policymakers," she says.

Phillip C. Schlechty, the president of the Center for Leadership in School Reform in Louisville, Ky., also notes that each new policy creates a constituency and that that very fact makes it more difficult to revise or abolish policies as needs change.

Teacher-certification rules, for example, were created to insure that teachers and administrators are competent, he points out. But they also restrict schools from redefining teachers' roles or restructuring to improve student outcomes.

"Those who develop certification and licensing laws," he writes in *Schools for the 21st Century*, " ... should also be aware that their decisions may so straitjacket teachers and schools that the harm done to students may be greater than if the certifying agencies had been more flexible in their views."

Other educators contend, however, that individual schools need not be hampered by the multiple layers of authority and the resulting "overload" of reform. If teachers worked together to make changes in their own schools, Mr. Pauly of the Manpower Demonstration Research Corporation says, the "multiple-policy issues would go away."

"The problem of overlapping policies is toughest for people trying to impose top-down change," he says. "They have to rationalize each connection, or lack of connection."

Deeply Held Beliefs Fuel Reluctance to Change

Both policymakers and school-based reformers also face another serious obstacle: the deeply held beliefs of people in the system. Despite the best intentions of reformers, few people want to change.

"In a lot of communities," Mr. Sizer says, "change is something everybody else is going to have to do."

In part, the reluctance to change reflects the nature of schooling, which is at its heart a "conserving institution," notes Ann W. Lieberman, the co-director of the National Center for Restructuring Education, Schools, and Teaching at Teachers College.

"School is the only institution people think of as stable," she says. "The idea that a school would look different and that kids would be engaged in different ways of learning is very threatening to people."

As a result, Ms. Lampert of Michigan State says, policymakers often block curriculum reforms because they are " 'not the way I learned.' "

Educators are also reluctant to change because they think what they are doing is right. Getting them to change, argues the Yale University psychologist Seymour B. Sarason, takes more than a simple command that they do so.

Reformers "assume that change is achieved through learning and applying new or good ideas," he writes in *The Predictable Failure of Educational Reform.* "They seem unable to understand what is involved in unlearning what custom, tradition, and even research have told educational personnel is right, natural, and proper."

Milbrey W. McLaughlin, the director of the Center for Research on the Context of Secondary School Teaching at Stanford University, says her research has found that teachers tend to fall in one of two groups: those who are eager to innovate and those who view problems as intractable. The latter group, she suggests, is by far the most common.

Mr. Sizer believes that the public, at least, can become convinced of the need for change. He points out that his coalition's reforms, once considered "radical and out of fashion," are now more accepted.

In part because previous reform attempts appear to have failed, Mr. Sizer says, "there has been a relative warming of the climate for suggesting bold changes."

Mr. Cohen of Michigan State is optimistic that educators can change as well. "History is not destiny," he says. "I think we can do and think differently."

Lack of Capacity: Money, Leadership, Infrastructure

In order for improvements to occur, however, schools must have the built-in capacity to change. Teachers need time to plan and learn new methods. Leadership to foster innovation is essential, as is an infrastructure that allows ideas about new practices to flow throughout the system. In most schools, each of these three essential conditions is in short supply.

Lack of money can also undercut a school's ability to reform itself. And inequities of funding among schools have been well documented.

While there are some well-publicized instances in which schools have transformed themselves despite these financial constraints, a serious effort to restructure teaching and learning throughout the system requires a considerable amount of teacher time—and time is money.

As Mr. Sizer writes in a past issue of his coalition's newsletter, Dennis Littky, the principal of Thayer High School in Winchester, N.H., the first coalition school, estimated that his small school needed an additional $125,000 a year just to start its reform program. By now, that sum would be much higher.

"That would pay for two to three weeks' additional time a year for teachers, summer stipends for a quarter of the faculty, a few overstaffed 'empty chairs' during the year to allow for teachers to travel and learn," Mr. Sizer says.

Even narrow reforms can be curtailed by a lack of funds. Ms. Darling-Hammond notes that a study she conducted for the RAND Corporation found that the computer revolution failed to sweep the schools for the simple reason that not all schools could afford the hardware to introduce computer-based instruction.

But in addition to money, reform also takes leadership, and not all schools possess the kind of leaders who are willing to foster innovation.

"It's not that the principal does it all, but he has to help make it possible," Ms. Lieberman of Teachers College says. Principals "can control time, and what comes in to a school. They can stop an idea if they want to."

Successful reformers face this problem as well. Hard-won reforms in a school often disappear when the leader suddenly leaves and a new leader comes in with a different set of ideas.

But that fact simply points up the difficulty all reformers face, Ms. Resnick of the University of Pittsburgh says. "I don't think there are villains," she says. "The system is constraining what they can do, what they think is possible. Within the constraining system, almost everybody, most of the time, is trying to do well."

In addition to financial and leadership constraints, schools lack an infrastructure for reform, a factor that has enabled medicine, for example, to implement widely ideas brought about by new technology.

"There is a huge infrastructure for knowledge diffusion [in medicine]," Ms. Darling-Hammond says. "New things known, like bypass surgery, are immediately brought into training in medical schools, so that interns and residents very quickly internalize the change."

"There are also widespread vehicles for disseminating knowledge to practicing physicians," she continues, "from what we would call in-service courses to journals."

"In education," Ms. Darling-Hammond points out, "in such literature as we have, researchers read each others' research. Teacher magazines tend to avoid the knowledge base."

She and others also point out another important shortcoming of the educational infrastructure: the fact that teachers are isolated from one another.

"Most teachers have never seen another teacher teach in their own building, much less gotten out of their building to look at practices in other schools," Ms. Darling-Hammond says. "You can't change to something you've never seen."

Ms. McLaughlin of Stanford found that teachers who were the most innovative were ones who visited one another's classrooms and shared materials. "Most teachers are neither trained nor used to talking to one another," she says.

Even if the infrastructure of schools is rebuilt, change in education can only come about if other institutions change as well. But so far, Mr. Cohen of Michigan State says, higher education, by maintaining admissions policies that fail to demand high student-performance standards, and businesses, by refusing to hire students based on their academic performance, have thwarted schools' goals.

"If schoolpeople are the only people who take reform seriously, then it doesn't have a chance," Mr. Cohen says. "It is implausible to imagine that K-12 educators could swim across currents generated by higher education and business."

State Policy Tools Fall Short of Goals

As the experience of the 1980's makes clear, even the most ardent reformers can fall short of their goals if the tools at their disposal are not up to the job of overcoming the obstacles in their way.

During the past decade, state after state and district after district adopted policies that assumed that, if they moved a few levers at the top of the system, the rest of the system would fall into line. In fact, though, those levers caused barely a ripple in most classrooms.

"Few people [in the 1980's] understood the extent to which any change is going to require thinking about American education as a complex social system," Ms. Resnick says. "The way they went about trying to fix it showed that: entrance requirements, course structures, minimum-competency tests."

"The governance system took the tools it had—like Carnegie units—and the assumptions it had—that those kinds of regulations have something to do with the content that is learned—and used them," she adds. "[Then] we become surprised that the outcome as a whole doesn't improve much."

Despite the record, however, the attitude persists that all that is needed is for state policymakers to pull some levers.

"Some [corporate] C.E.O.'s say to me, 'You have an easy delivery system— 19 districts,' " says Pascal D. Forgione Jr., the superintendent of public instruction in Delaware. "No. I have 6,000 professionals."

In part, the policy reforms took the shape they did because policymakers lack respect for the teaching profession and for teachers' part in changing classroom practice.

"It seems that people jump to the conclusion that teachers are not smart enough to transform knowledge into curricula and instruction," Ms. Lampert of Michigan State says. " 'We have to do it for them.' "

Ms. McLaughlin's research on teachers, though, shows graphically that the policies don't affect what happens in the classroom. She and her colleagues surveyed teachers about their practices in California—a state that adopted a broad range of reforms, including curriculum frameworks and teacher-training networks—and in Michigan, which adopted few such reforms. The teachers' responses were virtually identical in the two states.

Some teachers, like Mrs. Oublier in Mr. Cohen's article, persevered and attempted to change their practice. But all teachers are not like Mrs. Oublier, and many have either ignored the new policies completely or turned cynical as they have seen much-trumpeted reforms make little difference.

"People have been disaffected over the past 10 years," Ms. Lieberman says. "There was no money, no thrust, no support for change. There has only been a lot of headlines and neon lights."

In looking at ways to bring about what they see as real change, several reformers have suggested new strategies that schools and policymakers can employ. The strategy may not require a detailed map for reform—as long as it recognizes the problems with past strategies.

"Americans, standing on the near shore of huge change, don't have much sense of how to get to the other side," Mr. Cohen says. "But if you organize your trip like ones you've taken [in the past], you'll not get there."

Mr. Pauly contends that finding "pressure points" in the system offers opportunities to bring in changes without requiring "high intensity" efforts to get a whole school to change. As examples, he says, reformers could focus on revamping the first year of high school, or beginning-reading instruction.

Large-scale reformers "are trying to take on so much that they run the risk of failing," Mr. Pauly says. "If you focus on pressure points, you may be able to accomplish changes."

Other reformers suggest that large-scale change is possible if policymakers redefine their roles so that they "enable" changes to happen, rather than mandate it.

Under such a system—which Commissioner of Education Thomas Sobol of New York State has called "top-down support for bottom-up reform"—states would set standards for schools, and allow local schools the flexibility to come up with ways of meeting the standards. But the state would also provide assistance to help schools build their own capacities to change by providing training and encouraging them to create networks to share ideas.

"If you think systematically, you realize we must do it school by school, but, at the same time, we can't do it [only] school by school," Ms. Resnick says. "We can't do it boutique-fashion."

Ms. McLaughlin says that such a strategy would enhance the power of such state policies as curriculum frameworks and testing programs by insuring that schools are able to implement them. "Once you've got the culture and the environment of a school as a learning community," Ms. McLaughlin says, "that's when all the stuff at the top of the system can have a positive effect."

Whatever the strategy, Mr. Sarason of Yale University argues, it must change power relationships—between teachers and students and between teachers and administrators—or it is doomed to failure.

Mr. Sarason likens the changes that are needed to the founding of the United States government. The Founding Fathers, he says, didn't merely tinker with the Articles of Confederation, which they knew were inadequate; they reconstructed the system.

"As long as they allowed themselves to stay within the confines of these articles, the major problems would be intractable to remedy," Mr. Sarason writes. "Confronting that intractability, they entered history."

THE FUTURE OF SCHOOL

By Lynn Olson

When educators were invited to design schools of the future for a nationwide competition in the fall of 1991, the most striking thing about the results was not their diversity but their similarity.

Ungraded, multi-age classrooms; assessments based on performance, not guesswork; students who graduate based on what they know and can do rather than the time spent in class; activities that engage children's hands as well as their heads; and learning done in teams instead of alone at desks were ideas that permeated the hundreds of proposals.

They are all elements of what one researcher describes as an "emerging oral consensus" about what schooling should look like in the 21st century.

It is a far cry from the authoritarian image of one teacher standing at the front of the classroom and pouring information into 20 or 30 waiting heads.

And it represents nearly a 180-degree turn from what policymakers were calling for just 10 years ago. Back then, reformers were nearly single-minded in advocating policies designed to crack down on students and teachers.

Indeed, if there was a consistent message in *A Nation at Risk*, it was to do more of what we'd been doing, only better: More homework. Longer school days and years. More rigorous grading. Better textbooks. More tests.

The only problem was, it didn't work. The performance of American students, by and large, has remained lackluster on national and international measures of achievement. And young people are just as bored and turned off by schooling as they were before the call to action was sounded.

As Lauren B. Resnick, the director of the Learning Research and Development Center at the University of Pittsburgh, noted in a 1987 address to the American Educational Research Association, American schools have become simultaneously one of the most important elements in our society and

The atmosphere at Stanton Elementary School in the Appalachian foothills of Kentucky appears playful. But, according to Principal Faye King, the children are all actively engaged in learning—a sharp contrast with most schools, where the most conspicuous performer is often the teacher.

one of the most irrelevant.

That's not surprising, given that much of what passes for education in schools violates what both research and common sense tell us about how people learn best—and contradicts the way we expect them to live and work as adults.

Everyone knows that human beings learn at different rates and in different ways. Schools, on the other hand, insist on treating all children of the same age alike, expecting them to progress in lock-step fashion and to learn mainly by listening.

We know that humans are social by nature and increasingly work in situations that demand collaboration. But our schools ask students to sit most of the day without speaking to each other and to compete rather than to cooperate.

Businesses and colleges complain that high school graduates are limited in their thinking and problem-solving abilities. But schools stress getting the "right answer," rather than asking the right questions or devising multiple approaches to a problem.

Rarer still do we cede enough power to students to let them take on the fundamental responsibility for their own learning.

Now, a growing recognition of the mismatch between the worlds inside and outside school has launched a quest for a new model of schooling—a different kind of learning environment to replace the one that has characterized American education for two centuries.

"To say this is a consensus, I think, would be to press the case," says Ms. Resnick, who has become a leading advocate for this new vein of thought. "But it's something like a consensus among both the leading researchers and educational practitioner-philosophers."

In the schools that these futurists envision, understanding and intellect would be as valued as athletics are today. Students would become active learners who assume an increased responsibility for their own education. And learning would occur in context, in environments that are laden with stimulating and resource-rich materials and that enable students to learn through a variety of avenues.

The emphasis would be on applying and using knowledge to solve real-world problems, not just on regurgitating facts. And the traditional walls between education and the broader community would come tumbling down.

In such schools, every student would be expected to meet high standards for what he or she knows and can do. And the vision of what a successful high school graduate should look like would drive both the curriculum and the assessments.

Most of all, these schools would be communities of learners—in which as much attention is paid to the intellectual and developmental needs of adults as of children. Decisions would be made as close to the classroom as possible. And teachers and principals would have a far greater say over curriculum, budgets, and hiring.

Despite this "emerging oral consensus," however, there is no agreement about how to get from here to there. It is a lofty vision that could produce as many different kinds of schools as there are students and communities. And few schools—to date—have managed to achieve it.

Indeed, after 10 years of reform, the struggle to create a new generation of schools on a broad scale has largely just begun.

Nonetheless, the harbingers of change may already be among us.

Student Learning at Heart of Vision for Schools

The first thing a visitor notices about Stanton Elementary School in the Appalachian foothills of Kentucky is the lighting. There are real incandescent lamps here, not fluorescent tubes.

Rocking chairs and cushions reside where desks have been. Children aren't all doing the same thing at the same time. Some are reclining to read. Others listen to recorded books on headsets. There are children typing and writing in journals. Some youngsters are working independently, others are working in groups. They aren't all the same age, or the same size, or the same ability.

"It's a much more relaxed atmosphere," says Faye King, the school's principal. "And, initially, it might be construed as playful, because children are so engaged in their work that it hardly has the appearance of work."

Most of all, the students are active. It is a school focused on performance—where children are doing things, not just watching someone else. In the past, the biggest performer in too many American classrooms has been the teacher.

The implications of this shift to schools focused on students' work are enormous. "As soon as you say that performance is the key," notes Theodore R. Sizer, the chairman of the Coalition of Essential Schools, a national network of reform-minded educators, "then things like mandatory attendance and always being in a school building are going to become less and less important."

"If the kid can do it," he adds, "then I really don't care how she learns it. So I think the notion of school as a place with a bell at the beginning and a bell at the end, with four walls and a day that starts and a day that ends, that's going to start evaporating."

Much of the theory for such shifts stems from cognitive research on how people learn. By observing both children and adults in real-world settings, researchers have found that human beings are perpetual "meaning-makers." Put simply, people constantly try to make sense out of their environment by fitting new information into what they already know.

Isolated facts, flung at children with no connection to how they will be used or why they are important, have little staying power. Rather than being told about history or about math, such research suggests, children should be immersed in an environment where they can see adults modeling the kinds of activities that real historians or mathematicians do; practice some of those activities themselves, with adequate support and supervision; learn to reflect on what they have done; and engage in closer and closer approximations of such complex, real-world experiences.

"What you learn," Ms. Resnick argues, "is not just a body of subject matter, but a whole way of being with respect to knowledge or skill."

Within this broader context, students master individual skills—like multiplication or sounding out words—as they need them, rather than in isolation. And children are encouraged to think about challenging and complex problems from the start.

In such schools, youngsters explore real things that matter to them. Materials—not textbooks—line the walls.

"Primary classrooms are brimming with children's books, blocks, string, cardboard scraps, plants, animals, rocks, paints, and assorted theater props," writes George H. Wood, the author of *Schools That Work: America's Most Innovative Public Education Programs*. "For older children, there is hands-on equipment—tape recorders, cameras, science apparatus, good novels, charts and graphs, and objects of art."

In one Apple Classroom of Tomorrow a few years ago, a 6th-grade learning-disabled student used a computer to gain access to hour-by-hour satellite maps from the National Weather Service to track the progress of a hurricane up the East Coast.

"That was impressive enough from our point of view," recalls David Dwyer, the principal scientist for ACOT, a research project sponsored by Apple Computer Inc. that investigates how learning changes when students and teachers have immediate access to technology. "But he was actually then overlaying other kinds of data on top of those maps and trying to make a determination about what forces of nature control the path of a hurricane."

"In the process," he adds, "the kid was using scientific visualization tools that real scientists use. And he had a teacher who was comfortable with that kind of information."

In such schools, activities tend to center on long-term projects that cut across disciplines—not work sheets. These longer and more complicated tasks require larger blocks of time, and the 50-minute class period is giving way to accommodate them.

The Goal of Creating a 'More Permeable Membrane'

As the ACOT example demonstrates, a central characteristic of the new generation of schools will be the ability of students to draw on the world outside the classroom for knowledge and information.

"I think we're going to end up with a more permeable membrane between school and nonschool in educating children," predicts Chester E. Finn Jr., a founding partner of the Edison Project, a multi-million-dollar initiative that is designing a network of for-profit schools from scratch.

"I think we'll begin to fashion arrangements in which more learning takes place off-site," he continues, "and, maybe, in which more noncognitive things take place on-site."

In some instances, schools are trying to replicate the larger world inside the classroom through the creation of "micro-societies," complete with their own legislatures, courts, banks, post offices, newspapers, and businesses. In others, schools are reaching out into the community to offer instructional opportunities for students—while giving them a chance to make a difference. At Belle Fourche (S.D.) High School, students write for the town newspaper and make drawings and photographs of local buildings for a project to renovate and revitalize the downtown business area.

At the Rindge School of Technical Arts in Cambridge, Mass., students in Cityworks are using the community as their laboratory, investigating its industries and trades, services and people, neighborhoods and architecture, as a way to learn both academic and vocational skills.

Ninth and 10th graders in the program, which began in 1991, take numerous expeditions out into the city and re-create it back in the classroom, using maps, photographs, tapes, oral histories, two-dimensional drawings, and three-dimensional models.

Last year, the teenagers made an 8-foot-by-14-foot wall map of Cambridge, lighted up by recycled batteries. They designed a restaurant, picked a building they wanted to renovate, made a model, met with the zoning department to find out whether they would need a variance or permits, studied the nutritional issues involved in designing a menu, and used the graphic-arts studio to produce menus, place mats, business cards, and T-shirts. They also argued strenuously about where in the city to place the restaurant to attract a diverse clientele.

"The message that we want to give kids," Principal Lawrence Rosenstock says, "is to take chances and try new things, to work hard, and to do high-quality work."

Setting High Standards for All Students

In schools like these, the focus is on raising the standards and expectations for all students, not just the college-bound. *A Nation at Risk* implied that a "rising tide of mediocrity" was dragging down the performance of America's best students. The new conventional wisdom is that, in the future, all students will have to learn to think for a living.

Indeed, one of the few requirements of the fall 1991 competition by the New American Schools Development Corporation to design "break the mold" schools was that they enable all children to reach "world class" standards in English, mathematics, history, geography, and science.

Exactly what world-class standards are and who should set them remains the subject of an intense and often acrimonious debate. But there is little disagreement that schools need to focus more on student outcomes than they have in the past, and that those outcomes should be sufficiently rich and challenging to engage all youngsters.

"If you don't know what you're aiming for," notes Howard Gardner, a professor of psychology at Harvard University, "you're never going to be able to make any progress."

As the first chapter in this book notes, our failure as a nation to coalesce around a clear and compelling mission for schools in the 21st century may be one of the primary impediments to reform.

Schools that have taken this charge seriously are trying to define what their graduates should know and be able to do, beyond requiring that they sit through four years of English and three years of math. Such schools are shunning multiple-choice tests in favor of a much broader set of measures to let students demonstrate their accomplishments.

At Littleton (Colo.) High School, teachers have defined 19 performance-based graduation requirements for their students, beginning with the class of 1995. These range from "the Littleton High School graduate speaks and writes articulately and effectively" to "the Littleton High School graduate has actively contributed to community or school-service organizations," and "the Littleton High School graduate effectively applies mathematical principles and operations to solve a range of problems."

Thirty-six different "demonstrations," or assessments of a student's performance, are tied to these graduation criteria. In one instance, teenagers complete an impromptu, timed writing assignment in a controlled setting. In another, students amass a portfolio of different writing samples over time.

Each of the "demonstrations" specifies which of the graduation requirements is being met, what the task entails, the criteria for completing it successfully, the rubric that teachers will use to score the project, and the testing conditions—such as whether a student can use a spell checker or a calculator.

"Keeping the end clearly in sight," argues Littleton High's principal, Tim Westerberg, "you move backward to ask, 'What does that mean for the curriculum? How do we need to repackage, or maybe even rewrite and reorganize and redesign, our curriculum for the students to engage in learning experiences that logically lead to performing well on these assessments?'"

"The goal," he adds, "is to have what you test be very much a part of what kids are learning on a day-to-day basis in the classroom."

Over time, as students assume more responsibility for these assessments, they become their own best critics. They get better and better at pinpointing both what they know and what they don't, what good performance looks like, and where their own performance falls short.

A Community of Learners: For Teachers and Students

But schools must insure that everyone has equal access to knowledge if they are to sustain clear and high expectations for all students.

The Humanitas program in Los Angeles, for example, is designed to provide all youngsters with the kind of challenging, intellectual curriculum traditionally reserved for the very few. Teenagers in the program, which operates in 37 high schools, are recruited from a cross section of the student body. The program goes after the "average kid," which in Los Angeles includes a large percentage of children from poor and minority families.

The curriculum is organized around central concepts—"the roots of prejudice" is one example—that draw from an array of disciplines that are taught separately at the vast majority of schools.

Students read original source materials, rather than textbooks. And they write a lot, with a focus on the interdisciplinary essay that concludes each unit.

According to an assessment of the project by the Center for the Study of Evaluation at the University of California at Los Angeles, Humanitas students write better and have a surer grasp of abstract concepts than do other students. They were also absent less, and a smaller percentage dropped out of school.

But "as rich as our curriculum is, and as engaging as the work is," hypothesizes Cris Gutierrez, a Humanitas teacher at Thomas Jefferson High School, "the fundamental difference is that we hold [students] responsible to a community within a community. And because they're so well known in it, and because we're so well known to them, it's easier and more feasible to take risks with them intellectually. And for the faculty to do the same with each other."

As Ms. Gutierrez's comment illustrates, the needs of teachers in such settings are crucial. Their intellectual development and that of their students go hand in hand. According to one principal, shifting the teacher's role from that of expert to coach requires the "highest level of expertise imaginable."

Teachers in these learning environments must have a firm grasp of educational research; an understanding of their subject and how to teach it; knowledge about child development and individual learning styles and how to apply them; a willingness to work in groups; and the ability to structure lessons so that students can help determine the direction their coursework will take. Most of all, they must have the time and opportunity to learn from each other, and to take risks together.

In Humanitas, for instance, teachers can enroll in a two-week summer academy. And during the school year, those new to the program are released from their teaching duties to attend workshops at one of three Humanitas Teachers' Centers.

But in most schools, teachers rarely have the chance to catch their breath, let alone engage in such self-rejuvenation.

Deborah Meier, the founder of the Central Park East Secondary School in New York City—one of the few schools consistently cited as an example of where education should be headed—argues that schools "must create a passion for learning, not only among children, but also among their teachers." Both, she asserts, have become "passion-impaired."

"At the very least," she writes in a provocative article in *Teachers College*

Record, "one must imagine schools in which teachers are in frequent conversation with each other about their work, have easy and necessary access to each other's classrooms, take it for granted that they should comment on each other's work, and have the time to develop common standards for student work."

There is also a growing recognition that if educators are to feel a sense of ownership over their schools—and if we are to take advantage of their knowledge and expertise—then most decisions regarding budgets, hiring, and curriculum should be made at the school site.

"What is certain," Ms. Meier adds, "is that this kind of collegiality works best in settings that are sufficiently small and intimate that self-governance and staff-development schemes don't exhaust teachers' energies or divert them from their central task."

Pulling It All Together Into a School That Works

The challenge is to pull all of these elements together into a school that works. Within education circles, Central Park East is widely viewed as one of the few places that have managed to achieve this vision. As a result, the school has taken on a mythical stature fast approaching that of Camelot. Its prominence speaks as much to the difficulty of creating truly innovative schools as it does to the program itself.

The school, located in East Harlem, looks like any other public education facility from the outside, perhaps more rundown than most. But it is what happens inside that counts.

At Central Park East, children stay with teachers for two years, so that they know each other well. In the high school, Ms. Meier notes, most students see no more than two or three different teachers a day, including an adviser who spends an hour a day with a small group of 15 teenagers.

Every teacher is responsible for one interdisciplinary course, such as literature and history or math and science. And the typical class is about two hours long, providing enough time, according to Ms. Meier, to include whole-class seminars, small-group work, independent study, and one-on-one coaching by teachers and students.

Working with one set of students, teachers teach in collaborative settings, with four or five teachers working in close proximity. This approach, Ms. Meier argues, means that teachers can easily make decisions, alter plans, rearrange schedules, regroup students, share ideas, and observe each other's work.

Most decisions are made as close to the classroom as possible. And teachers collectively decide on content, pedagogy, and assessment.

As Ms. Meier also notes, the whole staff is "not enormous." Neither Central Park East Secondary School nor the district's elementary schools that are modeled on the same concepts include more than 450 students, and most are limited to 200 or 300. "That means," she wryly observes, "a faculty that can sit in a circle in one room and get a chance to hear each other."

The result is that students succeed in far greater measure than their socioeconomic, ethnic, and racial backgrounds would predict. About 90 percent of those who attend the schools graduate from high school, in a city where nearly half of all students drop out. Half of those who graduate from Central Park East elementary schools go on to college, and the numbers are even higher for those who attend the high school.

Reform Architects Still Wrestling With Barriers

To many, Central Park East is a beacon. But how the components of the modern learning environment come together may differ from school to school, based on its students and its community. And while there are many elements of good schools to be found, places like Central Park East that have succeeded in putting most of the pieces together remain a rarity.

As the preceding chapter on the barriers to school reform notes, researchers are just beginning to understand how complicated it is to change entrenched beliefs and practices at the school site, and how weak our previous interventions have been.

For the past two years, Fred M. Newmann and his colleagues at the Center on the Organization and Restructuring of Schools at the University of Wisconsin at Madison have been engaged in a nationwide search for reinvented schools.

"It's been very difficult to find them," he laments. "We've received nominations from over 300 schools, and we've made phone interviews to all of those, and then site visits to close to 40 of them. And at this point, we've only been able to find 15 [schools] to study, and the schools we're studying actually don't combine all of it."

"We sort of chose those that we think are highly promising," he says, "even though they may meet only some of [our] criteria."

What's more, once you move beyond the small group of educational researchers, practitioners, and policymakers who run into each other at conferences and on national commissions, whatever consensus there is quickly dissipates.

If there is a radically new vision of schooling emerging, it has yet to grab hold in the vast majority of schools and classrooms—or in the hearts and minds of many American schoolteachers.

"This is one of the really depressing things, I find, about American education," says Sue E. Berryman, an education specialist with the World Bank in Washington. "In some ways, there's a group of us who just really end up talking to ourselves. That's a little hard, but I'm afraid that's more true than any of us really wants to confront."

Even among the cozy crowd of educational insiders, areas of ardent disagreement remain.

Should standards and assessments be developed at the national level or by individual schools and communities? People howl and scream at each other on that issue. Questions about what constitutes the "canon" of cultural literacy, or whether there exists a core body of knowledge that all students should possess, provoke a similarly visceral response.

Who should be allowed to teach in schools? And to what extent should schools be the site for, if not the provider of, the many non-educational services that students and their families need, ranging from health care to counseling? Although few people continue to profess that the school can do it all—absent the support of families, the mass media, and other nonschool institutions—there is more rhetoric on this topic than action.

Visionaries also differ widely on the role that technology should play in the schools of tomorrow. In a world where virtually everyone has access to a television set and a telephone, and may soon have access to a computer on the same phone lines, it would be ludicrous to think that schools can retain their role as the sole—or even the primary—purveyors of information in our society. In many ways, they forfeited that role long ago.

In his book, *School's Out: Hyperlearning, the New Technology, and the End of Education*, Lewis J. Perelman argues that rapid advances in technology will soon make existing schools obsolete, and that any attempts to revamp or revitalize them are doomed to failure.

Others concede that technology will play a far more ubiquitous role in the schools of tomorrow, but suggest that that day may be a long way off.

"If you ask me, do I expect the Apple or I.B.M. or A.T.& T. school of tomorrow to be filled with technology and long-distance satellites and that sort of thing, certainly not in my lifetime," Mr. Gardner of Harvard says. "That's at least in part because I think it's too expensive."

But the most fundamental disagreement centers around just how radical a change is required to make schools more productive.

Albert Shanker, the president of the American Federation of Teachers, says,

"I used to think we basically had to abandon what we have now, because it doesn't work." But his view changed, he says, when he realized that students in Germany, Japan, Canada, and France seem to learn very well in more traditional learning environments.

So the A.F.T. now has two objectives, he continues: "One is to take those pioneers who want to build the world of tomorrow, and experiment with that, and give them the wherewithal and the resources to do it."

"But that doesn't take everybody else off the hook," he adds. "They've got to figure out how do we get our schools to be as good, in terms of student outcomes, as schools that look fairly traditional in other countries."

Attention Turns to Task of Getting From Here to There

Indeed, despite recent attempts to house schools at the worksite or in giant shopping malls, few people expect that the school—as such—will disappear.

"When you talk about the school of the future," says Roger Semerad, the president of the RJR Nabisco Foundation, which has underwritten an effort to create "next century" schools, "my guess is we will still have a building. And we will still have teachers and administrators. But I hope that we have an entirely different process, like we have a new process for building cars or making steel."

The real question, then, is whether we know how to get from here to there. Because while stories abound about the dynamic teacher or the dynamic principal who turned a school around, the future of public education rests with the thousands of ordinary individuals who populate the 80,000 public school buildings in the United States. Somehow, they need to own a vision that only a few principals and teachers now share.

"There really is not any good understanding of how to propagate changed schools," Ms. Resnick says, quite humbly.

If nothing else, the last decade has stressed for educators the need to maintain a little humility about the pace of change and how to bring it about. "Every single school must become a revolutionary cell," Ms. King of Stanton Elementary School argues. "It's not something that can be done from the outside. It is a synergy that arises among the staff and cannot be imposed."

But in a soil that has proved, until now, so inhospitable to the widespread growth and nourishment of good schools, a consensus is growing that something must be done to provide a framework in which communities of learners can flourish.

PART TWO

THE BALANCE OF POWER

By Ann Bradley and Lynn Olson

In this chapter, we explore the balance of power within schools and districts and the efforts to shift authority so that those at the school site are empowered and encouraged to use their resources in behalf of greater learning for students.

DENVER—At 6:30 on a cold winter evening, nine people sit down at pushed-together tables in a carpeted community room at Thomas Jefferson High School. For the next two hours, this diverse group—the school principal, three teachers, a counselor, two parents, a businessperson, and a student—will hash out a plan for their school's budget.

A short time ago, such input would have been the principal's alone to give. Now, in schools throughout this city, Denver residents gather routinely to share in such judgments.

Since 1991, when Gov. Roy Romer of Colorado gave sweeping authority over educational decisions to committees in each of Denver's 112 schools, the balance of power in the city's schools has shifted.

The Governor's resolve to create the committees reflects a growing national sentiment that one key to improving schools lies in harnessing the energy and ideas of the people who work in them, pay taxes to support them, and send their children to learn in them.

"I want everybody to look down the street," Governor Romer said at the time, "and see that school building and say, 'That's ours. We are responsible for it.' "

Indeed, the twin ideas of giving greater decisionmaking authority to individual schools (often known as site-based management) and dispersing it more widely within schools (commonly known as shared or collaborative decisionmaking) have become two of the most widely adopted reform tools of the 1980's and 90's.

The collaborative-decisionmaking council at Thomas Jefferson High School meets to hammer out a plan for the Denver school's budget. Site-based management has become one of the most adopted tools of the reform movement.

The strategies have been endorsed by such varied groups as the National Governors' Association, the Business Roundtable, and the National Education Association.

At least five states—Colorado, Florida, Kentucky, North Carolina, and Texas—have mandated some form of participatory decisionmaking at every school. And hundreds of districts in other states claim to be engaged in the process.

But the initial burst of enthusiasm—during which such large urban school systems as Chicago, Miami, Los Angeles, San Diego, and Rochester, N.Y., waded into site-based management—has given way to an intensive re-evaluation of its efficacy.

Many agree that it has provided a vehicle for greater parent and community involvement in schools, and that teacher morale has improved in those districts that have adopted the strategies.

In general, though, they haven't resulted in the kinds of dramatic gains in student achievement or in the innovations in classroom practices that their advocates had hoped for.

And while some argue it is simply a matter of time before such changes occur, others question whether there is any necessary link between changes in governance and deeper changes in teaching and learning.

Too often, site-based councils have gotten mired in trivia and in the mechanics of making decisions. Many districts have failed to create a framework in which school-based management can thrive. And frequently, little, if any, authority has actually been delegated to the school site.

"It's real hard to find locations where, for the lack of a better term, the reality meets the rhetoric," observes Betty Malen, an associate professor of educational leadership and policy studies at the University of Washington.

Creating a 'Greater Commitment' to the Overall Enterprise

The rationale behind school-based management is that, by empowering those at the school to make decisions, teachers and others will be better able to meet the needs of their students and will gain greater ownership of proposed school improvements.

In addition, if schools are to be held accountable for student performance, it seems only fair that they be given the resources and the responsibility to determine how they operate.

The idea first took hold because it was also felt that schools—like businesses—had become dominated by top-heavy, top-down management and had overlooked the expertise of their front-line workers.

Research from the private sector suggested that companies that adopted formal worker-participation schemes, at least in the short run, experienced improvements in worker satisfaction, commitment, quality, or productivity, and saw decreases in their worker-turnover and -absenteeism rates. In almost no cases did the programs make things worse.

More than a decade of research on effective schools also suggested the importance of allowing schools to set their own goals and develop their own cultures.

"When a process makes people feel that they have a voice in matters that affect them, they will have a greater commitment to the overall enterprise and will take greater responsibility for what happens to the enterprise," Seymour B. Sarason argues in his book *The Predictable Failure of Educational Reform.*

"[T]he absence of such a process," he continues, "insures that no one feels responsible, that blame will always be directed externally, that adversarialism will be a notable feature of school life."

But these days, it is hard to pinpoint exactly what "school-based management" means or where it exists.

As Priscilla Wohlstetter, the director of the school-based-management project for the Consortium for Policy Research in Education, notes, "School-based management is everywhere, but nowhere."

Districts vary greatly in the kinds and number of decisions that are turned over to schools, in whether such decisions are final or merely advisory, and in how many schools participate. There is also wide variation in who makes the decisions within schools and the process that they use for doing so.

"My sense is that the term became, in some circles, a slogan," Ms. Malen says. "When you'd try to track what, if any, policy changes were formally adopted in a district, it was hard to track them."

Such diversity has also made it difficult, if not impossible, to evaluate school-based management's effectiveness.

Early findings from case studies of individual districts and from larger national and regional surveys have found decidedly mixed results.

A study of the Jefferson County, Ky., public schools and its professional-development academy recently found that students in schools committed to sustained and comprehensive reform were more likely to show consistent improvements from year to year than those in schools that moved from one reform to another or saw no need to innovate.

Among other things, the study found that the more successful schools had principals who "truly believe" in the need to change and in the role of participatory management in bringing it about.

A survey released in January 1993 in Chicago—where substantial power for making decisions has been turned over to local school councils—found that the percentage of principals, teachers, parents, and community representatives who felt that their school had improved since the councils were established in 1989 has increased markedly.

Donald R. Moore, the executive director of Designs for Change, a Chicago-based citizens' advocacy group, says that some 300 of the city's 540 schools are "either cooking or making significant change." But in about 30 or 40 others, he says, conflicts between individuals have rendered the councils ineffective.

A 1991 evaluation of school-based management in Dade County, Fla., one of the first big urban districts to adopt the strategy as a primary reform tool, concluded that "teacher status" had definitely improved. There was more collegial decisionmaking at the school site. And Gerald Dreyfuss, then the assistant superintendent for school-based management and now the principal of Arvida Middle School, reported that applications for teacher openings in the district had quadrupled since the program began in 1986-87.

Other districts report changes in at least some schools that could eventually lead to improved student learning. In New York City, an early evaluation of 12 schools found that they had introduced such innovative measures as team teaching and a greater voice for teachers in textbook selection and development.

In Denver, several schools have adopted performance-based assessments in place of standardized tests—a "significant change" that some teachers have wanted for years, says Judie Mitchell, a 1st-grade teacher at Greenlee Metro Lab School.

In general, however, the relationship between school-based management and changes in the classroom, including gains in student performance, is tenuous at best.

"There's little necessary connection between school-based management and improving teaching and learning," argues Susan H. Fuhrman, the director of the Consortium for Policy Research in Education. "There are a lot of intervening factors."

The evaluation in Dade County found no significant change in standardized-test scores over the period of the pilot program. A similar evaluation in San Diego found "inconsistent results." And a study in Los Angeles found that the first year of shared decisionmaking "did not generally result in major changes at the schools we studied."

Of course, standardized-test scores may be particularly inappropriate for measuring the kinds of educational innovations that school-based management is meant to foster—such as greater problem-solving skills and the ability to work in groups.

Such test scores also ignore many of the other benefits that collaborative decisionmaking might reap, like higher staff morale and a better school climate.

More disturbing in the minds of many is the fact that the ingrained relationships among parents, teachers, and principals within many schools participating in collaborative decisionmaking appear to be unshaken. Principals tend to take the lead role, parents play a supporting one, and many teachers remain hesitant to question established practices.

More rarely still has school-based management made any inroads into changing the authoritarian relationship in the classroom between teachers and students.

But, as Mr. Sarason warns, "To alter the power status of teachers and parents, however necessary and desirable (and problematic), without altering power relationships in the classroom, is to limit drastically the chances of improving educational outcomes."

Simply changing the participants in the decisionmaking process, he suggests, won't necessarily "improve the quality, innovativeness, or creativity of educational decisions."

School-Based Management: What's the Point?

One problem is that many districts embarked on site-based management without defining what was expected of the councils or linking the management strategy to the district's long-range plans for improving student learning.

"School-based management for what sort of gets lost in the conversations," Ms. Wohlstetter of CPRE says.

Observers here in Denver charge that, because Governor Romer mandated the school-governance changes, the central administration has dragged its feet in implementing collaborative decisionmaking. No formal goals have been established for it, for example, and there are no plans to evaluate its effectiveness.

"The district has not embraced collaborative decisionmaking as a primary reform strategy," charges Adele Phelan, the chairwoman of Citizens for Quality Schools, an advocacy group supporting the reform.

A report by the group on the first year of the process noted that many council members perceived the administration as reluctant to relinquish power to individual schools, and that progress toward tangible results had been sluggish.

"The district has major goals for achievement and attendance," observes Michael Murphy, a professor of educational administration at the University of Colorado at Denver. "If they had linked this reform to those and said, 'That's the focus, and we're going to check on how well you do it,' it would have been very different."

In contrast, Superintendent Evie Dennis claims that the district is supportive of school-based management, but that changes in the bureaucratic culture will take time. The district has a court-ordered desegregation plan, she notes, and the councils must work under other mandates as well.

According to the superintendent, the district's priority is longstanding: to graduate more children who possess more skills. Like many of her colleagues nationwide, she cautions that, if collaborative-decisionmaking councils "don't translate into that, then I don't know if they are of any value."

Part of the confusion is that proponents of school-based management are really advocating two reforms at once: one of the governance of schools and districts, and one of the teaching and learning process itself.

But many districts that embarked on school-based management put more energy into deciding who would be on the councils and how they would make decisions than in creating a vision for reinvigorating schools or in providing schools with the support needed to do so.

"When you stop short of process, we've got nothing," says Patrick O'Rourke, the president of the Hammond (Ind.) Federation of Teachers. The Hammond schools adopted school-based management as a reform tool in the early 1980's. "When you spend a lot of time putting in place a new method of governance," he adds, "you get hung up on the governance question."

In Denver, many school councils that have made progress have done so in such relatively noncontroversial areas as school attendance, discipline, and tardiness policies. The same is true for schools in other districts.

Ann Lieberman, the co-director of the National Center for Restructuring Education, Schools, and Teaching at Teachers College, Columbia University, says school councils "start with real grubby issues."

"They don't do highfalutin things like everybody wants," she adds.

Gary Martyn, a media technician and a member of the decisionmaking committee at George Washington High School in Denver, says, "You get bogged down in micromanagement: The bathrooms are dirty, the lights are out somewhere, the intercom doesn't work."

Similar minutiae have frustrated members of the committee at North High School, also in Denver.

"When we started, our concerns were that, up in the second-floor men's restroom, there's not enough toilet paper," recalls Fidel (Butch) Montoya, a parent member of the council, "or that room 102 is 108 degrees. That's not the responsibility of [the council]. Our goals are student achievement and expectations for students and teachers. But it took months to reach that point."

Uncertainty surrounding the goals of school-based management has allowed politics—and who wins and who loses in the struggle for power—to dominate the shift to collaborative decisionmaking.

"When we first started out," observes Loretta Johnson, the assistant superintendent in Rochester, N.Y., "the shared decisionmaking and collaboration, for some teams, appeared to be just a new brokering of power, and they played it out like that. And they lost sight of the reason these things were put into place: to improve instruction for kids."

In Los Angeles and Dade County, for example, principals voted to become unionized after school-based management gave teachers an increased voice in setting school policy.

And a report by the RAND Corporation asserts that, in adopting school-based management, most districts "transfer the politics of interest-group bargaining from the school district to the school building."

Even Citizens for Quality Schools in Denver acknowledges the difficulty in reaching consensus among diverse groups. "It is hard to find a shared vision—about anything—among a group of people purposefully elected to represent different interests," the group says.

Only Limited Authority Has Shifted to Schools

In many districts that profess to be engaged in site-based management, little real authority has been shifted to the schools.

At a minimum, site-based management implies giving schools control over how they spend their money, who works in their buildings, and how instruction is delivered.

But studies have found that districts often relinquish authority over one area and not others. They are likely to give schools power over their budgets first, their personnel second, and their curricula last.

Frequently, schoolpeople are confused about what power they actually possess because it's not spelled out. And in practice, labor agreements, court orders, categorical programs, and district tradition combine to mute schools' authority over their operations.

Many districts enable schools that want to deviate from established practices to secure waivers both from the school board and the teachers' union. But the process for doing so, Ms. Malen of the University of Washington observes, puts the "burden of proof" on the schools and can be cumbersome.

Meanwhile, the hierarchical structure that exists above the schools changes little.

In Denver, the teaching contract appears to be quite specific in terms of the power that schools have. The school board keeps responsibility for finance, curriculum goals and evaluation, the school calendar, bargaining, desegregation, construction, and maintenance. Schools manage their budgets, select teachers and principals, and organize the content of their courses and programs. They also have complete freedom to organize and assign staff members' time—including the amount of instructional time, preparation time, lunch time, student-contact time, the number and length of classes, and the frequency of meetings with parents.

Nevertheless, ambiguity remains.

"These are not mini-school boards," Superintendent Dennis says. "This is not Chicago."

Shortly after the contract was signed, she recalls, a principal called her to ask if his school could eliminate its bilingual-education program. "I had to say, 'You can't do that,'" she says. "'That's a court order.'"

For their part, schools complain that the central office has been reluctant to loosen its controls. A number of schools that needed to hire principals in 1992 were sent only three or four people to interview, instead of being given access to the district's entire list of job candidates.

According to Citizens for Quality Schools, some councils have been reluctant to exercise their authority because of "mixed messages" from the central office.

Even with the latitude enjoyed by the Denver councils, many haven't made substantive changes in instruction—such as in the use of time within the school building.

More Training and Access to Information Needed

The intensive, ongoing training needed to make school-based management work has also been largely absent.

Members of a school council need to understand the technical issues, such as budgeting, that will enable them to contribute to the school. And they need help with the personal and group skills required for collective decisionmaking, such as the ability to resolve conflicts.

Carol H. Weiss, Joseph Cambone, and Alexander Wyeth, all researchers at the Harvard Graduate School of Education, note that shared decisionmaking requires teachers to confront their colleagues and other adults face to face to resolve important problems that aren't directly linked with their classrooms. Sticky problems can arise—such as what to do about a colleague's poor performance—that threaten teachers' relationships with one another.

"Very little in their background or training has prepared [teachers] for this kind of democratic politics," the researchers argue. Teachers "have been socialized for so long to compliance with orders from above (leavened with sub rosa griping) that they do not have the mental set to participate and take responsibility."

School councils—and, particularly, teachers—also need help in understanding the issues involved in curriculum and instruction and some of the alternatives for restructuring their schools. And teachers need training in new pedagogical techniques and in their subject matter.

In Denver, Ms. Phelan of the advocacy group Citizens for Quality Schools says, "even though [school councils] have the authority, if you haven't been able to establish a vision for a school, you don't know what to do. Schools need a lot of help in understanding the menu of possibilities."

Frequently, however, districts lack the time, money, or commitment to provide enough training to set school-based councils firmly on their feet.

Some states that have mandated school-based management have also failed to provide money for training.

In Denver, the teaching contract mandated that a board of directors be created to offer training programs for members of the collaborative-decisionmaking teams. Initial training was provided to all 1,500 council members, and ongoing training and support is also being offered. But some committee members say the needs are so vast that far more assistance is needed.

"There does not appear to be a wide range of dispute-resolution skills inside a high school," says Wyatt McCallie, the business representative on the team from Thomas Jefferson High. "I get the impression that there is not a great reservoir of skills and techniques that can be used to resolve things, like brainstorming."

To make good decisions, schools also need access to information, including budgetary data and feedback on student performance.

But such information isn't always available—in part, because districts aren't used to providing it. Information in hierarchically structured school systems most commonly flows upward, not vice versa.

In Denver, councils were asked to make recommendations about cutting their budgets. But there was a problem, Mr. Martyn at George Washington High School says. "We got a list of services [provided by the central administration], but no dollar amounts and no numbers of people," he recalls.

And when he called the central office for an organizational chart of the district, "They seemed mystified. They had a generic one, but no names and numbers."

"There's a complete absence of data in the school community about what it really costs for these programs," Mr. McCallie complains.

School-based councils also appear hungry for information on ways to evaluate their own progress and for indications that they are doing what they should.

A Lack of Rewards for Time-Consuming Efforts

But perhaps the biggest complaint by teachers and others is the amount of time that shared decisionmaking takes—and the lack of rewards for their efforts.

Such criticisms stand in stark contrast to successful worker-participation schemes in business, note Susan Albers Mohrman, the deputy director of CPRE's school-based-management project, and Rodney T. Ogawa, an associate professor of educational administration at the University of California at Riverside.

"Performance-based rewards are considered by many in the private sector to be a key element of high-involvement management," they point out. In some cases, individuals are paid more as they gain skills that are needed by the organization. In other instances, entire units are rewarded for improvements in productivity and performance.

"In the long run," David T. Levine and George Strauss write in a review of employee-participation schemes in the business community, "psychic benefits are not enough. Workers see themselves doing supervisors' work without supervisors' pay. Further, if participation contributes to increased profits, employees want to share the benefits."

The Denver contract set aside $100,000 for an annual incentive program. But schoolpeople say the criteria for success are unclear. Marrama Elementary School won $2,000 for its efforts, but members of its council weren't sure why.

"It wasn't necessarily the best schools that got awards," Rae Garrett, the president of the Denver Classroom Teachers' Association, says.

For teachers and others, the intrinsic benefits of serving on the committees may be at least as important as any monetary rewards. But even here, the slow progress that many councils are making has proved frustrating.

Because of the time involved, collaborative decisionmaking "has taken some time to adjust to," says David Strodtman, the principal of Thomas Jefferson High School. "It takes so much longer to do things."

"We have all these great plans, and we meet forever and ever, and we never do anything about it; we never follow through," laments Audra Sandoval, a senior at North High School in Denver who serves on her school's committee. Although the North High council set up an advocacy program to pair incoming freshmen with groups of teachers, she says, the program is "in limbo."

Other participants on site-based councils in Denver and elsewhere say the amount of time and energy they have expended may eventually cause them to drop off their committees.

During the first year of collaborative decisionmaking in Denver, according to Citizens for Quality Schools, there were resignations from every category of council membership except principals. The turnover was especially high among business representatives, 25 percent of whom quit.

"I want to have a say, but I don't want to have to do the work," Bernie Lopez, a teacher at Rishel Middle School, says. "It's affecting my teaching negatively. There's got to be a happy medium so that we can do a good job making decisions and in the classroom, and have a life outside."

Warren Wheeler, a history teacher at North High School, complains, "It's messing up my family life. We meet every week. I'm going to have to resign."

Some school councils have simply imploded under the strain of politics and time pressures.

In Rochester, for example, former Superintendent Peter McWalters placed Franklin High School in receivership and replaced its principal and some of its staff members after a site-based council was unable to reach consensus about how to make improvements at the school.

And at the Rosemary Hills School in Montgomery County, Md., teachers voted to withdraw from a shared-decisionmaking experiment after they concluded "there was a lot of work put into something that accomplished very little," Principal Linda Weber says.

But the more common pattern identified by researchers is a gradual diminishment in participation and a growing level of cynicism over time.

"The exhaustion will create a pullback," Ms. Malen says. "Not in the sense that they announce they're not doing it anymore, but in the sense that it becomes a much more routine kind of matter that is quite different from how the concept was cast. They meet less often or not at all."

'Unrealistic Promises' and 'Unbelievable Expectations'

In retrospect, reformers may have overestimated what school-based management by itself could accomplish and underestimated the amount of change needed elsewhere in the system to make it work.

Union leaders, in particular, seized on shared decisionmaking as a way to empower teachers and establish their unions' role in education policymaking, only to be brought up short when it began to threaten some of their most sacrosanct protections, such as teacher tenure and transfer rights.

"People put unbelievable expectations on school-based management/shared decisionmaking," concludes Pat Tornillo, the executive vice president of the United Teachers of Dade. "They expected us to turn the world around overnight. That isn't the way it works."

"There were so many ambitious and, in my judgment, unrealistic promises attached to school-based management," Ms. Malen says.

Of course, many of these problems aren't unique to schools. The same issues that have plagued the implementation of site-based management in education are true of business as well.

In their study, Mr. Levine and Mr. Strauss note that not all employees want the added responsibilities or enriched jobs that participation provides. Many would prefer their secure routines to remain unchanged. Participants' input may be confined to matters of only modest importance, such as the color of walls or the food in the cafeteria. And the democratic atmosphere of the participative group may be so inconsistent with ordinary managerial practices that workers suspect management of hypocrisy and insincerity.

As in education, the authors also note that first-line supervisors (principals, in the case of education) often feel discriminated against.

"They are forced into a system that typically they had no part in designing," they write. "They are forced to share their own power, but don't see their bosses sharing theirs. In some cases, they see guaranteed job security for employees, but not for themselves."

Finally, they observe, saving management money, rather than making workers happy, has been the major purpose of many shared-decisionmaking schemes.

The advent of shared decisionmaking in education has also coincided with a time of huge budget shortfalls, leaving many teachers suspicious of its motives and despairing about the prospects for improvement.

"Faculties are not wrestling with issues of renovation, but wrestling with issues of retrenchment," complains Edward J. Doherty, the president of the Boston Teachers Union. "And they were not excited about spending long hours together deciding what to cut out of their schools."

In Denver, collaborative decisionmaking coincided with one of the worst budget crises in the district's history: In the spring of 1993, the school system faced a shortfall of up to $46 million for the 1993-94 school year.

In 1992, the decisionmaking committee at the Greenlee Metro Lab School in Denver was forced to cut an instrumental-music position. "Before, our principal or downtown would say, 'This is what you've got, and live with it,' " says Ms. Mitchell, the co-chairwoman of the committee. "But some of those decisions, I would rather not have up to me."

Indeed, advocates of school-based management are realizing that, unless it is linked to reforms elsewhere in the system, substantial results are unlikely.

"We're convinced school-based management in and of itself does not lead anywhere," concludes Albert Shanker, the president of the American Federation of Teachers. "Outside of a system of curriculum frameworks and assessments and incentives, and a whole bunch of things like that to tell school-based managers what to do ... school-based management is just another level of governance, and, potentially, another level of bureaucracy."

For many school systems, the adoption of school-based management means major changes in organizational structure, management style, and the allocation of power and resources, Karin M. Lindquist and John J. Mauriel of the University of Minnesota wrote in a 1989 paper.

There is also a need for new accountability systems, and a serious renegotiation of the respective governance roles and authority of the school board, the teachers' union, the central office, and the community stakeholders, they state.

"If these global changes are not made," they argue, "school-based management will be just another moderately helpful public-relations and communications vehicle tinkering with the peripheral issues of school governance and management."

But right now, too many plans appear to be grafted onto systems and schools that remain fundamentally unchanged.

In Denver, says Sue Wilson, a parent at the Knight Fundamental Academy: "Site-based management is an innovation, yet it is trying to fit into an administration and a school board that were made 92 years ago. It doesn't fit together. ... We need to look at a new system."

There's No Going Back: 'The Genie Is Out of the Bottle'

Despite all of the concerns about site-based management, however, few think that the idea of providing schools and the people who work in them with greater authority over their professional lives should be abandoned.

"There is a broad cultural change in what's going on in the American workplace, and it does not exclude the schools," contends Samuel B. Bacharach, a professor of organizational behavior and educational administration at Cornell University. "It can't be right for everything but the schools."

The same sentiment is voiced by those in Denver. "This is something that parents here had been looking forward to for a long time," says Kathy Marci, a parent who serves on the Thomas Jefferson High committee, "so that we would have a bigger role in making some decisions."

"The genie is out of the bottle," Mr. Murphy of the University of Colorado says. "It would be hard for the district or the union to stuff it back in the bottle again. Whether it will ultimately make a difference remains to be seen."

The issue now is how to make school-based management work—how to provide the conditions that would give it a fighting chance.

Most important, experts suggest, school-based management should be part of a broader systemic strategy for improving teaching and learning.

"In architecture, they say that form derives from function, and we violated that with site-based decisionmaking," argues Doug Tuthill, the president of the Pinellas Classroom Teachers' Association in Pinellas County, Fla. "What we didn't do is first develop a common vision of student learning and then talk about changing the focus of decisionmaking based on that vision."

Some experts believe that districts should provide schools with guidance, perhaps in the form of a list of national organizations and groups involved in school restructuring with which they could work.

Many people are also calling for a clearer devolution of authority to the school site that, in many ways, goes beyond what was initially advocated.

The most effective school-based-management programs, according to CPRE, would be ones where schools are given lump-sum budgets to allocate according to local needs and the authority to hire and fire school staff members.

States, CPRE suggests, could devise a time line for transferring budget and personnel authority to school sites and require full transfer by some date. Local districts could exercise oversight over outcomes rather than process and redefine the role of the central office as supportive rather than compliance-oriented.

The growing interest in "charter schools" as a new means for providing public education highlights the frustration with the current regulatory climate in which schools operate. Under such arrangements, groups of teachers and others can form independent public schools under contracts with local school boards. As long as they meet the outcome standards specified in the contracts, the schools retain control over their budgets, hiring, and curriculum.

Advocates in Boston, Detroit, and other big cities are also arguing that the traditional relationship between the schools and the central administration be reversed and that schools be allowed to purchase services from the central administration—or elsewhere—rather than be forced to take what's given. In both Chicago and Edmonton, Alberta, for example, schools can purchase staff-development services from experts outside the district.

Experts have also highlighted the critical role of the superintendent and the central office in supporting the shift to school-based management and in changing their own responsibilities from insuring compliance to creating the incentives for reform. Once authority is delegated to the school site, its distribution within the school needs to be re-evaluated.

Some now suggest that school-based management pays too little attention to the key role of the principal and puts in place too unwieldy a decisionmaking structure. They even question whether group empowerment is the most effective means of running a school. A few districts, such as Edmonton and Prince William County, Va., have empowered principals, rather than committees, under site-based management.

"We may have a faulty model here, where we've confused management responsibility for a school with the core work, which is teaching, curriculum, and instruction," says Jane L. David, the director of the Bay Area Research Group and an expert on school-based management.

"A school-site council is a very appropriate group—with parent and teacher and administrative representation—for the management of the school and, perhaps, for decisions about allocating resources within the school," she adds. "But the actual work of making decisions about schedules regarding teaching and learning and materials and curriculum rightly belongs, I suspect, to a work team of teachers."

In Chicago, the law assigns three key policy decisions to the local school councils—the selection of the principal, the development of a school-improvement plan, and the allocation of the school's budget—but places day-to-day operations firmly in the hands of the principal, who can be fired by the council if he or she doesn't do his or her job.

In fact, educators may need to create different kinds of decisionmaking structures in schools that are more closely tied to the core work of teaching and learning.

Again, CPRE suggests that teams of teachers, defined by grade level or academic department, could be given the authority to make resource tradeoffs and to manage the way they perform their jobs. A second option would be to create schools within schools, or "houses," where teams of teachers would have greater control over how their time, resources, and instruction are managed.

Third, as districts move to site-based management, more attention and effort must be invested in training both for those at the school site and for central-office personnel.

Over a five-year period, CPRE advocates, states should set aside 2 percent to 3 percent of their total education revenues for professional development, a sum that is more in line with the training budgets at the most productive private companies.

Paul Hill, a senior social scientist with RAND, suggests that schools be given total control over their training budgets so they can buy services as needed. Others suggest that outside facilitators be used to help teams learn to relate to one another and to connect with training opportunities.

Franklin High School in Rochester, for example, now has a facilitator from the Eastman Kodak Company. And Mr. Hill notes that districts can create their own cadres of facilitators from the ranks of both union and management to quietly intervene in schools before problems become severe.

As part of site-based management, school districts are also beginning to provide sites with the information needed to develop school-improvement plans.

Again, CPRE suggests that states could develop a prototype information system of budgetary, student, teacher, and outcomes data that includes all the key elements needed to engage in site-based decisionmaking. States could also devote resources to disseminating information about educational innovations throughout the state. And districts or consortia of districts could design the computer systems needed to make such information readily available to schools.

The point is for schools to understand their weaknesses and be able to act on them. For example, Mr. Hill says, if a school is given information showing it has a weak reading program, it could decide to double the amount of time devoted to the subject.

Within schools, better strategies are needed to share information at the site among all parties.

But one of the stickiest topics for schools remains the system of incentives and rewards that will make it worthwhile for teachers, in particular, to come out of their classrooms and engage in creating schoolwide improvements.

States, CPRE suggests, could develop model pay systems that reward groups based on their performance. Districts, in turn, could pilot the new pay systems, for which they could waive personnel regulations, including union contracts.

In addition to monetary rewards, CPRE suggests rewarding teachers with sabbaticals, prestigious mentor positions, and opportunities to attend professional conferences, take classes, or become involved in teacher networks that are focused on some aspect of the curriculum, teaching, and assessment.

Despite the fitful progress to date, site-based management has revealed a reservoir of both schoolpeople and community members who are willing and interested in playing a greater role in the direction that learning will take within their particular buildings.

"As teachers," Pat Pryor, a teacher at Marrama Elementary School in Denver says, "we have never had a say in the running of our schools. This has been given to us, and what we do with it is up to us."

"It's a frustrating process," Mr. Martyn of George Washington High School agrees, "but it's valuable. And we are desperately trying to make it work."

TIME AND SPACE

By Meg Sommerfeld

In this chapter, we examine the time-bound and time-conscious nature of schooling and the rigid use of building space. It is becoming increasingly apparent that such norms and conventions stifle educator creativity and student achievement. But some schools, at least, are discovering that there are alternatives.

MURFREESBORO, TENN.—At 6 each morning, about 50 children begin their school day at Northfield Elementary School here. Many will remain until 6 P.M. as part of an extended-day program offering academic and enrichment activities.

Although students at the City Magnet School in Lowell, Mass., don't start off quite as early, their school day isn't conventional either. Mornings are spent learning the principles of publishing, economics, and government; in the afternoon, students put such skills into practice at their "jobs" at mock newspapers, banks, and courthouses within the school.

Some 3,000 miles across the country in Chula Vista, Calif., students in an alternative program attend school for only two hours a day. They spend the rest of their week completing independent assignments and working at jobs. The "learning centers" they attend are open year-round from 7 A.M. to 9:30 P.M.

These are the exceptions to the rule. Each is trying to confront one of the most implacable barriers to school reform in the United States: the rigid use of time and space that affects teachers' working conditions, the kinds of projects that students can pursue, and the ties that schools have with their communities.

Ten years after *A Nation at Risk* recommended extending the length of the school day to seven hours, instituting a 200- to 220-day school year, and establishing 11-month contracts for teachers, most schools still use a 6 1/2-hour day and a 180-day year. And most teachers still work on a September-to-June calendar.

Students at the City Magnet School in Lowell, Mass., apply what they learn in class to "jobs" they hold at the school. Recognizing that the rigid use of time and space can constrain teachers, students, and the learning process, some schools have begun to reconfigure their schedules and redesign their structures.

Moreover, the physical setup of the typical American classroom and school has changed little. The sight of a single teacher lecturing to 25 pupils in uniform rows of desks remains the norm.

However, a small but growing number of schools are re-examining the amount of time in the school year and, perhaps more importantly, questioning the unwritten rules that govern how schools use time and space. In some cases, they are turning the traditional school day on its head.

Some schools have shifted to a year-round schedule. Others have extended their hours before and after school and into the weekend. Still others have instituted flexible schedules for both students and teachers, with time set aside for large- and small-group instruction and for teacher planning.

In some instances, school buildings are being opened up to the community. In other cases, the use of space within schools is being reconfigured to make room for team teaching, peer coaching, and "schools within schools."

"I happen to believe that time is the uncracked nut," said Milton Goldberg, the executive director of the National Education Commission on Time and Learning. "It's a prism through which we can look anew at teacher time, student motivation, and curriculum."

Rethinking the School Day: An 'Absolutely Essential' Task

The standard academic calendar has its roots in the 19th century. The first compulsory-attendance law was enacted in Massachusetts in 1852 and required students to attend school for 12 weeks. With the rise of industrialism, the need for a more skilled workforce became more pronounced. By 1890, as a result, the average school year had increased to the current standard of about 36 weeks.

Currently, 32 states, the District of Columbia, and two territories require 180-day school years. Two states require more—Ohio's school year is 182 days, and Kansas' is 181—and the rest mandate 174 to 176 days.

State legislatures usually set minimum standards for school calendars. But as a briefing paper to the national commission created to study the use of time in schools has noted, schools and districts usually do not exceed the minimum required.

Nonetheless, rethinking the structure of the school day is "absolutely essential" to address the demands on education in the 1990's, says Theodore R. Mitchell, the dean of the graduate school of education at the University of California at Los Angeles.

The previous emphasis on quantity over quality of instruction, he argues, "is why *A Nation at Risk* continues to be problematic, with its demands for harder, faster, and more of the same."

In traditional, regimented school schedules, time has been the constant and learning the variable. Each student is expected to spend roughly the same number of hours in school, complete the same number of courses, and attend school for the same number of years. But what students learn in school has been allowed to vary widely.

But more recently, says Gary D. Watts, the senior director of the National Education Association's National Center for Innovation, support has emerged for the notion that learning should be the constant, and time the variable. "There isn't a teacher in the world who won't say some kids may need three minutes [to learn something], some may need three hours, and some may need three days," he observes.

Proponents of a more student-centered approach believe that schools need more flexible structures to enable students to take as much or as little time as necessary to master their coursework and to give teachers more control over the time they need to prepare and teach their lessons.

Indeed, as the call goes out for all students to engage in higher-order thinking and to learn through hands-on activities and teamwork, the use of time and space in schools must be reconfigured.

Greater collaboration and decisionmaking among the adults in a school building, as well as the use of schools to train future teachers, conduct research, and serve broader societal needs, also cry out for a re-examination of how time and space are structured.

While actually translating these concepts into widespread practice could prove both tremendously expensive and a logistical nightmare, signs are emerging that the public is willing to accept a greater degree of variation in how schools organize their calendars and facilities.

In 1991, the annual Gallup Poll on education found that 51 percent of respondents endorsed a 210-day school year—the first time that a majority had supported a longer school year since the poll began including the question in 1981. Last year, the percentage favoring such a shift increased to 55 percent, and even larger majorities advocated keeping educational facilities open after school, on weekends, and during vacations.

Other indicators also suggest that the rethinking of how schools use time and space is gaining momentum as a central element in the restructuring movement:

- The federally sponsored National Education Commission on Time and Learning is compiling data on how schools across the country use time.

Its report to Congress in 1994 will include recommendations on the length of the school day and school year, the time allocated for various academic subjects, and how to make better use of the time available by improving student motivation.

- Many reform-minded projects and networks have sought to shatter the status quo of how time and space are apportioned within a school building. Several winners of the design competition sponsored by the RJR Nabisco Foundation, for example, have used their grant money to extend the school day or year, compensate teachers for additional professional-development time, or open their buildings to the community at nights and on weekends. And similar ideas permeate the blueprints for "break the mold" schools now being developed by contractors with the New American Schools Development Corporation.

- A longer school day and year have been mentioned as possible elements in the blueprint for the Edison Project, the proposed network of 1,000 private, for-profit schools that the entrepreneur Christopher Whittle has set out to design.

- Researchers at the RAND Corporation recently interviewed more than 40 organizations involved in school-level reform and published recommendations for how to create more time in schools.

- Slightly more than 600,000 children in kindergarten through 8th grade were enrolled in 13,500 public school-based before-school and after-school programs in 1991, a study by the U.S. Education Department reports.

- Some schools are reaching out to children and their families before age 5 and forming closer ties with community colleges and employers for teenage students to insure that youngsters start school ready to learn and leave school ready to enter the workforce or higher education.

In 1914, George Bernard Shaw penned this diatribe against the enterprise of schooling: "There is, on the whole, nothing on earth intended for innocent people so horrible as a school. To begin with, it is a prison. But in some respects more cruel than a prison. In a prison, for instance, you are not forced to read books written by the warders and the governor ... and beaten or otherwise tormented if you cannot remember their utterly immemorable contents."

While most educators would probably balk at Shaw's observations, the analogy is not without its grounding in reality.

In the traditional school day, students follow highly regimented schedules punctuated by buzzers or bells, and their movement is restricted as they go from one compartmentalized space to another.

Challenging these deeply ingrained orthodoxies can be a formidable task.

"I think that there is a sense that the school day is a part of some kind of natural law of the same symbolic weight as gravity," Mr. Mitchell, the U.C.L.A. dean, observes. "We have lived with the system for so long, and become so accustomed to it, that it's one of the basic identifying characteristics of the school, and when we attempt to change those basic underlying structures, we threaten people's familiarity with the very institution."

The main problem with the traditional school day, he asserts, is that it was designed to meet the social goals of an earlier era. "It was built around an industrial model," he explains, "in which teaching children to respond to differential tasks by moving in an orderly fashion at different points according to a well-structured and fragmented day was precisely the type of schooling that was required by a society that was highly industrialized, mechanized, and routinized."

Such a structure, however, no longer meets the needs of today's students. Our highly technological world both enables and demands a more flexible use of time in school.

But here's the rub: Introducing such changes runs smack up against the fact that the entire system of accountability in American education is itself anchored in seat time.

"Just about any student who logs enough time at a school desk will get his diploma," Edward B. Fiske, the former education editor of *The New York Times*, writes in his book, *Smart Schools, Smart Kids*. "What counts is not so much what you know as how fast you can deliver it."

Similarly, he observes, teachers earn pay raises by accruing seniority—not by improving their performance. And states use student-attendance rates as a factor in calculating the amount of aid that each district receives.

'We Have Met the Enemy, and They Are Hours'

A retired administrator at a Long Island high school once kept a sign on his bulletin board that caused many of his colleagues to chuckle knowingly. It read, "We have met the enemy, and they are hours."

At all points on the political spectrum, there is agreement that educators do not have enough time to do all that is expected of them.

"Teachers don't usually have time to go to the bathroom, so they don't have very much time to think," observes Joan Lipsitz, the education program officer at the Lilly Endowment in Indianapolis. "What has been called the 'dailiness' of teaching is so time-consuming that to find any time in the school day for reflection and planning and dreaming and asking questions like 'what if?' has been very difficult."

Part of the problem, most every educator would agree, is that there has never been enough time for meaningful professional development in the schools in the first place. The prevailing belief that teachers are only working when they are standing in front of a room full of children makes the designation of time for staff development difficult.

In fact, schools often need the credibility of external organizations—such as joining a restructuring network or winning a foundation grant—to leverage enough resources from within for professional development or for other noninstructional time.

Carl Glickman—an education professor at the University of Georgia who coordinates the League of Professional Schools, a network of 60 restructuring schools in that state—says the teachers he works with often find it "easier [to get time off] to go to a conference 180 miles away ... than to spend time in their own districts to do that planning."

Now, new demands on teachers—ranging from their participation in school-based decisionmaking to their role as curriculum writers and developers—are making the need for more and better training sorely felt. Indeed, such noted educational scholars as John I. Goodlad have frequently suggested employing teachers year-round—not to be with students, but to engage in continued professional development and planning.

Proposals by many to transform schools into "professional development" sites akin to teaching hospitals also emphasize the need for new configurations of time and space. In those schools, future educators are trained, university professors and classroom teachers collaborate on research, and innovations are constantly tested and refined.

Schools also need additional time to meet the increasing demands placed on them by a society undergoing profound changes in the workplace and within the family structure. As more women have entered the workforce and single-parent families have become more commonplace, many schools are feeling the need to open their doors earlier and stay open later.

At the same time, because the basic amount of knowledge that students are expected to master has increased exponentially, the pressure on the existing school day is greater than ever. There are more years of history to teach, more works of literature to read, and more mathematical theories to understand.

One indicator of the expanding curriculum can be seen in how textbooks have swelled in size over the past 10 years. A typical 11th-grade American-history textbook from one of the major publishers, for example, has increased from 800 pages in 1983 to 1,100 pages in editions going to press this year. "The books now weigh five to six pounds," observes Gilbert T. Sewall, the director of the American Textbook Council. For students to tote just one of these hefty tomes, he notes, is like carrying three quarts of milk.

Not only is the amount of information greater, but the kinds of skills that a well-educated graduate is expected to possess—such as computer literacy and higher-order math skills—have both changed and increased over time. The curriculum has expanded over the years to include other nonacademic subjects as well, such as sex education and driver's education.

Indeed, the ever-expanding nature of the "shopping mall" high school, as many have come to call it, has led to a push to streamline and rethink the curriculum to emphasize a "less is more" approach, a curriculum in which fewer subjects would be taught, but in depth.

Finally, the reform movement itself is part of the problem. While prior reform efforts emphasized mandates from on high, the collaborative nature of the current restructuring movement requires much greater levels of participation from both teachers and administrators.

In schools that have implemented shared-decisionmaking councils, for example, the time of many teachers and community members, rather than just one principal, is now needed to set policy.

Changing pedagogical strategies places further demands on teachers. First, time is needed to learn the new skills; in addition, the techniques themselves are more time-consuming to execute than those they replace.

Planning lessons that actively engage children and teach problem-solving skills requires substantially more time than preparing a lecture. Similarly, portfolio assessments are considerably more time-consuming to conduct than standardized tests that can be scored by a computer.

Ironically, the more a school is engaged in reform, Mr. Watts of the N.E.A. observes, the more time becomes a problem for teachers, many of whom devote long unpaid hours to sustain restructuring efforts. "They're trying to maintain 'System A' while they're inventing 'System B,' and they're doing System B on their own backs," he says.

As the RAND Corporation's recent "Time for Reform" report notes, "Unlike retail stores that display notices in the window proclaiming themselves closed for inventory, repairs, or remodeling, schools must continue to provide services for their customers."

Opinions Vary for Remedying the Time and Space Dilemma

But while educators and policymakers may agree that schools cannot do all that is expected of them within the current structure of the school day, there is a wide range of opinions about how to respond to the problem. Some advocate extending the length of the school day or year; others think a greater emphasis should be placed on making more effective use of existing time.

In a widely cited 1990 cover story in *The Atlantic* magazine, Michael J. Barrett, a Massachusetts state senator who is also a member of the National Education Commission on Time and Learning, makes his case for lengthening the school year by citing the superior performance on standardized tests by students in countries with longer school years, such as Japan (240 days), then-West Germany (226 to 240 days), and Israel (216 days).

"The United States faces a time-in-school deficit every bit as serious as the trade deficit and the balance-of-payments problem," he writes. "Each year, American children receive hundreds of hours less school than many of their European or Asian mates, and the resulting harm promises to be cumulative and lasting."

To back up his hypothesis, Mr. Barrett cites the data of such researchers as Herbert Walberg, an education professor at the University of Illinois at Chicago. In a review of more than 100 studies of time and learning published since *A Nation at Risk*, Mr. Walberg found that increased classroom and homework time was correlated with moderate gains in academic achievement.

But others say many of the international comparisons are deceptive. A 1987 report of the International Association for the Evaluation of Education Achievement, for example, concluded that the length of the school year was unrelated to levels of achievement among 20 countries participating in an international math study. While Japan ranked first and the United States placed 14th in achievement, the United States actually devoted more school hours to math instruction—an average of 144 hours each year—than did Japan, with 101 hours annually. In addition, 11 of the 13 other nations that ranked higher than the United States also allotted less curricular time to math.

"Without other kinds of reform, the longer school year does not guarantee greater quality time on task," argues Curtis C. McKnight, a professor of mathematics at the University of Oklahoma at Norman and a co-author of the 1987 study. "The solution is not that simple. I think it has a lot more to do with how we use the time than how much time we have."

Mr. McKnight speculates that mandating longer school years without first examining these other questions will produce a Parkinson's Law effect: The existing work will expand to fill the time available for its completion.

Detractors of the comparisons of the United States and Japan also say they fail to take into account the impact of widespread ability grouping in the United States. In Japan, they note, classes are largely untracked, and students spend many hours outside of school studying at a private "juku," or cram school. They also charge that such theories fail to explain why students in countries with shorter school years, such as Belgium, still outperform the United States.

Although Mr. Barrett acknowledges the need for changes in both the quality and quantity of instruction, he strongly believes that lengthening the school year is still necessary. He pictures an extended year as a "big tent," a larger superstructure within which schools could have greater scheduling flexibility.

"A number of things may go into the tent to make it a better place," he writes. "To accommodate them all and to arrange them in proper order requires the space the tent provides."

In any case, because of the tremendous barrier posed by cost, the arguments for and against extending the school year may be moot. Time is money, as the cliche goes, and the adage is particularly true for schools. Schools, after all, tend to be more personnel-intensive than other institutions. On average, 85 percent of a district's budget is devoted to staff salaries, the Education Commission of the States reports.

Using an estimate of $27.45 for daily per-pupil costs, lengthening the school year to 210 days could cost an additional $33 billion a year, according to the N.E.A. and the National Association for Year Round Education. Total government spending on education is estimated to be $445 billion a year, so that action alone would require a 7.4 percent increase in education spending at a time when many states are cutting school aid.

Such cost barriers notwithstanding, a few states have already moved to increase the length of the school year. A reform act enacted in 1992 in Oregon, for example, included a plan to lengthen the school year to 220 days by 2010. With Oregon schools currently facing a major budget crunch brought on, in large part, by a recently passed property-tax-limitation law, however, the fate of the plan remains unclear.

Recent proposals to lengthen the school year by 20 days in Maryland, North Carolina, Georgia, and Missouri have also been shelved because of a lack of funding.

More modest proposals have fared somewhat better. In 1991, Kansas passed legislation increasing the school year in incremental portions to reach 186 days by 1995, and Minnesota plans to add two days each year to reach 190 days beginning in the 1994-95 school year. These two initiatives are more likely to be fully funded and implemented, according to Melodye Bush, an information specialist at the E.C.S.

'Moving Away From Cells and Bells'

Even though the total length of the school year is likely to remain the same for now, an increasing number of schools are changing how they use their existing time and space. As Mr. Watts of the N.E.A. puts it, schools are "moving away from cells and bells."

One approach gaining in popularity is year-round schooling, which is often confused with extended-year schooling. The overwhelming majority of year-round schools still use a 180-day calendar, but divide it into different segments, usually with the end result being that the long summer vacation is eliminated.

Slightly more than 2,000 public schools now use year-round schedules. Of those, only 21 also employ an extended-year schedule, defined as 205 or more days of instructional time.

The bulk of year-round programs were initiated because schools lacked the facilities needed to accommodate increasing enrollment, says Charles Ballinger, the executive director of the National Association for Year-Round Education.

In the districts that implemented "multi-track" year-round education, such as Los Angeles and San Diego, the student body is divided into several groups. Each group attends school for 180 days a year, but not all groups are on campus at the same time.

But recently, Mr. Ballinger says, more schools have adopted year-round schedules as a way to curtail the "drop-off" in learning that occurs when students are out of school for a long stretch of time. The North Rock Creek, Okla., district converted its elementary school to the state's first year-round program in August 1992, for example, after being convinced of the new calendar's educational benefits.

"A large part of our reasoning was that we wanted to cut down on the length of time these kids had on their own," Alisande Porter, the president of the district's board, says, adding that the community was easily sold on the notion that long summer breaks hamper the potential of the district's large contingent of Native American and disadvantaged students.

As for the extended year, Mr. Ballinger asserts that, until the economy improves, it will remain a local initiative. "California had a bill [to extend the calendar] introduced this year," he notes. "But it didn't go anywhere because [the state] can hardly pay for 180 days right now."

Still, he contends, longer years are likely to become a more common feature in schools of the future. "The question is not whether it will happen, but when it will happen," he says. "I think we'll see quite a few more pilot schools over the next few years, and around the turn of the century ... I see the economy recovering enough to support some serious change in that direction."

Although a longer school year may still be off on the horizon, other schools are already experimenting with longer days.

For instance, 35 percent of all children enrolled in before- or after-school programs are served at public schools, the Education Department's new study found.

In Murfreesboro, a city of about 50,000 located about 30 miles south of Nashville, the local schools have tossed aside the notion that school must start at 8 or 9 in the morning and end at 3 in the afternoon. Children may spend as many as 12 hours in school as a part of the district's extended-day program.

Parents can drop off their children as early as 6 at each of Murfreesboro's eight elementary schools. The youngsters "usually come in half asleep, and we take them into the gym and wake them up," says Peggy Bell, who directs the extended-day program at Northfield Elementary School, where she also has a full-time job as a guidance counselor.

Looking remarkably exuberant and energetic at this early hour, Ms. Bell describes the morning's activities as she gives a visitor a tour. Following some vigorous and playful exercise in the gymnasium, the children will head to the cafeteria for breakfast. Afterward, they play with building blocks, draw, or engage in other small-group activities until their regular school day begins at 7:45 A.M.

Later that day, a significantly larger group—about 280 to 300 students— will participate in the after-school portion of the program. Offerings here and at other schools in the district include hands-on science instruction, homework tutorials, private music lessons, art and foreign-language classes, and sports and recreational activities.

Providing services for children while their parents are at work should be a critical item on the agenda of American educators, says John Hodge Jones, the superintendent of the Murfreesboro schools and the chairman of the National Education Commission on Time and Learning. "We must look at the total needs of children, the needs of the modern home, the needs of our labor force," he says.

About 2,000 children, just under half of the district's students, elect to participate in the program—a clear indication, Mr. Jones says, of the need for schools to offer such a service.

Parents in the community sing its praises. "I've been real high on the program," says Mike Pirtle, the managing editor of *The Daily News Journal* in Murfreesboro, whose 4th-grade son is a regular participant. "If we didn't have [the extended-day program], I don't know what we would do.'

And despite the long hours, many students say they enjoy the program. "It's better than just being home and watching TV," says Joshua Robinson, a 6th grader at Mitchell-Neilson Elementary School.

Parents foot the bill for the majority of the program's costs—about $26 per week per child during the school year and $40 per week for a summer session that runs from 6 A.M. to 6 P.M.

The district is able to offer the program at a relatively low cost primarily because a substantial portion of the staff members are students at Middle Tennessee State University in Murfreesboro, and they are paid only about $4.35 to $5 an hour.

Each of the eight program sites is overseen by an administrator or teacher, who earns an extra $9,000 a year on top of his or her regular salary. The staff is rounded out by full-time teachers—who take on the additional duties voluntarily for slightly lower pay per hour than they earn in the class-room—and by other licensed teachers who only want to work part time or who are in between jobs.

For the student staff members from Middle Tennessee State, most of whom plan to become teachers, the program is a valuable opportunity to learn positive discipline techniques, says Sue Bordine, the assistant principal and the program site director at Mitchell-Neilson Elementary.

"I've had student-teachers for 25 years, and [classroom management] is their number-one problem," she says. "The kids just carry you out the window your first year; they're so skilled at being difficult." In contrast, she says, the student-teachers who work at the extended-day program will be far more prepared when they enter the classroom.

Another district that has pioneered an innovative school calendar is the Sweetwater Union High School District in Chula Vista, Calif., just outside San Diego. About 1,380 of the district's 28,500 students are enrolled in an alternative program in which they attend school for only two hours a day.

The program was created in 1986 to decrease the district's high dropout rate and, in particular, targeted students who had dropped out because of financial problems. It offers both a more personalized atmosphere and a flexible schedule that enables teenagers to work at a job, part time or full time, while completing their diplomas. For teenage parents, child care is also available while they are in class.

Students at the center attend school in groups of 20 for two-hour time slots, about half of which is spent working independently at computers on individualized assignments. Once a week, they meet one on one with their teacher for about an hour. "We're trying to get to kids before they drop out," says Tom Williams, the district's director of alternative programs. "They take the same curriculum, but it's just delivered in a different way."

In addition to their classes and jobs, students complete about 15 hours of independent-study assignments each week.

Students take two or three courses of their choice at a time, using as little or as much time as they need to complete them. Many find it easier to focus on completing one course credit every three weeks than to work on six credits simultaneously for a semester.

"You go at your own pace," remarks Beatriz Cendejas, an 18-year-old student who has been enrolled at the Sweetwater center since 1991. "It's a lot of work, [but] it's on you if you want to finish. You can go faster if you want."

And thanks to the program's flexible schedule, Ms. Cendejas is able to spend several hours a day working at the Del Rey infant-care center, which in turn is helping her become better prepared to seek employment as a child-care specialist after she graduates.

Others praised the physical layout of the learning centers, which, with their conference tables and computer stations, are designed to look more like offices than traditional classrooms. All the teachers have telephones at their desks to facilitate communication with both students and their parents.

Since the program was instituted seven years ago, the district's annual dropout rate has declined from 9.9 percent to 4.1 percent.

"It seems that [most] schools are set up to fit students into institutions instead of saying, 'What do we have to do to meet the needs of kids?'" Mr. Williams remarks. The success of the learning centers, he maintains, is rooted in their flexibility. "We've shown [students] that schools and teachers can be human," he adds.

A variety of other, less revolutionary changes in how schools structure their day are under way elsewhere in the country.

The RAND Corporation's "Time for Reform" report found that some schools are "banking" time by starting 10 minutes earlier each day so that, over the course of a month, they can accumulate an extra day for teacher professional development and planning.

Others are exploring new avenues for assisting at-risk students or others who need extra time built into the day. Schools in San Diego County set aside time for tutorials rather than pull students out of their regular classes. And the Carl Sandburg Intermediate School in Alexandria, Va., a winner of an RJR Nabisco grant, has instituted a two-hour after-school program three days a week for at-risk students. Other schools are offering optional courses—such as computer or foreign-language instruction—before or after school.

Still other schools have chosen to break into the sacred ground of the weekend. Hull (Mass.) High School conducts a "Saturday School" for freshmen and sophomores in need of extra help on their homework.

And even schools that still operate on 8:30-to-3, Monday-through-Friday, 180-day calendars are experimenting within the confines of the traditional school day. Many of the schools involved in the middle-grades restructuring movement, for example, have replaced the traditional 40- to 45-minute periods with a "block scheduling" format.

At the C.C. Capshaw Middle School in Santa Fe, N.M., students are assigned to teams, each of which has between five and seven teachers—one in each of the core academic subject areas. Guidance counselors, administrators, and special-education or Chapter 1 representatives are also assigned to each team. Teachers on the same team share a common planning period and have control over how to use large blocks of their students' time each day, allowing them to vary the amount of time devoted to different lessons as needed.

Similar approaches have been used by many schools in the Coalition of Essential Schools, a reform-oriented network begun by Theodore R. Sizer, a professor of education at Brown University.

In his most recent book, *Horace's School,* Mr. Sizer outlines a master schedule for a hypothetical "Franklin High School" based on his work with the coalition schools. It sets up roughly two-hour blocks for classes and groups students and teachers in "houses." A rotation plan allows classes to meet at different times of the day; the schedule also incorporates daily planning time for teachers, as well as opportunities for students to perform community service.

But as educational entrepreneurs have sought to reconfigure how the school day is used, their progress has been hindered by an extensive array of state requirements. Twenty-four states, for example, even mandate the number of minutes spent on math and science instruction each week in elementary and middle schools, according to the Council of Chief State School Officers.

"Realistically, you can say that many of the requirements fly in the face of common sense," Mr. Sizer argues. "Each one of us learns at different rates, and how many minutes doesn't tell us very much."

The guiding principle behind such mandates, says Sophie Sa, the executive director of the Panasonic Foundation, is that schools can achieve educational equity by imposing equal requirements.

"There's a sense that people want to feel that they're getting the same, that equality means equity, and [thus having] the same number of hours means no department is being slighted or no student is being slighted," she muses.

But Ms. Sa and a growing number of educators contend that such approaches miss the point and that it's the actual outcomes of student performance that must be compared.

Likewise, whether a student is 15 or 16 or 19 "is irrelevant" to the issue of what he or she should be studying at any given time, Mr. Sizer says. Rather than delineating exactly what courses a student should study at various grade levels or ages, he suggests, schools should concern themselves with defining what a well-educated student should know by the time he or she graduates.

"You have to be clear [about] exactly what you want her to learn," he says. "It's much easier to say 'four years of English' than to define what English is."

Different Spaces for Different Functions

As schools begin examining how they use time, they are also re-evaluating other aspects of their organization, such as how they use physical space.

At the City Magnet School, a middle school in Lowell, Mass., the school's adoption of a "microsociety" curriculum 12 years ago led to a complete renovation of the school's facilities. Today, the school has numerous nontraditional spaces—among them a mock courtroom, a bank, a marketplace, and a newspaper office—where students learn about the "real world" by running their own in-house versions of grown-up institutions.

The goal of the school, Principal Sue Ellen Hogan says, is for "children to become independent learners, to become more responsible for what they're doing and more engaged in what they're doing."

Instead of the "chalk-talk model" in which the teacher is always the authority, Ms. Hogan argues, "the children become authorities or reference points for each other," and teachers become coaches or facilitators.

"The microsociety schools are one example of how dramatically schools can change on the inside," observes Peter Samton, a partner in the New York City architectural firm of Gruzan Samton Steinglass.

But while a small number of innovative institutions are thriving, Mr. Samton cautions, the status quo has remained largely unchanged. "Most architects are not aware of these questions," he says, "and they are dealing with school boards ... that are not willing to put it into concrete yet." One reason, he notes, is that they have been burned in the past for such reform failures as the open-classroom movement of the 1960's.

A handbook of model designs compiled by the school of architecture at the New Jersey Institute of Technology notes that the failure of the open-classroom experiments "has unfortunately resulted in a retrenchment in terms of school design, with schools of the 1980's being constructed in the most traditional of modes."

What killed the open-education movement, Mr. Glickman of the University of Georgia argues, "was that schools were built without any walls but [also] without ... discussion about the serious principles of learning."

In contrast, educators say, the current changes in education are not fleeting fads; instead, they say, they are part of a fundamental evolution that will require changes in how schools are designed. Greater emphasis on collaborative work means schools need differentiated spaces within classrooms that will allow students to work together without disrupting other small groups. Meanwhile, collaboration among teachers means schools will also have an increasing need for professional workspaces outside the classroom.

And, as the New Jersey Institute's manual notes, the more widespread use of technology not only requires changes in how schools are wired, but also affects lighting levels and cooling systems. Most schools being built today—even in districts that do not yet possess an extensive array of computer equipment at the outset—are being wired with the assumption that computers will eventually be in every room, Mr. Samton says.

Another key factor in how schools use space is the fact that learning may not always take place at the school itself. "When we look at our own memorable learning experiences," Mr. Glickman observes, "those do not always occur within four walls and with 25 other people of the same age and with a teacher."

More and more, education in the future may include such off-campus components as student internships, community-service programs, and instructional segments offered through such community institutions as museums and libraries. Technology can also serve as a window on the outside world by connecting students with information and opportunities far from their home communities.

Changes are also afoot in how existing facilities use their physical resources. While few cities can afford to build many new and smaller schools right now, educators have become increasingly concerned that the impersonal nature of large urban schools has caused many students to fall through the cracks.

The nation's largest school system, the nearly one-million-student New York City district, plans to create at least 50 smaller, theme-oriented schools that would provide a "more personalized, caring environment" for students. Efforts to create smaller "schools within schools" are also under way in Philadelphia and Chicago.

In many cases, such schools break with the traditional notion that a school building and an educational program are one and the same. By creating smaller, autonomous units within existing school buildings, educators hope to create a more cohesive faculty and student body.

"This generation of reform is about community-building between administrators, teachers, parents, and students," says Michelle Fine, a consultant to the Pew Charitable Trusts' reform project in Philadelphia.

The impact of the absence of stability in many large urban schools has often been underestimated, she continues. High staff turnover and low student morale often serve to nullify the impact of other reforms, such as lengthening the school year or extending the school day. "Simply adding more time will not yield improvements in student outcomes if people don't feel committed to the community," Ms. Fine remarks.

Moreover, a recent report by the Public Education Association, an independent civic group, and the Architectural League of New York maintains that larger schools are more expensive in the long term because they require a disproportionately large management structure and incur higher security costs.

"No research evidence supports a claim that large schools ... achieve operational-cost scale efficiencies significant enough to justify their existence or to offset other related, educationally damaging inefficiencies," the report adds.

Paying Attention to Dewey's Call

As Ms. Sa at the Panasonic Foundation notes, many of the changes currently in vogue in the restructuring movement—such as creating longer blocks of time for classes or sending students out into the community to learn about "the real world"—are far from new. As early as the turn of the century, educators like John Dewey were touting many of these ideas.

In *The School and Society*, first published in 1899, Mr. Dewey decries the structure of the "ordinary schoolroom," with "its rows of ugly desks placed in geometrical order, crowded together so that there be as little moving room as possible, desks almost all of the same size with just space enough to hold books, pencils and papers ... it is all made 'for listening.' "

Instead, he suggests, classrooms need places for children to work, to "construct, create, and actively inquire."

Nearly 100 years later, it remains to be seen whether the majority of schools will be able to adopt and sustain significant changes in how they use time and space, given the political and economic climates in which they operate.

What is clear is that it will take a long time to rework the deeply rooted structure that characterizes schooling in America.

Many observers note that it is extremely difficult to change the culture of a school. "I don't think as a society we have an appreciation of the complexity of schools as organizations and the delicate nature of the teaching-learning exchange," Ms. Lipsitz of the Lilly Endowment observes. "I think if we did, we would know it takes a lot more time to grow a child than to grow a car or a drug or a building."

THE COHERENT CURRICULUM

By Debra Viadero

In this chapter, we examine what many consider the centerpiece of reform efforts: the attempt to define what should be taught and how to teach it.

SAN DIEGO—It is "math choice" time in Jane Fulkerson's combined kindergarten and 1st-grade class here, and there is an audible buzz in the air.

Children are sprawled around the room as they engage in a wide range of carefully chosen activities. In one corner, tiny hands spin a number on a cardboard spinner and count out colorfully painted beans. On the floor, two small girls connect colored plastic cubes to make patterns repeat. Three children at a table nearby color in rows of seven blocks each on a worksheet.

"You have to make different patterns," explains one of the three, a pigtailed girl in a spotless pink sweatsuit. "But they all equal seven."

Ms. Fulkerson herself is working with a group of children as they move the hands on a clock and discuss the time of day they go to school and then the time they go to bed. As the children become excited, their voices rise and then fall again. The buzzing sound resumes. To Ms. Fulkerson and other teachers like her here at Elizabeth Freese Elementary School, that buzz is the sound of children learning. "I think," the veteran teacher says, "that this is the right way to teach."

The "right way," to Ms. Fulkerson's way of thinking, means giving students plenty of hands-on learning opportunities and helping them begin to think critically, talk with one another, and work together to solve problems. She wants to expose her students early on to a wide variety of mathematical elements—patterns, measurement, even some geometry. And she wants to instill in her pupils a basic sense of what numbers mean

At San Diego's Elizabeth Freese Elementary School, Antaleise Lewis, left, and Yolanda Sepulvada learn basic math by adding and subtracting the plastic bears they are playing with. To many working to improve the schools, the central task reformers face is defining what students should know and be able to do.

and how they feel.

A teacher for 18 years, Ms. Fulkerson has come to this new view of teaching through the California mathematics framework.

California's subject-matter frameworks—there are now eight in all—are the focus of a pioneering effort in this state to improve schooling for every child in every classroom.

Unlike most state reforms, which tinkered around the edges of schooling, California started by aiming directly at the heart of the educational enterprise: the teaching and learning that goes on in the classroom every day. And the frameworks lay out the blueprint for a fundamental overhaul in curriculum.

Where state curriculum guidelines have traditionally been lists of topics schools should cover at each grade level, California's curriculum frameworks seek to articulate a more comprehensive—yet, at the same time, less specific—view of what teaching in a particular subject should look like.

Rather than simply specify content, the frameworks call for changes in the way subjects are taught. They urge educators to move away from the traditional "drill and skill" approaches to teaching and to stress, instead, teaching children to think critically and to problem-solve. They advocate teaching fewer topics in greater depth. And, rather than lay out topics by grade level, they only broadly state the concepts, themes, or "big ideas" students should master in, for example, grades 3 through 6.

To be sure, officials here recognize that reforming the curriculum alone won't improve schools, and they see reform as a complex jigsaw puzzle that also includes the kinds of tests students are given, the quality and availability of training for teachers, and the kinds of educational materials available to schools. But the key piece of the puzzle is the curriculum.

"The whole reform effort needs to be driven by what you want to teach and how you want to teach it," says Bill Honig, who spearheaded the frameworks as the state's superintendent of public instruction. "Some of the other reforms never get to that."

While California led the way, a number of other states—Connecticut, Maine, Rhode Island, and South Carolina, among them—have also begun to use curriculum documents to anchor their school-reform efforts.

Similar efforts are under way at the national level as well. In 1989, the National Council of Teachers of Mathematics published national curriculum standards.

Now, national standards for what students should know and be able to do at key points in their schooling are also being hammered out in seven other subjects.

Most of these new standards-setting efforts came after then-President Bush and the nation's governors, in a historic "education summit" nearly four years ago, agreed that one goal for education should be that American students meet "world class" standards for learning in major academic subjects.

Reformers are also hoping to convince federal lawmakers that a national system of examinations is needed to reinforce those standards.

All of this activity is remarkable for a nation that has long cherished the notion that control of the content of schooling belongs largely in the hands of local communities.

"Local control met its Waterloo at the October 1989 education summit of the President and the governors," says Allen R. Odden, an education professor at the University of Southern California. "Ten years ago, this would never have happened. Now we're saying, 'Yes, it's possible to have national standards, and it is desirable.'"

Those efforts, however, are still new, and disagreements remain about how to proceed.

While California and the national efforts seek to define the curriculum subject by subject, other states and some educators argue for a more holistic view that would look at the full range of student learning and foster interdisciplinary instruction.

Educators in Maine, for example, point out that learning is naturally interdisciplinary, and that what students learn in one subject is inextricably linked to what they learn in another. Part of educators' task, they say, is to help pupils see the connections. Thus, that state's curriculum-reform document divides learning into much broader areas, such as "communication" and "personal and global stewardship."

And as California's experience shows, putting the entire puzzle together is a daunting enterprise. If there is a lesson here for other, similar efforts nationwide, it is that change is complicated and it moves at a glacial pace.

Although California has been working at curriculum-centered reform for eight years now, the effort has reached, at most, only two-thirds of the teachers in the state. The state's assessment system, which many say drives instruction, is only this year fully implementing a redesign that more closely matches the frameworks. And efforts to provide professional development for teachers to help them reorient instruction along the lines of the frameworks—particularly pre-service education for prospective teachers—have fallen far short of the need.

"The framework is the push, and then you have to ask yourself, 'How do you get that done?' " Mr. Honig says. "How you get that done is a very difficult, very complex question."

Nevertheless, the experience here has provided a beacon for educators nationwide. If the largest and most diverse state can define what it is students ought to know and be able to do, many say, surely other states and the nation as a whole can do the same.

Curriculum Reforms From Sputnik to Basics

To a degree, the curriculum has always figured in efforts to improve schooling. In the 1950's, Americans' fear of losing the space race led to the "Sputnik revolution." Schools nationwide beefed up math and science teaching. But education historians say those changes weren't widely implemented and had all but disappeared from schools by the mid-1970's.

In more recent decades, the "back to basics" movement fueled a renewed emphasis on basic arithmetic and reading skills. States also began to require "minimum competency" tests as a condition of high school graduation.

That movement achieved one of its central aims: It made strides in closing the achievement gap that separates African-American students from their white peers. But there were also drawbacks.

"I think it created an artificial ceiling for children and teachers, and when the minimum becomes the ceiling, it doesn't allow for stretching all children," says Barbara S. Nielsen, the state superintendent of schools in South Carolina. Her state, one of the first to adopt a basic-skills curriculum, is now working to develop frameworks modeled on the California approach.

The emphasis on basic academic skills also reinforced what many claimed was wrong with education in the first place. There was too much "drill and skill," too much emphasis on rote learning, and too few opportunities for students to learn to think.

Throughout most of the current education-reform era, however, few efforts have dealt directly with what is taught in schools.

A Nation at Risk, the landmark report that spawned the reform movement in 1983, called only for students to take more courses—four years of English, three of math, three of science, and so on—without saying what should make up the content of those courses.

"As if," George Leonard writes in *The Atlantic* magazine, "four rather than three years of English for students already turned off by the present system would make much of a difference."

In the end of the 1980's, however, 42 states had raised high school graduation requirements in response to the report.

"In fact, what happened was that people took the same courses they were teaching anyway and retitled them," says Diane S. Ravitch, a former U.S. assistant secretary for educational research and improvement.

In contrast, Ms. Ravitch says, reform should start with a definition of what students should know and be able to do, and work backward from there to redesign the system to achieve those ends.

And no place took that idea more seriously than the Golden State, she notes. "California led with the key to systemic reform," Ms. Ravitch says. "That is, if you want to change curriculum, where do you start?" The answer, she says, is "with the curriculum."

In addition to leading by example, California has also had a direct influence on national efforts to redefine curricula. Ms. Ravitch, for example, who as assistant secretary sponsored the national standards-setting projects, was the co-author of California's history and social-sciences framework. And her co-author, Charlotte Crabtree, is directing the national history-standards project.

Moreover, Ms. Ravitch's deputy, Francie M. Alexander, oversaw the development of California's frameworks as the state's deputy superintendent of public instruction.

'Dean of Instruction' Leads the Crusade

Educators in California credit Mr. Honig, the exuberant and outspoken former superintendent, with having spearheaded the state's crusade to overhaul the content of schooling. "He really has been the dean of instruction here in California," says Michael W. Kirst, an education professor at Stanford University.

In the early 1980's, when he was elected superintendent for the first time, Mr. Honig set out almost immediately to remake the state's curriculum frameworks. He has been an aggressive advocate for them ever since and has taken a direct hand in their development. At times, Mr. Honig says, he sent drafts of the frameworks back for revision up to nine times.

Although curriculum commissions were set up to put together the frameworks, Mr. Honig had a substantial say in choosing the teachers, subject-matter experts, and business people who were appointed to the panels.

Mr. Honig's continued participation in the frameworks process, however, appears unlikely. He was removed from his job in February 1993 following his conviction on four felony conflict-of-interest charges. Mr. Honig has said he will appeal those convictions.

As a result of Mr. Honig's stewardship, however, almost all of the frameworks have "a philosophical edge," Mr. Kirst says. The superintendent's leadership enabled the state to "get a document with specific content and pedagogical philosophies without watering it down to satisfy every special interest," he says. "Some groups are happy with that, and some are not happy."

One of Mr. Honig's specifications for the frameworks was that they have what he calls "pitch."

"You want them to be not too general so that there is no focus and not so specific that everybody can't buy into it," he says. Members of the curriculum committees said that balance was often difficult to strike.

That, coupled with the guiding principle that "less is more," also meant that tough decisions had to be made about what to keep in the frameworks and what to throw out. Much of what was cut or de-emphasized were topics that were once commonly taught in schools.

In math, computational skills were played down in favor of exposing students to what the document calls the "strands" of mathematics—geometry, statistics and probability, logic, measurement, algebra, patterns and functions, and number sense.

Some educators still contend that the emphasis in the language-arts framework on having young children read literature and whole texts came at the expense of instruction in phonics.

And the history-social sciences framework remains controversial among educators in that field partly because some social-studies educators contend its emphasis on history shortchanges economics, political science, sociology, and other subjects that traditionally fall under that umbrella.

Moreover, when it came time to choose textbooks reflecting the history-social sciences framework, a heated debate erupted over the proper emphasis on the history of various racial and ethnic groups. While the books, in keeping with the framework, attempted to strike a balance between stressing diversity and the common heritage, some argue that they didn't go far enough in presenting the multicultural view. In Oakland, for example, school officials refused to purchase any of the textbooks adopted under the framework.

Some of those philosophical shifts remain controversial. In the math framework, for example, parents still question the diminishing emphasis on drilling addition, multiplication, subtraction, and division skills into children.

"I still hear stories about people going into McDonald's, and the kids there can't make change," says Susan Braun, a school board member in San Diego. "People are very concerned their children won't be able to add."

And parents and teachers alike worry that their children won't learn phonetic skills in classrooms where literature is emphasized.

Indeed, these concerns highlight one of the fundamental conflicts in standards-setting and curriculum reform—the issue of depth over breadth. As teachers begin to stress long-term projects and deeper understandings for children, they touch on fewer topics. Why, parents who have become familiar with the curriculum through older children ask, does my younger child seem to be learning less in school?

In San Diego, Transforming a Vision

Of the eight visionary frameworks created so far, the math document was the first. Since then, reform-minded frameworks have been completed in language arts, science, health, history and the social sciences, foreign languages, the arts, and physical education. Completed in 1985 and updated again in 1992, the math framework brings the state's framework process full cycle.

The second revision, math educators say, was largely a fine-tuning aimed at making the state framework more compatible with national math standards. The 1985 framework, in contrast, marked a significant leap from traditional classroom instruction practices.

In San Diego—Ms. Fulkerson's district—administrators began to acquaint teachers with the coming changes a year before the frameworks were released.

"The frameworks are not something you can just give out to teachers and forget about it," says Vance Mills, the district's instructional-team leader for math, science, and education technology.

Teacher workshops and in-service sessions were held. The district also made an effort to link the frameworks with other reform efforts already going on there. San Diego is a district noted for its willingness to experiment with educational reforms, and many of those projects, such as the New Standards Project, a privately funded effort to develop what could become a national system of standards and assessments, were compatible with the changes called for in most of the frameworks.

District officials also have begun in recent years to take steps to make sure teachers have the equipment they need to teach in the new ways called for in the framework.

For example, in an effort to move students beyond arithmetic and into mathematics, the framework recommends extensive use of calculators in school. Now, every time the district buys a textbook, it buys a calculator as well.

"I can't say that ... you're going to see these in 100 percent of the classrooms," Mr. Mills says. "But what we've done is take away the excuse that we don't have the equipment."

The district also began "selling" the new approach to parents at every opportunity. San Diego schools have a "family math" program aimed at helping parents and children work together to improve their math skills. And many schools used the program as a vehicle to explain the framework to parents.

"Few parents were taught in these ways, and they think their kids are playing," says Susan Manning, a resource teacher at Ms. Fulkerson's school, where the "family math" program was used to great advantage.

In other districts, such as those in surrounding San Diego County, administrators have begun to hold "fairs" where examples of students' work are displayed to ease parents' concerns.

Despite the San Diego district's efforts, implementation of the frameworks at the classroom level has been uneven—as it is, observers say, across the state.

"You find that one-third of teachers are willing to go to volunteer sessions and look to make changes," Mr. Mills says. "Another one-third are not necessarily willing to volunteer, but they're willing to make changes, and you have to conduct the in-service [training] during school hours."

"The last third are the ones who will never change, and you just have to hope they'll retire," Mr. Mills says.

Statewide, even Mr. Honig estimates that no more than 7 percent of teachers have fully adapted their teaching styles to the frameworks. He adds, however, "I met a teacher, a guy in Los Angeles, who told me that in the last three years he has really shifted his teaching in the classroom to give a lot more problem-solving."

"Is he teaching the full framework? Probably not," Mr. Honig says. "Are his kids getting some benefit? Yes."

Ms. Fulkerson is a teacher who might fall in the first two-thirds of teachers described by Mr. Mills. She requested a copy of the math framework when it was published, and she uses it when she plans her course of instruction for the year.

Elsewhere at her school, there is evidence that other teachers are making similar efforts to transform the frameworks' philosophies into practice.

In one 1st-grade classroom, students have compiled a bar graph comparing all the sunny days of the year to the rainy days. In every class, there are boxes of manipulatives—interlocking plastic cubes, and beans, barrettes, and buttons to count—all tools intended to help students feel and see the math concepts they are learning.

Students in a 4th-grade classroom use calculators to work out story problems. Then, they put them aside to do some "mental math," figuring out methods to make computations quickly in their heads.

The problem they are given is $30 \times 4 + 5$. When a boy volunteers an answer, the teacher, Kristina Wenger, replies: "I want to know what Jared did in his mind to figure that out." Several methods for solving the equation are suggested.

As is called for in the framework, one lesson implicit in this exercise is that there is no one "right" way to solve a problem.

In a high school in another part of the city, however, the intractable nature of more traditional instructional practices is plainly evident.

One of the biggest changes for high schools in the math framework is the introduction of a course of study known as Math A. The course is meant to replace such traditional courses as general mathematics or consumer mathematics and to serve as a bridge between arithmetic and algebra.

Among its features are an emphasis on giving students authentic problems, rooted in real-life experiences. It recommends long-term projects for students to undertake collaboratively, and it incorporates some "higher mathematics," such as algebra and geometry.

The state provides five days of specialized training—more than is usually the case—for teachers of Math A and its successor course, Math B, for students who don't immediately go on to algebra.

In this high school, however, students are seated at individual desks in neat rows. They work alone on worksheets that keep them busy only as long as the 45-minute class period. The worksheets depict household items with three prices listed above them. The task for students is to guess which of the prices would have been correct in 1900.

To find out if their guesses are correct, the students are told to find the mean of an unrelated group of numbers listed in a corner near each picture.

While the exercise employs some practical information, it is hardly the kind of real-life problem that students might encounter outside school.

"We're trying a lot of things, and we're trying to learn from them, but we don't have it all figured out yet," says Thomas W. Payzant, who was the district's superintendent of schools before being named assistant U.S. secretary for elementary and secondary education.

Enough Training and the 'Right Kind' of Training

Like many observers of the California effort, Mr. Payzant believes the biggest obstacle to implementing the frameworks is the lack of professional development to support the kinds of fundamental changes teachers must make to teach in the ways the frameworks intended.

The state allows schools to set aside eight noninstructional days each year for training. The 1992 math framework, however, suggests that teachers need at least 10 days of in-service training just to teach it correctly.

Moreover, funds to pay the cost of such training or for the wages of substitute teachers are scarce.

"It's hard when you get into budget-cutting, and if you have to make tough decisions," Mr. Payzant says. "Very typically, staff-development time is the first thing that goes."

San Diego has had to make some of those tough decisions. The school system's budget declined by $22 million last year and is expected to decrease by up to $9 million more this year, Mr. Payzant says.

The budget cuts force schools such as Freese to pick and choose among the professional-development opportunities available to their teachers. The question for Freese's staff this year was: Should teachers attend a countywide language-arts conference or go to a similar two-day event in mathematics? The school opted for the former.

The same kinds of financial pressures are working against schools statewide.

Hit hard by the recession and cuts in federal spending on defense, state spending for education deteriorated sharply in the late 1980's. The state slipped from 31st in the nation in 1982-83 to 43rd in 1992-93 in per-pupil expenditures, according to Mr. Kirst.

It isn't, however, just a matter of getting enough time or money for professional development. Having the right kinds of training opportunities is equally important.

"Even the best skill-training workshops are insufficient for the kind of major changes we want to get out of the frameworks," says Mr. Odden, who, with Mr. Kirst, directs Policy Analysis for California Education, a state policy-research consortium.

What is also needed, says Milbrey W. McLaughlin, the director of the Center for Research on the Context of Secondary School Teaching at Stanford University, are "learning communities" that support teachers as they attempt to unlearn old methods and construct new practices for themselves.

Ms. McLaughlin conducted research comparing California teachers with teachers in Michigan, where little state-level reform activity was taking place.

In schools where teachers could observe their colleagues' classrooms or meet to talk about practice, she found, the frameworks were "strong stuff that forced productive, good discussions around issues of content and pedagogy." In both states, however, such discussions never took place in schools where those kinds of opportunities were unavailable.

To address some of those concerns, a handful of comprehensive professional-development programs are now under way throughout the state.

The California Math Project, for example, operates at 17 sites across the state and links teachers with university math educators for three to four weeks of training. The teachers then return to their schools to provide support and training for their colleagues. Those "teacher leaders" also receive follow-up attention over a period of three to four years, according to Nicholas Branca, who directs the effort.

"Teachers need to take the time to understand the mathematics involved," Mr. Branca says. "It's almost like having a different mind set about what mathematics is and how you're teaching it."

Most elementary school math teachers, he adds, have had little—or no—training in the subject before becoming teachers.

The California Mathematics Project was launched in the early 1980's, even before the 1985 framework was in place. Two years ago, similar projects were put in place in the seven other subject areas.

Another program, which is supported by a grant from the National Science Foundation, draws teachers together from middle schools to discuss ways to improve math education. The program, known as the Mathematics Renaissance Project, has so far provided support for more than 200 teachers statewide.

Experts point out, however, that those numbers are still very small, representing only a portion of the more than 200,000 teachers who could benefit from them.

Moreover, at the college level, state officials concede, there is no mechanism for making sure that education-school students are exposed to the frameworks' concepts and philosophies before they become teachers. Those universities and colleges that are providing such training for students—and there are some—are doing so on their own.

Efforts by states to implement curricular standards are also thwarted by standardized tests that bear little or no resemblance to the kind of teaching called for in standards-setting or curricular-reform efforts.

In 1987, California began an ambitious redesign of its assessment that was aimed at matching the tests to the frameworks' goals and at measuring, for the first time, what students are able to do with what they know.

That effort came to an abrupt halt in 1990, however, when then-Gov. George Deukmejian, embroiled in a feud with Mr. Honig, cut off funding for the California Assessment Program, known less formally as CAP.

Some schools across the state that had adapted their teaching to the frameworks saw their students' test scores dip—particularly in the area of language arts.

In the spring of 1993, however, the state was finally poised to put that puzzle piece in place. The state's newly redesigned assessments were to be administered to nearly every student in reading, writing, and math in grades 4, 8, and 10. The assessments are also expected to be expanded to include history and science in grades 5, 8, and 10 next year.

"If anything drives the curriculum in California," Mr. Mills says, "it is the CAP. School-by-school results are published, and they get a lot of attention. When we get that CAP in place, I think you'll see a major change."

Textbooks and curricular materials—another piece in the state's systemic reform effort—have also been slow to change.

California is the second-largest market among the 22 states that approve textbooks at the state level for use in classrooms; only Texas buys more books. Most states permit local districts to choose their own textbooks.

The state hoped to use its considerable clout with the textbook-publishing industry to pressure publishers to produce materials that would complement its frameworks.

In math, the state board of education set out to make those intentions known early on by rejecting all of the textbooks submitted by publishers after the 1985 framework was adopted. Publishers were permitted to try again but, Mr. Honig says, their next efforts "were still only about 20 percent there." As a result, teachers went for years with either old texts or new ones that didn't match up with the framework.

"All of the new books are really heavily into the manipulatives, but they don't do the business of teaching math," said David Crum, a bilingual 2nd-grade teacher at Euclid Elementary School in San Diego. "I actually keep my framework in my room to refer to because the books are so weird."

For other teachers, administrators say, it was easier to simply rely on whatever textbooks were at hand. To plug the gap in textbooks and materials, the state has been developing curriculum units that teachers could insert into their teaching. That effort, however, is far from complete.

There are signs, however, that the next round of math textbooks may represent a significant improvement over the previous generation.

The Glencoe division of Macmillan/McGraw-Hill in 1993 published the first textbook designed for California's Math A course. Designed as a resource book for students, the new book contains suggestions for long-term projects and activities and, in appendices at the back, lists the concepts, applications, formulas, weights, and measures students will need to know to carry out the suggested activities.

Noting, for example, that a person of average metabolism will gain a pound of weight after consuming 3,500 calories more than normal, one such activity asks students to work with a partner and keep track of the calories they consume each day. Then, pupils are asked to find their average daily calorie consumption and to determine how many calories they must consume to gain or lose weight.

For City Schools, 'Pie in the Sky'?

Even if they support curricular frameworks, classroom teachers face practical problems in implementing them—problems, they contend, that were never anticipated in systemic reform efforts.

Patricia Climes, who teaches Math A at Crawford High School in San Diego, points out that, on average, one-third of her students are absent from class on any given day. The high absentee rate, she says, prevents her from assigning long-term projects to her students.

Often, Ms. Climes and other teachers say, the students in Math A classes are those who have the most difficulties in school. Many are poor, and some are also recent immigrants with poor command of English. The teachers contend that many of the students have become indifferent to their efforts.

"Sometimes, I feel many of us in the city schools feel some of these materials are a little 'pie in the sky' for our kids," she says.

But, if the frameworks are to be truly successful, district administrators say, they must work with all students.

Moreover, other teachers say, they tend not to undertake cooperative-learning tasks with their students simply because the desks in their classrooms are not suited for that purpose. The desks vary in height, for example, or books tend to slide onto the floor.

For the most part, however, California educators say, the pieces of the puzzle are beginning to fall into place. "What has not been the biggest complaint has been the unwillingness of the system to respond," Mr. Kirst says. "There's widespread recognition of the frameworks. A lot of districts are briefing teachers on them, and a lot of teachers are trying them."

Among those who are trying them, many say the new content and methods are making a difference. "I think it's making a difference in their self-concepts, in their risk-taking, and in their math," Ms. Fulkerson, the kindergarten and 1st-grade teacher in San Diego, says. "In my classroom this year, I'm not seeing kids who are feeling bad about themselves in math."

Ms. Fulkerson's students, it should be noted, come from what the district calls a "minority isolated" school. More than 43 percent of the students at Freese are African-American; another 22 percent are Hispanic, and 15 percent are Filipino. Between 65 percent and 75 percent come from families poor enough to qualify for the federal free- and reduced-price-lunch program.

It has also helped California's curriculum project, educators say, that the state's math framework and the N.C.T.M.'s national standards share some common philosophies.

"We're all moving in the same direction," Jack Price, the co-director of the Center for Science and Math Education at California State Polytechnic University in Pomona, says. "In fact, all of the subject areas are all singing out of the same hymn book."

The existence of the national standards, he adds, may have been the primary reason publishers of math textbooks are beginning to make major changes in their materials.

The national standards have now been incorporated into curriculum guidelines of one sort or another in 40 states and the District of Columbia, says Mary Lindquist, the current president of the math teachers' group.

Perhaps more important, in a nationwide survey conducted last year, 48 percent of high school teachers and 22 percent of elementary school teachers said they were "well aware" of the national math standards.

However, real classroom-by-classroom change may still be years away. Mr. Price predicts it may not come until the turn of the century.

And, all the while, new discoveries are being made in the sciences, history is growing longer each day, and new works of literature are becoming classics. The definition of what students should "know and be able to do" may necessarily grow and change as a result.

"One half of the mathematics we know today," says Iris Carl, a former president of the N.C.T.M., "has been invented since World War II."

California updates its frameworks every seven years. And educators in this state warn that national standards-setting efforts also must insure that their standards are fluid while, at the same time, working to put them into common practice.

However, until real change begins to occur at the classroom level, Mr. Payzant says, "everyone has to be vigilant on keeping the focus on improving teaching and learning for all students."

"If not," he says, "this will run the risk of being viewed as one more misguided reform effort in the history of American education."

TAKING ACCOUNT

By Robert Rothman

In this chapter, we examine states' efforts to overhaul the way they hold schools accountable for student performance. Concluding that more traditional practices of regulating school "inputs" have failed, states are moving to set outcomes for student performance, developing new ways of assessing such outcomes, and freeing schools to determine how to attain them.

TALLAHASSEE, FLA.—In the paneled Cabinet room of the modern state Capitol here, a group of educators and public officials earlier this year laid out the future of Florida education.

Known as the Florida Commission on Education Reform and Accountability, the panel approved a set of measures to assess the progress of schools toward seven performance goals set in a 1991 state law. Schools, which under the law are required to develop their own plans for meeting the goals, must show "adequate progress" on such standards as insuring that all students can communicate and can solve mathematical problems. Schools that fail risk intervention by the state.

The new system holds schools responsible for results, but frees educators from mandates about how to achieve them. And it represents a 180-degree shift in the way that Florida governs its schools.

Florida's bold action places it at the leading edge of a national movement on school accountability that is essentially shifting the emphasis in schools from "inputs" to "outcomes."

To accomplish their educational goals, states have traditionally dictated in considerable detail how time and resources should be used in schools—from the number of teachers and books in the school library to the academic schedule and the content of every course. As a way of holding schools accountable for meeting the goals, students were required before graduation to take a basic-skills test to demonstrate their levels of achievement.

Pennsylvanians rally against the state board of education's controversial plan to implement a system of outcome-based education. States are finding it is a lot more difficult in practice than it is on paper to overhaul the way they hold schools accountable for student performance.

This approach resulted in more students mastering the basic skills and passing minimum-competency tests, but it didn't do much to foster higher-order thinking skills. And it severely limited innovation and creative teaching.

Now, states are developing a new compact—a new arrangement in which broad standards are set for what students should know and be able to do and schools are free to determine how to get their students there. In return, though, schools will be held accountable for results.

Charles W. Fowler, the superintendent of the Sarasota County public schools and a member of the Florida accountability commission, says the new approach is much more likely than the previous effort to lead to high levels of student performance.

"It's a welcome opportunity for professional educators, who for years functioned under the handicap of having other people tell them how to do their job," Mr. Fowler says. "Now we're saying, 'We will not tell you what to do, but there is going to be accountability for what students ought to learn.'"

Not surprisingly, Florida and other states are finding out that putting these new accountability systems into place is a lot more difficult than designing them on paper. Among the most contentious issues are:

- Defining performance standards. Deciding what outcomes will be expected from students has sparked heated debates in a number of states, but particularly in Pennsylvania. There, the House in February 1993 voted to kill its entire outcome-based program, under fierce pressure from critics who contended that a set of outcomes adopted by the state board of education fostered the teaching of "values," rather than academic skills and knowledge.

- Eliminating existing regulations. Getting rid of the "process" regulations that until now have largely defined educational systems has proved equally controversial. In New Hampshire, education groups rebelled when the state board proposed to remove rules that specify how services are delivered in schools. They argued that, in the absence of such rules, districts would fail to provide equitable services for all students.

- Developing assessments. Performance-based systems demand that students exhibit abilities seldom measured by traditional tests and that they demonstrate they can actually use knowledge, not simply fill in preselected answers. In places where new outcome standards have been defined, the rich assessments needed to measure progress toward them don't yet exist. And, in the interim, states are using existing tests that are not aligned with the curricula and pedagogies being used in the schools.

- Creating incentive systems. To motivate schools to produce the desired results, states are developing systems of rewards and penalties. In the process, policymakers are struggling with questions of efficacy and fairness. Doubts are often raised about the power of such arrangements to motivate individuals at the school level, and about whether the school is the proper unit of accountability.

- Agreeing on delivery standards. Even those who support outcome-based systems argue that they could exaggerate the inequities that exist among schools unless all students have access to a high-quality education. In a report issued in the fall of 1992, Linda Darling-Hammond, the co-director of the National Center on Restructuring Education, Schools, and Teaching at Teachers College, Columbia University, argues that, for accountability to succeed, states must also insure that all schools have the capacity to provide the type of education that will enable all students to meet the standards.

"Outcome standards alone cannot guarantee accountable schools," Ms. Darling-Hammond writes.

'Outcomes' Mean Many Things to Many People

Like many movements in education, the idea of "outcome-based education" has swept through the nation rapidly. In addition to Florida, 26 states claim to have developed such systems, and another nine are moving toward them, according to the Education Commission of the States.

But the term has also taken on the characteristics of a buzz word, meaning different things to different people. Several states are using student outcomes as part of their systems for accrediting schools; others say they are outcome based if they have implemented performance-based assessments.

"Anything with a test on the end is 'outcome based,' " says Lauren B. Resnick, the director of the Learning Research and Development Center at the University of Pittsburgh.

In general, educators use the term "outcome-based education" to refer to a system that specifies the performance—such as an understanding of math concepts or an appreciation of different types of literature—that students must demonstrate. Such systems generally include new forms of assessment that enable students to demonstrate such performances.

By contrast, most education systems specify "inputs"—such as requirements that students study four years of English and three years of math—

and assume that requiring the inputs would lead to desired outcomes. Tests generally measure a survey of knowledge in such coursework.

As a document from Florida explains the shift, the new system asks not "How many students are enrolled in a class called Algebra I?" but "How many students can successfully apply algebra in solving a problem?"

Few places have adopted the outcome-based approach as comprehensively as Florida. And few states have taken such a long road to get there.

In an 11-page memorandum to the state's accountability commission, Sen. Bob Johnson, a former member of the panel, showed that Florida has had a 30-year history of attempting to hold schools accountable for student performance.

As early as 1971, the memo shows, the legislature passed a comprehensive "educational accountability act," which, among other provisions, required the state commissioner of education to establish educational objectives for each subject area and grade level. The law also directed the commissioner to develop a statewide assessment system to determine "the degree to which established educational objectives had been achieved."

In carrying out the law, the state department of education created a basic-skills test and required students to pass it in order to graduate from high school. In a landmark ruling that helped spur the spread of minimum-competency testing throughout the country, a state judge ruled in 1983 that the state could legally withhold diplomas from students who failed to pass the test.

Michael W. Kirst, a professor of education at Stanford University, says the accountability system of the early 1970's served its purpose at the time by insuring that all graduates attained a minimum level of knowledge and skills. That approach "may have been the right thing for that period of American history," he says. The newer program, however, in keeping with today's reform ideas, is aimed at raising student performance to a higher level.

Florida was not alone in attempting to hold schools accountable for student performance.

In a wave that began in the 1970's and intensified after the 1983 release of *A Nation at Risk*, most states adopted some type of statewide testing program. Today, 47 states have such a program.

States have also used the test results in a variety of ways. Thirty-six states now use "report cards" that show schools and the public at large how schools are performing. The report cards also include data on such other indicators of school quality as attendance and graduation rates.

The goal of such programs is to focus the attention of educators and the public on the results so they will strive to improve them. As a report by the Southern Regional Education Board states: "What gets measured gets taught. What gets reported gets taught twice as well."

And that is especially true when "high stakes" are attached to the tests. As a number of researchers have found, teachers have tended to focus almost exclusively on the narrow skills and knowledge the tests measure. And, as a recent study by researchers at the State University of New York confirms, schools have also attempted to boost their standing on the tests by placing large numbers of students in special-education programs or by retaining them in grade so as not to have to test those students.

Moreover, the published report cards have failed to stir the public to agitate for improved performance as much as their advocates had hoped. Nor have they prompted schools to change their programs, according to Mr. Kirst. "There is not any evidence that districts really paid attention to these," he says.

But Lynn M. Cornett, the SREB's vice president for state services, says more recent versions of report cards, which include information on each school in a state, are more likely to generate pressure for improvements.

"People think, where change has to occur, they need information," she says. "They need it at the school level."

In addition to issuing report cards, a handful of states have also attempted to hold schools accountable for student performance by rewarding schools that perform well and penalizing schools with high levels of failures.

According to a 1991 SREB survey, seven states—including Florida—had school-incentive programs, and, as part of its landmark reform package, Kentucky is scheduled to begin one in 1994.

But the survey found that the results have been mixed. A program in Pennsylvania, for example—which provided funds for schools where reading and math scores increased, dropout rates decreased, or the number of students taking the Scholastic Aptitude Test increased—had little effect on most schools. Teachers and principals in schools that did not receive awards were not familiar with the program.

In addition, in Pennsylvania and other states, budget problems forced states to cut funding for the incentive programs, which decreased their effect. In Florida, for example, 585 schools shared $10 million in 1989, compared with 343 schools that shared $19.5 million in 1986. The program was scrapped in 1990.

Similarly, programs to provide penalties for failing schools have had, at best, a mixed record.

A study by the Consortium for Policy Research in Education, which examined the effects of efforts in Kentucky and New Jersey to take over school districts that are failing academically, concludes that "takeover programs can have little to do with long-term educational improvement."

The report notes that, in Kentucky, which attempted to take over the Floyd and Whitley county districts, the state intervention was focused on complying with state rules, rather than raising student achievement. And in New Jersey, which took over the Jersey City schools, the state emphasized the need to alter the governance and management of the district.

"In our opinion," the CPRE report states, "if takeover fails to improve teaching and learning, it is not worth the stigma suffered by school personnel and communities."

Others question whether schools should bear the primary brunt of accountability measures, or whether districts and states should be held equally responsible for their roles in providing all students with access to a high-quality education.

A Growing Sense That Top-Down Measures Failed

In Florida, at least, educators contend that the accountability measures failed to do much to improve schools because the state imposed too many mandates to allow schools to educate students effectively.

"The previous accountability systems didn't work because they were largely top-down," says Mr. Fowler, the Sarasota superintendent. "When you're trying to do quality control on a system of two million children and 110,000 teachers—even if they are only in 67 school districts—you just can't do that from Tallahassee."

Mr. Fowler says the heavy degree of state control was not limited to education, and reflects the rapid growth in the state.

"As the population grew, and communities grew, the legislature stepped into the breach," he says. "If anybody had a problem, anywhere in Florida, it ended up on a legislator's desk."

"Education was not excepted from that," he continues. "If somebody tells a legislator kids don't write well, the next thing, there was a bill to improve writing."

But the effect of the mandates was to hamstring teachers and administrators, says Ruth Holmes, a Chapter 1 resource teacher from Pensacola and a member of the accountability commission.

"A lot of times, money was for a certain program, and you could only use it for that certain program," she says. "If you saw children needing services, you couldn't use the resources, because they were from a mandate from the state legislature."

By 1991, the message that Florida's accountability system had failed had reached the legislature.

"The legislature has mandated and mandated, ordered and ordered school boards, and it hasn't worked," says Rep. Douglas L. (Tim) Jamerson, the chairman of the House education committee.

In response, lawmakers agreed to a completely new system, known as "Blueprint 2000." The legislation establishes seven education goals, modeled after the national education goals. The goals address children's readiness to start school, the graduation rate, student performance, the learning environment, school safety, teachers and staff, and adult literacy.

The statute also directs each school to conduct a "needs assessment" and to create a school-improvement plan to meet the goals. Schools that fail to demonstrate adequate progress after three years of assistance and intervention will be subject to penalties.

To provide greater flexibility to schools, the measure also places more than four dozen statutes in abeyance and waives another 15. Certain laws, however, including those dealing with civil rights, student safety, and exceptional children, are not waived.

To carry out the plan, the legislature also created the commission on accountability and charged it with developing performance standards for each goal area and methods of assessing progress. Last year, the panel came up with 22 such standards, including one that states: "All Florida students graduate from secondary schools with a certificate showing mastery of the student performance standards and outcomes."

The 10 student-performance standards range from "Florida students communicate in English and other languages using concepts, prose, symbols, reports, audio and video recordings, speeches, graphic displays, and computer-based programs" and "Florida students use numeric operations and concepts to describe, analyze, disaggregate, communicate, and synthesize numeric data, and to identify and solve problems," to "Florida students display responsibility, self-esteem, sociability, self-management, integrity, and honesty" and "Florida students work cooperatively to successfully complete a project or activity."

Philip D. Lewis, a former state Senate president and a member of the accountability commission, says the legislation was born out of "total frustration" with the quality of education in Florida.

"The legislature came to the conclusion that something dramatic had to be done," he says. "This is dramatic. I don't even know if they know how dramatic this is."

But in Pennsylvania, critics of that state's outcome-based education program are well aware of how radical it is, and they don't like it.

There, the state board of education last year adopted a plan that, like Florida's, scraps high school graduation requirements and instead establishes statewide outcomes for student performance and requires districts to develop their own plans for how they will attain the outcomes.

In January 1993, after some delays and protests, the board adopted 55 learner outcomes that all students must attain in order to graduate from high school. They include: "All students demonstrate knowledge of basic concepts and principles of physical, chemical, biological, and earth sciences"; "all students develop and defend a position on current issues confronting the United States and other nations"; and "all students explore and articulate the similarities and differences among various cultures and the history and contributions of diverse cultural groups, including groups to which they belong."

But in February 1993, the state House voted overwhelmingly to nullify the rules. In part, the vote reflected the view that the system is untried and potentially disastrous.

"Those making a radical change have the burden of proof to show it works," says Bill Sloane, an aide to State Rep. Ron Gamble, the sponsor of the amendment to kill the rules. "Unless and until the proponents produce research showing it to be effective, I don't think the state government ought to be doing anything."

"If they want to experiment in a couple of places, that's one thing," Mr. Sloane continues. "But don't mandate an experiment statewide in 501 school districts."

While critics in Pennsylvania questioned the system as a whole, they particularly objected to a number of the outcomes adopted by the state board. To many critics, these outcomes imposed "values" on students by measuring their cooperation and tolerance, not simply their reading and writing skills.

"We believe the purpose of the public schools is to teach academics. Period," Mr. Sloane says.

Susan H. Fuhrman, the director of the Consortium for Policy Research in

Education at Rutgers University, calls the Pennsylvania House action "a real shame."

"You shouldn't throw out the idea because of a disagreement over the outcomes," she says. "In a sense, that's what we've been doing for 200 years."

Ms. Fuhrman acknowledges that the outcomes are controversial and lead to "culture wars." But, she says, "that's a healthy discussion. We ought to decide as a society what we want."

While states such as Florida and Pennsylvania have pursued broad outcome goals for students that cut across disciplines, other states, such as California, have chosen to define what students should know and be able to do along more traditional subject-area lines. In the coming years, which approach is more productive—as well as the details of what goes into such outcomes—will continue to be the topic of heated discussion.

Outcome Systems Demand New Methods of Assessment

The debates over outcomes in Pennsylvania and elsewhere have also focused attention on another potential problem in developing the new accountability systems: whether states will be able to measure the performance goals they have set.

Unlike traditional testing systems, which tend to measure students' knowledge of facts, the new outcomes generally demand that students demonstrate their abilities to use their knowledge, as well as other abilities that are seldom tapped by conventional tests. These demands require a new testing technology, which as yet hasn't been perfected.

"We know how to assess how kids are doing in math," Mr. Kirst of Stanford says. "It's not clear how to assess kids' management of time or if they work well in groups."

Eva L. Baker, the co-director of the National Center for Research on Evaluation, Standards, and Student Testing at the University of California at Los Angeles, says the new forms of assessment raise a number of issues that must be resolved if they are to be used in accountability systems.

One significant problem relates to equity. To demonstrate that they can understand historical events or solve math problems, different students may write different essays or submit a wide variety of materials in a portfolio. But how can states hold schools accountable for vastly different student work that is based on different background knowledge and interests?

"We're caught in a dilemma when we try to contextualize [assessment] and make things relevant, and, at the same time, make things uniform and comparable," Ms. Baker says.

Another problem is insuring that the new assessments are technically sound so that valid inferences can be drawn from them.

A recent RAND Corporation study of Vermont's pioneering portfolio-assessment program shows the technical problems that can arise in shifting to new forms of assessment.

Vermont's program, the first statewide program to include portfolios, measures 4th and 8th graders' math and writing performance on a range of criteria, such as students' writing "voice" and their understanding of math tasks.

But in analyzing the results from the first full year of implementation, the RAND researchers found that the "rater reliability"—the extent to which raters agreed on the quality of a student's work—was low. They recommended that the state report the results of the portfolio assessment at the state level only, where results were sufficiently reliable.

Ms. Baker notes that, if states report unreliable results, they can draw improper conclusions about the quality of schools—a serious problem if states intend to hold schools accountable for the results.

"When the technical stuff isn't close, people make bad inferences," she says. "They think schools are worse than they are, but maybe [that's because] the measures are straining to provide information people thought they wanted."

"What policymakers want," Ms. Baker says, "sometimes they can't have."

Florida officials, for their part, say they continue to want such information. Ms. Holmes, the Pensacola teacher, says the new assessments would provide a much better gauge of student abilities than conventional tests. "My students could do science, they could write, they could do math and work out problems," she says. "What they couldn't do was bubble in answers on a test."

Mr. Fowler, the Sarasota superintendent, also says that the new measures would help improve teaching by breaking down disciplinary boundaries in schools.

"Real life for students is not organized by academic disciplines," he says. "If you are hired by a bank, you are not going to, in the first hour, do math; in the second, economics; and in the third, write reports."

But while states wait for the new measures to be perfected, officials are building the accountability systems by using existing measures that they admit don't match the goals of the new systems.

When the Florida accountability commission selected the measures that will be used until the new assessments are ready, for example, members debated which test to use as a measure of student achievement—the basic-skills High School Competency Test, which is required for graduation, or a higher-level Grade 10 Achievement Test.

In the end, the panel decided to use both, even though members acknowledge that they do not match the standards in Blueprint 2000. "Are these perfect measures? No," says Michael C. Biance, the executive director of the accountability commission. "That's why it's a transition."

Mr. Biance notes, though, that the panel kept its eye on the higher standards. As evidence, he points out that it agreed to drop a proposed requirement that schools attain minimum proportions of students passing the competency test on their first attempt.

Although the panel's motivation was primarily to permit schools greater flexibility, its action also has the advantage of focusing schools' attention on the long-range goal, rather than the interim, lower standard, Mr. Biance says. "This gets us away from 'dumbing down,'" he says.

Mr. Kirst of Stanford also dismisses the concern that the interim measures would send a mixed signal to schools. "In the 70's, [minimum competency] was driving the whole system," he says. "Now, we've got the view that there is a difference between minimum competency and what we need to aspire to."

Loosening Regulations Also Stirs Controversy

In creating the new accountability systems, states have pledged to loosen regulations on schools to allow them flexibility to meet the standards for performance. But in practice, eliminating regulations has proved almost as contentious as setting outcomes for student learning.

Part of the tension has arisen because lawmakers, accustomed to keeping tabs on the dollars they send to schools, are reluctant to cut the strings attached to those funds.

"We have to let people at the local level earn their way out of that deal," Mr. Lewis, the former president of the Florida Senate, says. "Is the legislature going to send $8 million to $10 million to the local level and say, 'Go forth and do good'? That ain't gonna happen."

Educators are also quick to point to the reasons the rules were adopted in the first place, and are loath to abolish them.

"You can focus more on outcomes, but it's not necessarily desirable to think about getting rid of the process regulations," says Ms. Fuhrman, the director of CPRE, the policy-research consortium. "There are equity concerns."

Adds Pascal D. Forgione Jr., the state superintendent of public instruction in Delaware: "One has to remove them with purpose and direction. We're not here just to sweep the minefield."

The tension over eliminating rules reached a breaking point last year in New Hampshire, where the state board set off an outcry by proposing to abolish its standards for school approval.

Board members argued that, by eliminating numerical caps on class sizes and a mandated ratio of guidance counselors to students, for example, schools could have greater flexibility in providing services to students. Although elementary schools had been free under a previous regulation to petition to waive the regulations, few schools actually took advantage of that freedom.

But the move to abandon standards sparked a furor from education groups. "If you gut the regulations, what do you need a state department of education for?" asks Mel Myler, the executive director of the National Education Association-New Hampshire. "It's the only bastion within the state to provide some equality of educational opportunity."

In the end, the board agreed to reinstate some numerical requirements, which made the revisions "palatable" to groups like the N.E.A. affiliate. Nevertheless, a legislative committee voted to oppose the rule, which takes effect in June 1993.

Even in states that have agreed to relax rules, the tension between state control and local flexibility remains palpable.

In South Carolina, for example, where the legislature in 1989 adopted a plan to free high-performing schools from most regulations, the program isn't reaching all schools that can benefit from it, a study by CPRE found. In fact, the report states, it may be the low-performing schools that most need deregulation. "Unlike currently eligible schools," it points out, "they have not flourished under the prevailing rules."

And in Florida, teachers warn that the state standards themselves may restrict local schools. Although schools are theoretically free to come up with their own plans for improvement, the state measures may, in fact, direct what such improvements must address.

"I understand the need to set standards," says Brenda Emerson, a teacher of visually impaired students at Princeton Elementary School in Orlando, Fla. "But attaching standards to every goal area defeats the purpose of allowing everyone to create what they need."

Indeed, simply setting standards and measuring student progress won't, in itself, insure that schools improve. Schools must also have the wherewithal to bring about changes.

"What if you come up with some innovative things, such as technology, that cost a lot of money?" Ms. Emerson asks. "If we come up with a great plan, how will we fund it?"

Many schools, moreover, may be unable even to dream up innovative ideas, Mr. Kirst says. Without the proper professional development that would introduce teachers to new practices and assist them in teaching in new ways, schools will fall back on old methods.

"The assumption is, you let off input regulations, and 1,000 flowers will bloom," he says. "Our findings are that 1,000 flowers do not bloom without help."

As a result, the new accountability systems may reinforce the inequalities that exist among schools. Those with the capacity to innovate may thrive, while those that lack such a capacity will languish.

Noting such equity concerns, Ms. Baker of U.C.L.A. says, "What worries me is the mentality that tests, pretty much by themselves, will create educational nirvana."

Educators Considering Standards for Delivery, Too

To address such problems, some educators have begun to think about a new set of "school delivery standards" to accompany the standards for student performance. The additional standards would insure that schools have the capacity to deliver the type of instruction needed to bring all students up to the performance standards.

Such standards also reflect the legal requirement the Florida court imposed in issuing its ruling allowing the use of a test to deny diplomas. The test could only be used, it ruled, if students had been exposed to the instruction the test measured.

In her report, Ms. Darling-Hammond of Teachers College outlines a dozen "standards of practice for learner-centered schools." They include: all students should have access to the school funding necessary to fulfill standards of excellence; all students should have access to well-prepared, fully qualified teachers; and all students should have access to a rich and challenging curriculum.

"A focus on outcomes with unequal allocations of resources won't enable students to achieve the outcomes, or schools to organize themselves to give students a fair shot," she says.

In a similar vein, the National Council on Education Standards and Testing, a Congressionally chartered panel that called for national standards and a related system of assessments, also urged that delivery standards be developed to measure schools' abilities to provide high-quality instruction.

But that recommendation sparked a fierce debate in Congress. Although the council had recommended that states could select their own delivery standards from among those developed by groups of states, Democrats insisted on national delivery standards to hold all states equally accountable. But governors and the Bush Administration resisted the national standards, arguing, in part, that a system of school-delivery standards smacked of the same kind of input standards the new accountability systems were trying to get away from.

The debate over delivery standards was expected to recur in 1993, when Congress again considers the issue of national standards and assessment systems.

But whatever the outcome of the debate, those involved in setting up the new accountability systems see them as perhaps their best chance of improving schools. And they plan to take full advantage of this opportunity.

"We are going to have one chance to do this," Ms. Holmes, the Pensacola teacher, says. "If we don't [succeed], we'll see more and more mandates. We can't fail."

BASIC TRAINING

By Ann Bradley

In this chapter, we examine the importance of professional development in insuring that teachers become a vital link in transforming schools and supporting student learning.

MONTPELIER, VT.—In the summer of 1992, the state of Vermont virtually exploded with learning opportunities for teachers. More than 1,000 educators gave up a week of vacation—most of them without pay—to study math, science, geography, elementary education, and art, and to develop plans to improve their schools.

Vermont's ambitious overhaul of schooling for its 90,000 students—known as the Green Mountain Challenge and driven by the aim of nothing less than "very high skills for every student: no exceptions, no excuses"—fueled this intense interest in professional development.

In fact, says Richard P. Mills, the state's commissioner of education, the only way to achieve the state's goal is to make professional development an ongoing process for every teacher and principal in Vermont. "I believe that teachers will not only shape systemic reform," Mr. Mills asserts, "but if we share the risk with them, teachers will drive it."

In Vermont, teachers have been involved in redesigning the education system since the get-go. They put together, for example, the first statewide assessment that uses portfolios of students' work. Just as notably, the state has adopted innovative policies for teacher education and relicensure that officials believe could transform the teaching profession.

Both inside and outside the state, Vermont is winning high marks for recognizing that teachers must play a central role in rethinking schools and for supporting their work and professional growth. Unfortunately, such a vision is not universally shared. Too often, teachers and their needs have

At one of the state's math network meetings in Johnson, Vt., Kim Fellows, left, and Terry Johnson discuss the state's student portfolio program. Most reformers agree that the professional development of teachers must be vastly improved if the school-reform movement is to succeed.

been overlooked in the rush to make changes in schools.

Teachers' Learning: 'Centerpiece, Not Afterthought'

As far back as the 1840's, notes David K. Cohen, a professor of education and social policy at Michigan State University, Horace Mann wrote about the importance of providing teachers with adequate learning opportunities. The subject was also of concern to John Dewey, who organized his laboratory school at the University of Chicago with teachers' intellectual development in mind.

The current push to reform schools to foster students' problem-solving skills is placing incredible demands on the nation's 2.4 million public school teachers. Such changes are clearly no less revolutionary than those being urged for students.

But without serious attention to professional development, the reforms have little chance to take hold and succeed.

Complaints are already being voiced, for example, that the sweeping reform of Kentucky's education system hasn't provided enough learning opportunities for teachers. And in California, which has pioneered a set of curriculum frameworks, state officials acknowledge that the vast task of educating teachers has lagged behind.

Indeed, professional development suffers from a nearly universal poor image: one marked by undemanding after-school workshops attended by educators who see no connection to their daily working lives. Often, it is the first thing slashed in tight budget times.

Nothing short of a radical rethinking of the importance and role of professional development is what is needed. Opportunities to learn and experiment must be built into teachers' workdays and years. And powerful incentives must be created for teachers to pursue serious learning for the sake of their professional growth.

Attending to teachers' learning needs must be "a centerpiece, not an afterthought," says Marla Ucelli, a senior program adviser at the Rockefeller Foundation. "If we don't deal with the issue of ongoing training and renewal for people in the classroom, then none of the reforms we think are valuable are going to stick."

While the reform movement has coalesced around images of students as active learners, less attention has been paid to what teachers should know and be able to do in order to support such student enterprise.

"Serious reform has to involve serious learning" for teachers, Mr. Cohen warns. "There are relatively few people who have a sense of how enormous the learning is, and how difficult it will be to encourage it." In a new book, the Michigan State professor and several colleagues describe this new "teaching for understanding."

In stark contrast to the prevailing model of transmitting knowledge and facts to passive students, teaching for understanding means actively engaging students with concepts to promote deep understanding. It would require vast changes in what most teachers know and believe, Mr. Cohen and Carol A. Barnes, a doctoral student at Michigan State, say.

"Teachers would have to revise their conception of learning, to treat it as an active process of constructing ideas rather than a passive process of absorbing information," the two researchers write. "They would have to rediscover knowledge as something that is constructed and contested, rather than handed down by authorities. They would have to see that learning sometimes flourishes better in groups than alone at one's desk with a worksheet. And in order to learn, teachers would have to unlearn much deeply held knowledge and many fond beliefs."

"Such learning and unlearning would require a revolution in thought," they add. "Moreover, even if teachers' academic knowledge and conceptions of learning changed, they still would have to learn how to teach differently."

Researchers and practitioners are just beginning to explore what this new kind of teaching would look like.

While the back-to-basics movement stressed that effective teachers command center stage in their classrooms, "presenting, regulating, monitoring, and evaluating instruction," Mr. Cohen and Ms. Barnes note, there is no neatly packaged pedagogy to match the current reforms.

"There are all kinds of dilemmas and challenges in the reinvention of schools that don't have clear, practical answers to them," agrees Judith Warren Little, an associate professor at the graduate school of education at the University of California at Berkeley.

Typical professional-development approaches "assume that we have a practice to put into place," she says, "and many of the new reforms belie that assumption."

Creating new systems that can meaningfully support deeply intellectual work by teachers—with all of its messiness and false starts—won't be easy. Standing in the way are two of the most formidable barriers to school improvement of any kind: a lack of time and a lack of money. An even larger barrier, perhaps, is the powerful image of didactic teaching that would have to be cast aside to make way for "teaching for understanding." These barriers also go a long way to explain why professional development has typically been what Ms. Little calls "a remarkably low-intensity enterprise." Most workshop-type offerings, she complains, place teachers in a passive role. They are treated as consumers, not producers, of knowledge.

But if the goal of schooling is to help students become critical thinkers, then their teachers must also be active, engaged learners who continually reflect on and adjust their teaching. Just as important, Ms. Little argues, teachers must also be given chances to participate in, contribute to, and analyze the school-reform movement itself.

From a variety of disparate sources, a picture of promising approaches to professional development is emerging. First, meaningful professional-development programs break teachers' isolation by bringing them together, over extended periods of time, to struggle with significant issues. The focus is shifting away from what an individual teacher knows and is able to do to creating teams or groups of teachers in a school or district.

Second, teachers are linked with people outside of schools to help them understand the applications of what they teach and how to link their classrooms to the real world.

And, through it all, teachers are given regular opportunities to practice what they are learning, receive feedback, revise their work, observe other teachers, talk about their experiences, and reflect on what they have discovered.

"The notion is to think of schools as learning communities," says Susan Loucks-Horsley, a senior associate at the Regional Laboratory for Educational Improvement of the Northeast and Islands, "where adults are always asking questions, seeking answers, and investigating. If we want kids to do that, teachers have to do that."

To accommodate this richer view of teacher learning, the definition of professional development is broadening to encourage and reward teachers' participation in school-improvement efforts, individual and group research projects, and curriculum and assessment development.

In fact, new research suggests that teachers will not be able to transform their classrooms without the support of a network of like-minded colleagues. Left in isolation, concludes a five-year study by the Center for Research on the Context of Secondary School Teaching at Stanford University, teachers tend to fall back on old practices or quit their jobs.

"Those teachers who made effective adaptations to today's students had one thing in common: Each belonged to an active professional community which encouraged and enabled them to transform their teaching," the study says.

Professional communities—whether an academic department, a school, a network, or a professional organization—offer "powerful opportunities" for reform, it concludes.

Teachers Wrestle Together With 'Important, Difficult Issues'

In Vermont, the state's new assessment program for 4th and 8th graders in writing and math has fueled an intense demand for professional development that has been met in innovative ways.

"The need for training is enormous," says Susan Rigney, the manager of the assessment program, "which is why the assessments were undertaken in the first place: to impact instruction." Most of the budget for the assessment program, for example, pays for professional development.

In response to the clamor, the education department created networks of teachers for math and writing. Each of the 17 groups is led by a specially recruited and trained teacher.

Last year, the network leaders offered what Commissioner Mills calls "a takeout menu of options for training on demand." Teachers could choose what suited them: a series of workshops, full-day or half-day training, or short meetings. They scheduled their training after school, during release time, at faculty meetings, or during designated in-service days.

The network leaders were given long-distance calling cards and encouraged to check regularly to see how schools were faring.

"The point is, we were not just dropping a statewide test on a bunch of hapless teachers," says Geof Hewitt, the writing-network coordinator. "We are intent on making sure that their needs are met."

Network leaders provided some of the training. Sometimes, they acted as brokers, linking teachers with people who could answer their questions.

"Some of the most in-demand consultants are teachers," says Patricia McGonegal, a Vermont middle school teacher and a writing-network leader, "because they can say, 'Yeah, this works in my classroom.' The people who can speak with authority are teachers."

When teachers in the networks met, they examined real student work and talked about how to get their students to write and think mathematically to meet the scoring guidelines. They also discussed and debated how to reshape their teaching practice.

"The whole idea of shifting to problem-solving is a dramatic change for teachers," Jill Rosenblum, the math-network coordinator, says. "You can't succeed with students unless you do it yourself."

The best professional development, Ms. Rosenblum writes, took place spontaneously during the network meetings, "over lunch at a scoring session, around the copy machine while preparing an activity, on the road while car-pooling to a network meeting, in a faculty meeting when asked to report on your work with portfolios, and any time when colleagues get together to talk and think about these important, difficult issues."

Traditionally, in-service training and other staff-development workshops have been conducted by outside "experts": consultants, staff developers, or college professors. Now, the emphasis is on helping teachers to discover and develop their own expertise and share it with colleagues.

In New Mexico, 13 specially trained teachers are sharing their knowledge about educating disadvantaged students with schools throughout the state. The teachers will be released from their own classrooms for five days this year; so far, the cadre of teachers—which grew out of a leadership academy funded by the Rockefeller Foundation—has worked with 20 schools and is still receiving calls.

"These people are too valuable to just work in their own schools," Roberta Smith, the project's coordinator, says. "Teachers love to listen to other teachers. They feel like they are authentic and have something important to say."

The American Federation of Teachers' well-regarded Thinking Mathematics project also uses teachers to help others learn new ways of teaching math. The project is part of the union's educational research and dissemination program, which is designed to help teachers understand and make use of educational research on generic classroom techniques.

The project uses a teacher network in each of its 38 sites to train teachers and provide them with support. To participate, districts must guarantee to free the leaders from their other duties for two days a month. The project also tries to train groups of teachers from the same school—rather than individuals from many schools—so teachers can work together as they change the way they teach.

Teachers also worked closely with researchers to develop the curricula for the project.

"We go in, not to give teachers a bunch of activities," Alice Gill, the project's coordinator, says, "but to help them understand how kids learn math, so that they have a real good understanding of why kids ought to be doing this sort of thing."

One of the best ways for teachers to learn, says Keith Yocam, the professional-development manager for Apple Classrooms of Tomorrow, is for them to plunge right in to a new situation under the watchful eye of another teacher.

The ACOT project, using a three-year, $1.2 million grant from the National Science Foundation, is setting up three teacher-development centers in schools in Nashville, Cupertino, Calif., and Columbus, Ohio. Seven hundred teachers are expected to receive training at the schools.

In weeklong practicums throughout the school year and in summer institutes, the teachers will use technology under the tutelage of other teachers and will interact with students who are learning with computers. As teachers return to their classrooms, they will be supported by coordinators who visit them and help them reflect on the changes they are making. Like the Thinking Mathematics teachers, they will attend the sessions in teams.

Mr. Yocam hopes that the approach—which he calls "situated teacher development"—will be a model for further professional-development activities.

A preliminary study from ACOT's Nashville site, Mr. Yocam says, indicated that teachers left the program with an increased sense of their own efficacy and with a view of themselves as learners, capable of handling challenging material. "Every day that a teacher goes into a classroom," he says, "they should be as challenged as they want their kids to be."

Building on teachers' sense of themselves as learners and producers of knowledge is essential if they are to cultivate the same attitudes in their students. One of the best ways to accomplish that aim, many argue, is for teachers to grapple with the fundamental questions of what students and teachers should know and be able to do.

In districts working with the National Board for Professional Teaching Standards, for example, teachers are discussing and debating the board's vision of accomplished teaching. The board, a private organization governed by a teacher-majority board, is developing a voluntary national system to certify highly accomplished teachers. It is scheduled to begin testing its assessment system this fall.

With the board's standards in mind, teachers in South Brunswick, N.J., have analyzed videos of each others' classrooms. They are also designing portfolios to document their teaching.

Willa Spicer, the director of instruction for the South Brunswick township schools, calls the sessions "self-reflection as a method of staff development." "Groups of teachers are coming together to design portfolios, to say, 'What's important enough to assess, and how do we know if we're doing it?'

and to ask about accomplished teaching," she explains.

Similarly, teachers involved with the New Standards Project, a privately funded effort to develop what could become a national system of standards and assessments, are grappling with such questions for students.

Teachers in 19 states—including Vermont—and six districts are involved with the project and have created "performance tasks" for students and scored pilot assessments.

The project is drawing in as many teachers as possible, says Lauren B. Resnick, its co-director, because "the whole goal of this is to spread knowledge of and commitment to the standards throughout the whole education community."

Ms. McGonegal, the Vermont teacher, traveled to Dallas last November to help write performance tasks. Because New Standards has sparked so much teacher engagement, she describes the effort as a "reform project disguised as an assessment project."

"Teachers are showing each other some fabulous pieces of classroom practice," she says. "Good teachers are going to pick that up and say, 'I can do something like this.' "

As the work moves forward, the project plans to create teams of teachers in each subject in every participating school. These "assessment leaders" will be responsible for scoring and for helping their colleagues organize portfolios to be scored.

The lead teachers will, in turn, be part of a professional-development network coordinated by "senior leaders" responsible for about 10 schools, Ms. Resnick says. The senior leaders will be in charge of creating professional-development opportunities and for running the scoring in their regions.

The directors of the New Standards Project are also exploring the possibility of offering senior leaders some type of certificate that would be based on their proven ability to perform various functions.

The National Alliance for Restructuring Education—made up of a subset of New Standards partners and other groups—is also developing a network-type model for professional development. Curriculum associations and researchers will be part of the networks, Ms. Resnick says.

"There is a kind of continuous flow of interaction in both directions," she explains. "The model of teacher training we have had mirrors the model of one-way information flow and expertise."

"The idea that somebody else comes in and tells you what to do just has to go—it's not going to work," she asserts. "On the other hand, the notion that everybody has to make it up all alone, over and over again, without the jump-starting and stimulation of a community, is just a counsel of despair."

Embracing a broad view of professional development, some reform projects are forging national communities to share what they have learned about the difficult process of remaking schools. They recognize that focusing on teachers alone is unlikely to get the job done.

"The need to build capacity applies also to principals, central offices, boards, state departments of education, and even policymakers," Jane L. David, the director of the Bay Area Research Group, says. "The kinds of new thinking that teachers need in classrooms to reach ambitious outcomes for all students is paralleled in what administrators and policymakers need as well."

The National Re:Learning Faculty, created by the Coalition of Essential Schools, includes principals and other administrators. Its 150 members are trained to help coalition schools solve problems.

Teacher members of the faculty receive four weeks of intensive training in the summer in Providence, R.I., the coalition's headquarters, paid for by CitiBank. They learn how to observe other teachers' classes and make constructive suggestions, as well as how to help schools plan for change and solve conflicts.

They also teach summer school, putting into practice the coalition's "less is more" philosophy with integrated, cross-disciplinary courses.

The coalition then pairs the members of the national faculty with schools. Over the course of a school year, they offer seven full days of assistance, helping the schools develop strategies for change.

"That still isn't very much," says Paula Evans, the director of the National Re:Learning Faculty, "but it's a considerable commitment, and it's quite different from traditional professional development."

"This is practitioners working with practitioners over time," Ms. Evans says. "It's people who are really trying to understand what a school is all about and trying to help those in the school to define and come up with strategies to address their problems or their roadblocks or to celebrate their successes."

In addition to opportunities to solve problems together, teachers need professional-development activities that both broaden their own knowledge and help them improve their instruction.

One of the most powerful strategies is to link teachers with their real-world counterparts: English teachers with playwrights, social-studies teachers with museum curators, science teachers with scientists.

Introducing teachers to people who work in their disciplines, says Ron Thorpe, a program officer at the Geraldine R. Dodge Foundation, gives them a sense of participation in a broader, discipline-based community. In turn, they can expose their students to the real-world applications and methods of these fields.

"Teachers have not felt that these people were their colleagues," Mr. Thorpe says. "They have felt removed, lesser; yet they have to work symbiotically."

The Collaboratives for Humanities and Arts Teaching, known as CHART, links teachers in 14 locations with the arts and humanities communities. The goal of the program, funded by the Rockefeller Foundation, is to provide students with more diverse, multicultural arts and humanities curricula and experiences. The projects vary from site to site, but many are interdisciplinary, and all stress writing, says Judith Rényi, the director of CHART.

The programs begin with summer institutes that plunge teachers into intensive study of their subjects and create a sense of community. Teachers are encouraged to work in teams, so that lone teachers aren't left in isolation in their schools.

They work closely with museum curators, artists, playwrights, and the like to write curricula. During the school year, students regularly visit museums and theaters.

"There is a constant dialogue going back and forth between teachers and the collaborating resource people," Ms. Rényi says. "What a museum curator can do is say, 'Here's this wonderful collection of Chinese pots, right down the road from the school, and it teaches us something about world history.' But he can't tell the teacher what to do in the classroom; they need to figure that out for themselves."

After the "pure learning experience" of the summer, Ms. Rényi says, the sites try hard to sustain the energy and intellectual engagement by arranging for meetings of participating teachers.

By meeting on Saturdays, after school, during common preparation periods for teachers in the same buildings, or on districtwide in-service days, the teachers have managed to keep the sense of community alive despite the press of everyday school life, she says.

"It's very hard. Creating curriculum like that is very time-consuming and exceedingly difficult," she says. "The teachers who managed to do good stuff donated a huge number of hours."

As interest grows in freeing schools to develop their own distinctive approaches, so does the need for involving entire faculties in professional-development activities. School-based management, in particular, is creating a demand to build the capacities of school-level people.

In Dallas, the district increased its budget in 1992-93 by nearly $1 million to pay for "staff-development associates" in each school. These teachers will be responsible for identifying their schools' needs, arranging staff-development opportunities, and training two teachers as coaches for new teachers.

"For so long, because staff development was planned centrally, the principals and the entire staff just waited for somebody else to do it," says Pam Spruiell, the district's executive director of professional training and development. "It's been a slow process to get them to think, 'We're in charge of this now, and need to do what's best for the campus.' "

To take charge, however, people in schools need to be able to determine what kind of training or study would help them reach their goals.

Providing schools with the money and flexibility to meet their own needs is a central recommendation of an independent commission that suggested ways to improve the federal Chapter 1 compensatory-education program.

The commission suggested that schools be allowed to set aside 5 percent of their Chapter 1 money, increasing to 20 percent over a period of years, for professional development. The money could pay for release time for teachers so that they could visit effective programs or for teachers to engage in common planning, explains Robert E. Slavin, a member of the commission and the director of the elementary school program at the Center for Research on Effective Schooling for Disadvantaged Students at Johns Hopkins University.

Just as important, the panel recommended that schools be able to buy training or assistance from any source. And the entire school faculty, not just Chapter 1 teachers, would be eligible to participate.

The panel, which offered its recommendations in anticipation of Congress's reauthorization of the program next year, suggested giving schools increased amounts of money over time in order to allow them to learn new practices, Mr. Slavin said. It also called for setting aside 1 percent of the Chapter 1 money for research and development of promising approaches.

Today, he notes, schools that receive Chapter 1 money feel compelled to spend it on people, not on the information and training that could improve instruction.

"It isn't going to happen unless we give teachers, principals, and staff more effective strategies," he asserts. "We are not going to make big changes by having teachers teach harder—they've got to teach better. And that's not going to happen without a major investment."

Finding Time and Money: Innovation With 'Stolen Hours'

Educators complain that successful businesses, recognizing the value of investing in their employees, don't scrimp on their training and retraining.

While districts typically spend one-half to 1 percent of their total budgets on professional development, the American Society for Training and Development estimates that businesses spend about 1.4 percent of their payrolls on formal training and development.

Perhaps more important, private firms build time to learn into the salaried workday, rather than expecting employees to undergo training after hours.

Albert Shanker, the president of the A.F.T., asserted in one of his weekly columns that the key to General Motors' successful new Saturn line lies in its "impressive training program," offering 400 hours of initial training to members of the work teams that make the cars and a menu of 600 courses for further study.

"Imagine trying to change things as basic as the culture of a school and the way people teach with a couple of days of in-service training a year and some hours stolen from class-preparation periods," he writes. "But that's about what most teams that are trying to restructure their schools have in terms of time and resources."

Even districts that have made significant investments in teachers' learning have difficulty sustaining programs.

Some of the most innovative and promising practices are only possible because of grants from businesses and foundations. Typically, staff-development money is one of the first things to go—because its importance hasn't been recognized and because political realities make it an easy mark.

In Dade County, Fla., for example, the Dade Academy for the Teaching Arts, which gives teachers the chance for a nine-week sabbatical, has seen its funding cut in half. At one time, the district paid for 22 teachers to cycle through the academy each grading period; now, only 12 get the chance.

"The budget ax has been constantly over us," says Evelyn Campbell, the director of the academy.

The Pittsburgh school board eliminated that city's three teacher centers, mostly because paying for substitute teachers to replace those on leave was too expensive.

"The first thing they look at is what cuts the public wouldn't be aware of," says Albert Fondy, the president of the Pittsburgh Federation of Teachers. "If they eliminate the teacher center at a school, the school itself is still there, and the only people aware it's gone are teachers or administrators."

In Louisville, Ky., however, the Jefferson County Public Schools/Gheens Professional Development Academy has thrived, thanks to the district's decision to use professional development as "the instrument of school reform," according to a recent report on its impact.

The academy, which merged with the district's traditional in-service unit, now has a budget of more than $10 million, the report says, due to a "major reallocation of school district funds."

Although districts and states could undoubtedly make better or more creative use of existing time and money for professional development, many agree that the agenda for teachers' learning is likely to go unfulfilled unless new incentives are created.

The college and university courses that count for advancement on the salary schedule—and more pay—for teachers "do not seem to have appreciably advanced teachers' knowledge of pedagogy or academic subjects," Mr. Cohen and Ms. Barnes, the Michigan State researchers, say.

"As things now stand," they continue, "serious learning only counts professionally for teachers if they individually choose to make it count."

Because teachers need a much deeper knowledge of subject matter than many now possess, the A.F.T. has advocated modifying salary schedules so that teachers would only receive salary differentials for coursework in their subject, not for methodology courses.

At the same time, many people suggest that the range of activities that "count" for relicensure and salary-schedule advancement must be broadened to include work on school-improvement projects, study groups, reform networks, curriculum and assessment development, and standards-setting efforts.

Teachers in the Adams County (Colo.) 5 Star School District, for example, can receive credit for participating in school-improvement projects and for classroom research. They must demonstrate, however, that their coursework or project is directly linked to their work and the district's long-term plan.

New providers of professional development and new kinds of schools also could meet teachers' needs.

Some local teachers' unions, for example, are assuming greater responsibility for teachers' development. Members of the Rochester (N.Y.) Teachers Association have approved a dues increase to pay for such activities.

In addition, the burgeoning movement to create professional-development schools holds out the promise that teachers' learning could become a more integral part of their workdays. In these schools, teachers and their college or university counterparts collaborate on research, work with new teachers, and investigate promising teaching practices.

In the process, says Ann W. Lieberman, the co-director of the National Center for Restructuring Education, Schools, and Teaching at Teachers College, Columbia University, the idea of professional development shifts from a "deficit" model concentrating on teachers' weaknesses to a "growth and practice" model that produces new knowledge.

To help teachers wrestle with larger educational issues, Mr. Cohen and Ms. Barnes propose that education policy be made "truly educational" for teachers through the creation of special curricula that would parallel efforts to establish standards, frameworks, curricula, and assessments for students.

"The aim would be to undertake framework design such that it also presented a rich set of occasions for educators to learn," they explain.

The researchers suggest that an independent, nongovernmental body— perhaps the National Board for Professional Teaching Standards or the New Standards Project—could undertake such ventures.

Despite the slim resources devoted to professional development, many suggest that districts could make better use of their money and teachers' time. Categorical programs, for example, contain money for professional development that might be combined for more impact. "There are a lot of scattered ways that money is spent," says Ms. Ucelli of the Rockefeller Foundation, "and not a comprehensive sense of what it is all leading to."

Ms. Rényi of the CHART program recommends that districts bunch in-service days together to give teachers a chance to delve more deeply into curriculum projects and discussions. Others suggest that teams of teachers in a school be given common preparation periods.

Developing a cadre of trained, long-term substitutes can also relieve teachers' concerns about leaving their classrooms.

To allow for "alternative" forms of professional development, Ms. Little of the University of California at Berkeley advises that districts shouldn't spend all their staff-development money on packaged approaches. But eventually, she says, the public is going to have to invest in more salaried work time for teachers to learn new methods. That's not likely, she notes, as long as teachers are only considered to be working when they are with children.

Such an approach might mean lengthening the school year for some teachers to allow them to be paid for participating in summer institutes or for developing curricula. "Long term, we have to change our calendar," Mr. Mills, the Vermont commissioner, says. "We have to add more time without the kids."

New policies are also needed that recognize and value teachers' learning during their entire careers.

In Vermont, the state Standards Board for Professional Educators created local standards boards to make decisions on teachers' continuing education and relicensure.

Each teacher presents an individual plan for professional growth to a standards board. Teachers can receive credit for a broad array of activities, including participating in reform networks and teaching courses, instead of just formal coursework. The plans also emphasize the need for teachers to reflect on their current practice and consider their future learning needs, Vermont officials say.

"The whole thing is a shift to really looking at a teacher's needs and finding the appropriate professional development," says Betty Carvellas, the chairwoman of the state standards board. "In the past, you took three courses that were related sometimes, and sometimes weren't, or were at a convenient time."

The state also has created a consortium that plans to establish a data base of professional-development offerings and help teachers who are interested in learning the same things get together.

Eventually, the system should create "focused demand" for high-quality professional development, Commissioner Mills says. In turn, colleges and universities will have to respond to the demands expressed by teachers.

Finally, Vermont has adopted a new "results oriented" process for accrediting teacher education programs that calls for institutions to develop portfolios. Students in the programs also will have portfolios that document what they know and can do, rather than emphasizing what courses they have taken.

For Amy Moore, a math-network leader who has been teaching just five years, Vermont's emphasis on professional development has been a welcome one. "As a teacher," she says, "that's what I want to see: for all educators to be continuously learning."

DOLLARS AND SENSE

By Lonnie Harp

In this chapter, we examine the path of school funding and whether state and local officials can tie finance to reform priorities.

AUSTIN, TEX.—After three years of fruitless and contentious wrestling, people here would understand if Sen. Carl A. Parker compared the issue of school finance to a bottomless pit or, perhaps, a bed of nails. Instead, the powerful Texas lawmaker rocks back in his chair and calls to mind a much different image.

A sailboat race, he says.

Senator Parker gave up his seat as the chairman of the Senate education committee in 1993 hoping that a new face would bring results: specifically, a law sufficient to satisfy a court order to reduce school-spending disparities between wealthy and poor districts. But even once it clears that hurdle, Mr. Parker says, the state will be far from providing its districts with the fairly and efficiently funded education system mandated by the state constitution.

"It ought to be like how you handicap a sailboat race," he explains. "Everybody gets the exact same boat, the same wind, and they traverse the same course. The only difference between the winners and whoever finishes in last place is how the crew works together and how efficiently they use what they have."

"In Texas, we've got yachts racing against dories," Mr. Parker quips.

Across much of the country, attention to school finance remains a debate about which district has the best boat, not about how local officials harness the wind or navigate the course.

Funding for elementary and secondary schools is routinely the single largest pot of money that state lawmakers approve. Yet, distribution of that

A new analysis tool gave the Reynoldsburg, Ohio, school district a much clearer picture of how it spends money. A decade of school lawsuits has focused attention on the school-finance issue, but yawning disparities still remain between rich and poor districts.

money often bears only a distant connection to what policymakers say students need and what they expect schools to provide.

More often than not, the amount of state aid to schools represents little more than a historical buildup of money. The total gets run through tedious and cryptic formulas that adjust for economic and demographic factors and, in the end, usually provide districts with a bit more aid than they got the year before.

After fighting for increased state aid, districts in turn add that money to local tax receipts, which mirror local wealth or poverty. They take that total and pay for the same staff and programs as last year and, if the increase was higher than inflation, maybe more.

New Round of Lawsuits Forces New State Thinking

The recent success of state school-finance lawsuits has forced state officials to take a fresh look at local inequities, outdated formulas, and overall spending. Nevertheless, the court pressure has generally pushed states into political gridlock and produced variations on the existing funding system—not a wholesale rethinking of how the state might buy the kind of public schools it wants.

Critics complain that state and district officials treat public school funding—a total of about $252 billion from all sources in 1992-93—like fuel to stoke a hungry furnace. Instead of using funding increases to maintain the status quo, they say, it could be used as a powerful force to bring about real school change.

"School finance in the 1990's must push beyond fiscal inequities and determine connections among student outcomes, education programs, and education funding," Allan R. Odden, the director of the Center for Research in Education Finance at the University of Southern California, has written. "School finance ducked those issues in the past; the issues cannot be dodged in the future."

Adds Kern Alexander, a school-finance researcher at Virginia Polytechnic Institute and State University: "Court decisions are forcing a rethinking of the whole thing—focusing on the system when legislatures would just like to increase funding and go home. It is forcing them to think more about what they are spending and what they are buying."

Tremendous hurdles lie between today's entrenched political parochialism, with its skittishness toward budget reforms, and the goal of smarter spending.

"I have become discouraged that my fellow politicians in Texas are ever going to make the commitment to public education that they need to make," Mr. Parker says. "There is not a single group looking out for the long-haul interest of students. If that were the case, we wouldn't have 1,040 school districts in Texas, and we would have long since solved our school-finance problem."

Lawmakers, Mr. Parker and others say, can often be blamed for being blind to the good of the state because of their preoccupation with how it will play back home. But educators, too, are guilty of seeing school funds as they relate to their own needs and concerns, not the interests of the system as a whole.

After being bombarded by people speaking out for large districts, medium-sized districts, small districts, wealthy districts, poor districts, urban districts, suburban districts, rural districts, principals, superintendents, and teachers, Mr. Parker says, it is not hard to see why school-finance reforms are difficult to achieve.

Although the drive for greater equity has brought the school-finance system into the spotlight, lawmakers and public officials may have a hard time steering public debate away from the scramble for dollars to make some sense of the system—to define a vision, map out an action plan, calculate the costs, and fight to build it.

"The strongest force in the school-finance world is inertia," says John Augenblick, a Denver-based school-finance consultant. "Everything is based on what happened before and what people used to do."

The tide of state school-finance lawsuits that began in California in 1971 and was renewed in the 1980's in Kentucky, Montana, New Jersey, and Texas has served primarily to shed light on wide disparities in the spending power of local schools.

State courts have issued landmark opinions not only decrying the deplorable state of schooling for children who live in poor districts, but also reminding state officials in strong terms of their obligation to maintain a fair, efficient, and adequate public education system.

Many of the recent court decisions "are documents in true ethics," says Jonathan Kozol, whose 1991 book *Savage Inequalities* describes the circumstances of children in a host of wealthy and poor districts. "Some of these decisions are an avowal of all the good things America is supposed to be about, but there is a terrible falling off by the time it reaches the legislature, where they haggle and nitpick."

Indeed, observers say, many of the bold court opinions of the late 1980's and early 1990's have been followed by mundane state responses. Lawmakers in Texas have twice been ordered to try again, a New Jersey court is reconsidering the remedy adopted by the legislature, and the Montana case was back before a judge in early 1993. Even in Kentucky, where the state supreme court overturned the entire state school system, and lawmakers came up with a landmark school-reform plan that blazes many new trails, the finance system was not vastly changed.

"Despite the sweeping nature of their court cases, especially the Kentucky case," Mr. Odden concluded in a 1992 report, "the finance structures enacted are similar to those that many states have been using for years. For policymakers and analysts looking for innovative ways to design general aid programs, these state programs offer little guidance."

Gov. Roy Romer of Colorado adds, "People have been reacting to the pressure, but we haven't had a lot of creative thinking."

To date, much of the grappling with school-finance issues at the state level has been an exercise in finding a balance between local funds—mostly property taxes—and state revenues. Local funds still account for a sizable chunk of total spending, about 45 percent, compared with 49 percent from state taxes and about 6 percent from the federal government.

Many states are only now beginning to sort through the complicated issues raised by state courts on such issues as the role of property taxes and the definition of local control.

While legislators who have been drawn into the recent school-finance battles see an increasingly complex job before them, they contend that their first task must be to assert authority over the disparity problem.

"The issue is going to get resolved because the court has put the hammer on us," Mr. Parker says. "We have to focus on equity and get that in place, and then we need to unify people in seeking quality."

The equity problem can be traced to states' heavy reliance on local property taxes to fund education, and to district boundaries that tend to follow economic patterns. Using the same tax rate, a district with neighborhoods of $100,000 houses can raise five times as much revenue as a district filled with the same number of $20,000 homes. Even after state and federal aid is added, the poorer district usually comes out significantly behind.

The result is a gap in spending power that observers say translates into marked educational differences, with state finance systems giving wealthy districts a head start while dealing poor districts a weak hand.

For many poor districts, the results of state finance systems are displayed in the poor condition of school buildings, aging laboratories, bare-bones curricula, a dearth of foreign-language and arts courses, and a teaching corps made up of beginning and unprepared teachers, says Arthur E. Wise, the president of the National Council for Accreditation of Teacher Education. Mr. Wise was the author of a 1967 book, *Rich Schools Poor Schools*, that exposed many school-finance problems and triggered a decade of litigation.

"It isn't just that a child in a poor district is faced with one unqualified teacher; that child might go through a whole career without a good teacher," Mr. Wise says. "Well-off districts hire an ample number of well-qualified personnel, while poor school districts are stuck with the left-overs."

"It's not automatic that money is going to improve the system," Mr. Parker says. "But it's almost automatic that a lack of money will destroy or degrade it."

States thus far have pursued a variety of approaches to reduce the inequalities. In Kentucky, lawmakers provided incentive funds for authorities with high local tax rates, placed a cap on local spending to limit budget increases in wealthy districts, and raised state taxes to boost the buying power of poor districts.

Texas officials, meanwhile, are working to modify a plan that bypasses the politically explosive issue of district consolidation by creating regional taxing authorities that levy and collect a minimum property tax and spread the total local aid among member districts. Lawmakers in Kansas have moved toward a statewide property tax, while Gov. Mario M. Cuomo of New York in 1993 proposed giving districts the option of replacing local property taxes with income taxes.

Also in 1993, a Vermont task force detailed a host of tax-reform options and raised the idea of removing residential property taxes as a school-funding source. Property taxes currently account for 60 percent of school funding in the state.

"If you believe in equality of educational opportunity, we are not able to provide that under the current system," says David Wolk, the chairman of the commission on tax reform and the chief of policy for Gov. Howard Dean.

But reducing property-tax reliance is an area in which states have made more noise than change. "Local spending is not only an idea that people have held, it's an idea that's been reinforced," says Billy D. Walker, a finance researcher and the executive director of the Texas Association of School Boards. "Changing a tax system that has been in place for 150 years isn't easy."

The evidence is mixed on whether such a shift is under way. Researchers at the Center for the Study of Educational Finance at Illinois State University have found that states with pending finance litigation have seen greater school-spending increases than those without it. Where poor districts have won their cases, most of the new money has come from state taxes. Where the plaintiffs have lost, the funding increases have been drawn from local property taxes.

The move away from property taxes is slow and uneven, explains G. Alan Hickrod, the director of the center.

While many lawmakers see the need to increase funding for poor districts, they are not convinced that reducing the overall reliance on property taxes is wise. "It is advantageous to have locally applied taxes because it ties local taxpayers to local schools," argues John L. Myers, the education-program director for the National Conference of State Legislatures.

Others believe, however, that a stronger move away from property taxes is necessary to give all children the same opportunity for success and to galvanize support for school improvements.

"Reliance on a property-tax system has very deep traditional roots," Helen Hershkoff, the associate legal director for the American Civil Liberties Union, says. "But in a period where we're talking about change, it's important to revisit the ways we fund education in this country."

Complex Formulas Envisioned as Reform Reinforcement

After creating a balanced tax system that puts districts on the same plane, school-finance experts suggest, lawmakers should turn their attention to the formulas that sort and divide school money.

State formulas are often a hodgepodge of calculations that have grown up over time and usually involve a tangle of programs past and present.

Generally understood by only a handful of people in each state, the formulas convert total state spending into smaller morsels that go out to districts. Experts who have dissected the formulas bear witness to their complexity and inefficiency.

"The formula can be a very important statement of what a state's priorities are," says Steven Gold, the director of the Center for the Study of the States at the State University of New York in Albany. "But some of the most important issues facing the states now are not reflected in the formula; they're at the local level—questions of how money is going to be spent."

Current state formulas, which have been shaped by politics and demographic pressures, offer little help in speeding reform, Mr. Gold and others say. "Most of the discussion in the state legislatures with respect to school finance is about taxing and spending," Mr. Wise says. "It is not connected to reform."

Lawmakers could go a long way toward tying school finance to reform efforts by envisioning their distribution formulas as an instrument for underscoring policy aims and calculating sensible investments in students.

Since 1979, South Carolina officials have kept a close watch on their formula, which was written to provide districts with enough funding to support an agreed-upon pupil-teacher ratio and to pay for such necessary expenditures as supplies, personnel, and maintenance.

The $700 that the state earmarked for each student as a base cost in 1979 had risen to $1,576 by 1993. That calculation is modified by formula weights for disadvantaged and handicapped students, as well as for local property wealth, before providing the district allocation. Beyond that base, which accounts for about $850 million, $300 million more in state funding is portioned out to districts according to other criteria.

Unlike many states, where aid figures result from a division of whatever lawmakers have become accustomed to providing, South Carolina has set a reasoned bottom-line amount, according to Dan F. Chandler, the finance director for the state education department.

"We are confident the formula is a good tool for getting the money out, even though I don't think there is so much confidence that we're doing all that we need to do," Mr. Chandler says. "Like every state, we need to keep looking at equity and what the child's needs are."

Indeed, South Carolina and other states could do more through their funding programs to make sure schools meet their policy aims. "There's not a lot of thinking that links finance structures to program structures," says Mr. Odden of U.S.C.

In a 1992 book, *Rethinking School Finance,* Mr. Odden and his fellow authors recommend that states break sharply with current finance patterns. They call on state leaders to directly fund local schools in an effort to foster school-based management, revamp teacher-compensation strategies to reward experience and skills over tenure, create school-performance incentives aimed at achievement goals, provide funding for social services, and pay for expanded teacher recruitment and staff development.

Inspired by the new thinking from the state's tax-reform commission, Vermont legislative leaders in early 1993 unveiled a school-finance bill that would require the state to take over collective bargaining and become responsible for teacher pay.

Sponsors of the plan describe it as a natural outgrowth of the need for finance changes and classroom improvements. "As long as school boards and teachers are investing enormous amounts of time negotiating, not only do they not have the time and resources to deal with restructuring, but their attitude isn't there," says Rep. David C. Larsen, the chairman of the House education committee.

The bill has already drawn criticism from the leaders of the state teachers' union, who regard it as an attempt to cut teacher pay.

The plan would shift about half of the funding of local schools onto state shoulders and, Mr. Larsen says, increase equity among districts while freeing local administrators to consider policy and reform issues.

"This says your services are valuable no matter where you are teaching and levels the playing field for property-poor or income-poor towns," Mr. Larsen, a teacher and a union member, says. "They would be able to compete for teachers."

But reformers have learned that school-finance changes, even in the name of making sense of the system, come hard.

In the fall of 1992, 57 percent of Illinois voters approved a constitutional amendment that would have declared education a fundamental right in the state and charged lawmakers with funding the majority of the system. The state share of public school funding has dropped from a high of about 48 percent to nearly 33 percent in 1993.

The amendment, which would have replaced the vaguely worded education article of the Illinois constitution, fell short of the 60 percent majority needed. It was backed up, however, by a state task force's plan that defined the elements of an adequate education and set their cost.

But state education leaders, initially gleeful over the progress in a state that has some of the nation's biggest school-spending disparities, have quickly become pessimistic as political pressures have unwound the prospects for implementation of the task force's work.

"We have an education President, an education Governor, everyone elected to office says that education is their number-one priority, and 57 percent of the voters here said they were willing to change the system," says State Superintendent of Education Robert Leininger. "So the question is, What the hell is the problem here?"

A finance-equity lawsuit has run into an initial setback, and policymakers and legislators do not seem much interested in providing what officials have deemed necessary to maintain adequate schools.

The Illinois plan examines elementary, middle, and high school programs. It includes desired pupil-teacher ratios for classroom teachers (one for every 24 students) and other personnel, ranging from art instructors (one for every 500 elementary pupils) to district administrators (one for every 800 children).

For elementary schools, general aid—funds that do not include categorical state and federal programs—could range from $3,118 to $4,678 per student, depending on local cost factors. The average would be $3,898 per child, of which 54 percent would be devoted to school- and district-personnel costs.

Based on those targets, the task force concluded that about 80 percent of the state's districts fell below the funding necessary for an adequate education.

"In the beginning, it appeared our task was to tackle a technical, mathematical dilemma," Sen. Arthur L. Berman, a co-chairman of the task force, has written. "But task-force members quickly realized that it was children—not dollars—that were ultimately at stake."

Observers of finance-reform efforts in Illinois and other states wonder whether state leaders understand the weak foundations of their existing funding programs.

"We know the answers; we just don't seem to be able to crank up the political support," Mr. Hickrod says.

"A lot of people just haven't arrived there philosophically," notes Mr. Walker of Texas. "There are basic normative values involved in these things, and what people are talking about is a radical departure from the practice of 110 years. Plus, these people never understood school finance in the first place."

Local Spending Questions Add New Dimension to Debate

As state leaders have focused on broad questions of finance equity and formulas, buses have continued to roll, teachers to teach, and children to study. It is in the schools, observers say, that the most important chapter in the school-finance revolution may soon be written.

If many lawmakers have only a tenuous grasp of the real impact of their finance formulas, local school officials are also in the dark about how that money is being spent and whether their programs are worth the cost.

Whatever answer local educators might give when asked where their money goes, Bruce S. Cooper, a professor of educational administration and urban policy at Fordham University, says he would not believe it.

"It's all a load of rubbish and double talk, because you can't follow the money," says Mr. Cooper, who has come up with a method of doing exactly that. "When I first started, I thought that the educators knew where the money was going, but the truth is that they didn't. Everybody thought it was O.K. to be sloppy as long as they were not illegally sloppy."

Under the current finance system, the state apportions money to districts, which then combine it with local revenues and divide the funds among their central office, support operations, and individual schools. By the time the funds reach the classroom, it is hard to retrace the logic of how and why they got there or to know what the dollars buy.

"What's so stunning about the fact that we don't know this is how critical it is," says Sue E. Berryman, an education specialist for the World Bank and the chairman of the Consortium on Productivity in the Schools based at Teachers College, Columbia University.

"Somehow, the school and classroom are not in the view," says Mr. Cooper. "Historically, states were the fiduciary agent in every community, and, in exchange, the district agreed to make reports periodically. But in the end, the numbers don't tell you much because the state averages are just local averages that become national averages."

"It's an average of an average of an average, and then we wonder why we don't know where the money goes," Mr. Cooper says.

Mr. Odden, who also has initiated a study of school spending, says accounting for school funds has never been demanded of local administrators. Rather, the focus has been on winning greater funding to keep programs operating.

"Maybe some people could tell you where the money goes, but the orientation is, 'We want to keep what we've got now, and we want to do more,' " he says.

That attitude, some observers say, has led to the public education system's ability to swallow up any size funding increase without much hint of where it ends up.

Indeed, Mr. Odden says, for all the talk about making ends meet, public schools have been the beneficiaries of a windfall in each of the past three decades. Despite the tight education budgets of the early 1990's, he says, policymakers should expect that avalanche to continue.

Real expenditures per pupil rose from $1,621 in constant 1989 dollars at the end of the 1950's to $2,743 a decade later. By the end of the 1970's, the figure reached $3,345, and it rose by another 48 percent to $4,960 by the 1989-90 school year.

"*A Nation at Risk* called for higher funding, which we got," Mr. Odden says.

"It may be hard to think this way, but the question is, did we use that to fund those reforms?"

Much of the increase logged in the 1980's can be attributed to new programs, smaller classes, and salary increases. In addition, a sizable portion of the money has been devoted to special education and other mandated programs.

"Every time I hear people say they need more money, I think, if you only knew what you have," Mr. Cooper says. "Even though we know school is important, society hasn't had any way of tracking the money to the classroom."

Getting Information People Can Understand

The Reynoldsburg city schools sit on the east side of Columbus, Ohio. Once a quaint village of a few hundred people, the town has quickly become a popular suburb and home to 25,000. The school district operates seven schools serving 4,300 students on a budget of $29 million.

The district has been an eager and active participant in school reform.

Enrollments in Advanced Placement courses are booming, teachers work in teams, student mentoring is encouraged, multi-age classrooms are being tested at an elementary school, and the district is seeking grant money to expand its service-oriented program. Several courses have been integrated into concentrated double blocks, such as a senior political-studies class connecting high school English and government.

But Reynoldsburg officials discovered how little they really knew about their district only after Mr. Cooper studied their budget as a demonstration for Ohio officials, who are considering mandating the cost analysis state-wide.

"People need information they can understand, not a labyrinth nobody can read or decipher," says Richard A. Ross, the district superintendent.

After removing about $10 million tied to fixed costs from the budget, the analysis showed that the district spends 59 percent of its operational funding on classroom instruction, which includes teacher salaries. About 17 percent is spent on building support, including maintenance and transportation; 12 percent on student support, which includes such supplemental programs as sports and libraries; 11 percent on administration at the central office and schools; and 1 percent on teacher support and training.

Dividing the pie in another way, the analysis found that 6.4 percent of the district's funds are spent in the central office, with the remainder being spent at the school level.

The average per-pupil cost in Reynoldsburg, after subtracting fixed costs, is $4,363, the study revealed.

Digging a layer deeper, Mr. Cooper's analysis also enabled officials and residents to compare spending at individual schools, in the process sparking a number of management and policy discussions.

The figures show that per-pupil spending at the district's high school was $5,079 in 1990-91. That level dropped to $4,564 at the two middle schools, and $3,375 at the elementary schools. Spending on classroom instruction ranged from more than $3,000 per student at Reynoldsburg Junior High to just over $1,500 at Graham Road Elementary School.

While such factors as the seniority levels of teaching staffs and the concentration of kindergarten students readily explain some of the more glaring differences, the analysis also opened the district to new questions and to a new level of awareness and understanding about what it provides, officials say.

"We have found the whole exercise a very powerful stimulus for a lot of discussion," Mr. Ross says. "This allows the public to see where the money is going, and we need to show that."

"I would like to see it broken down even finer and tied to learner outcomes, and we also need to take a look at how our expenditures compare to how they are spending the same money in other countries," the superintendent says. "Then we can make comparisons, and I would imagine some things would really jump out at us."

Mr. Cooper says the cost comparisons he has undertaken so far have had a wide range of side effects. In many cases, they have raised community interest and shown that money is being used responsibly—news that has helped win bond elections in three districts. More important, however, the analyses have informed school decisionmakers and educators and helped shift school debates from raw amounts of money to the services and outcomes being bought.

"We're really beginning to compare schools, which sends up flags and forces questions about why some things are costing more than others," says Ms. Berryman. "Asking that question doesn't mean it is inefficient or that there is fraud or abuse. It may mean that in inner cities, with so many damaged students, you need more for support services."

In the 30 district analyses to date, spending on instruction has held near the overall average of 61 percent. For other categories, such as administration, the range swings more widely.

Mr. Cooper says that after the analysis, one district sold its expensive board headquarters and reduced the central-office staff by a third to improve efficiency. "I don't think there was a conspiracy not to tell people; they just didn't know what was happening," he says. "Once you turn the focus to schools and classrooms, it flips the whole school-finance system on its head."

The focus on school costs may lead to greater attention to program effectiveness and begin to force officials to rationalize overall school funding.

"I see school finance as the spine that runs through the system, but right now we're not using it to see how the system functions," says Ms. Berryman, whose productivity consortium hopes to find the links that turn funding and policy into action and achievement.

"We need to try to relate the variations to the learning that goes on, because that is the bottom line, and nobody has a clue on it," she says. "This is nothing complicated; it's very straightforward. But we can't do it right now."

Such a focus would begin to raise questions about the effectiveness of reform strategies, with the goal of determining how to build an efficient school system and figure its cost.

"It's amazing to me that the whole issue of student-faculty ratio is still unresolved, because it is big bucks," Ms. Berryman points out. "The dollars are a real way to get a handle on the system. Obviously, that can be misused—to just hammer away at money instead of saying what are we getting for our investment. We've got to be much more analytic."

School-based management and other reforms are almost doomed to dwell on trivia and be ripe for criticism without a good accounting system and an understanding of school spending.

"With this kind of direction, we can begin to answer questions like, Which is better: higher teacher salaries or lower class size?" Mr. Odden observes.

A productivity and investment focus "goes right to the heart of the matter," says Mr. Ross of Reynoldsburg.

"Right now, we've got programs operating that we don't ask are they worth the expenditure," he says. "We're doing that here now, and sometimes we don't like the answers. But we need to really look at whether we are being successful and not just adding layers."

Other observers suggest that the focus on spending and cost benefits should not obscure the mission of schools, which is to educate children well, not cheaply.

"We make the assumption that children are of equal worth, so we will have a difficult time talking about return on investment," notes R. Craig Wood, the chairman of the department of educational leadership at the University of Florida and a consultant to school-finance litigants in several states.

If educators and researchers succeed in discerning what strategies work and, by examining local costs, put a price tag on those ingredients, observers see the beginnings of a system where local school funding would be tied to policy goals and program outcomes. State officials, in turn, would have to begin to justify their current scattershot finance systems.

Assume, for example, that research showed that a low pupil-teacher ratio, new teaching and grouping strategies, longer school days, and increased professional development combined to produce a quality education. If analyses showed the cost of such a program in a given state was $5,500 per student, lawmakers would have an awkward time showing why they were budgeting $4,000 per pupil, while allowing local spending to range from $2,500 to $8,000.

Identifying and defining desired outputs better, Mr. Wood says, could force drastic changes in the way policymakers decide funding and other inputs.

"For state legislatures, most of the variables right now are input variables, things like what amount has been spent on students over a number of years," Mr. Wood explains. "Generally, we don't have any clear outcome measures. Once those are developed, then you really have a nightmare for legislatures because the question becomes are you going to spend it where you need to spend it."

"I see the courts saying equality of opportunity is still a question of inputs, but that could change with more reliable production-function studies," Mr. Alexander of Virginia Tech says. "Right now, the state of the art is that you cannot rely on them for public policy."

"The facts show that, in more cases than not, the calculation of the formula and level of appropriation is not the result of deliberations about what a child needs, but the result of politics, plain and simple," Ms. Hershkoff of the A.C.L.U. argues. "Legislatures are picking amounts out of a hat, which is the epitome of arbitrary and capricious action."

Political Obstacles Remain Despite New Ideas

In addition to being pushed from the local level through productivity studies and new cost-accounting programs, states may also be forced to alter their finance structures by the federal government, which is beginning to show interest in influencing the finance arena.

Early discussions about reauthorization of the Elementary and Secondary Education Act have brought suggestions from education advocates and lawmakers that equalization and finance reforms be encouraged by changes in the rules of the Chapter 1 and Chapter 2 programs.

In some cases, "federal aid may tip the balance, inducing states that would not have done so otherwise to adopt major school-finance reforms," says Iris C. Rotberg, a senior social scientist for the RAND Institute on Education and Training.

Ms. Rotberg suggests setting aside several billion dollars under the Chapter 2 block-grant program for equalization-incentive grants, which would be awarded to states that showed progress in closing local disparities. Current school-finance inequities have undermined efforts to raise the achievement of poor students with Chapter 1 compensatory-education grants, she argues.

Congressional leaders, however, are waiting for a sign from President Clinton. Although Mr. Clinton said during his campaign that he favored federal attempts to push state school-finance reforms, no specific plans have been mentioned. Even so, interest at the federal level appears to be gaining momentum.

Sen. Paul Simon, D-Ill., and Sen. Christopher J. Dodd, D-Conn., have mentioned a federal tax to offset some local property taxes as a funding source for education. Others have suggested that if the federal government opts at some point for a new value-added tax, a portion of the receipts could be set aside in a fund for local education improvements in poor areas.

Mr. Odden also predicts that increasing federal and state interest in open enrollment could push finance changes to make funding uniform among districts.

He suggests that states establish a foundation funding level sufficient to enable students to achieve the national education goals. On top of that base level, parents from individual schools could opt for an income-tax surcharge to fund enhancement. The aid would be sent largely to the school level and could be supplemented with federal funds.

The focus on national goals, standards, and assessments makes it almost inevitable that the federal government will take a stronger role in the issue.

"As we become increasingly interdependent as a nation, the problem will become apparent to national leaders and others," Mr. Kozol predicts. "It will become increasingly bizarre to say kids in Mississippi get $2,500 and kids in Connecticut get $8,000 and all of them have to take the same test."

"Even if Mississippi created the most egalitarian system, they are still going to have third-world schools compared to Connecticut," he says.

Mr. Kozol argues that state lawmakers should seize leadership of the finance issue, before local or federal pressure forces them to act, and begin making substantive changes. But it is a job that will take a large dose of political courage.

"I don't see anyone stepping forward to say we've got a system that doesn't work," says Mr. Leininger, the Illinois schools chief. "It's not the get-me-through-the-night problems that I worry about. It's the long range, the vision—saying here's where we need to be in three or five years."

In addition to balancing the demands of competing interest groups, state reform efforts must contend with the long-established tradition that dictates school funds be raised and spent locally.

"This is a big part of state budgets, and every single one of these legislators represents a school district," explains Mr. Augenblick, the Denver consultant. "Some can be statesmen, but every one of them is affected somehow by these decisions."

"Ultimately," Mr. Kozol argues, "this is not an issue for school-finance experts; it is an issue for civic heroes and heroines—people who can rise to the occasion. We need a good shot of transcendence in our legislatures."

Analysts express the hope that viewing school finance as a system that equitably invests in schools geared toward efficiency and performance could help realize a multitude of reform plans of the past decade.

"You see very little in the journals about accounting and costs and governance, but those may be the big issues in pulling the system around," Ms. Berryman claims. "Little things come out from the Education Department and other places about what works, but the bigger issue is, If you have a pot of money, where do you invest it?"

"These are decisionmaking issues that are not being addressed by anybody," she says.

Finance reforms are seen as holding the key to rationalizing education reforms, by tying funding to policy and achievement goals and lending purpose to the massive amounts of tax dollars spent each year.

"Much of the country thinks about education as our school or our project, and lots of teachers turn their noses up at the mention of what they think are cold notions of how the dollars are spent and the questions of are we getting results," Ms. Berryman says. "I wouldn't expect parents and teachers to see it all, but I would expect school boards and legislatures to. They need to think in system terms and ask where we invest our money."

Senator Parker agrees that it is time for state leaders to settle equity concerns and move on to performance issues and finance plans that focus all of the school players on the sailboat race he envisions.

As lawmakers strive to make sense of school finance, he says, education leaders and policymakers must also determine what strategies work and how to design local schools that better educate students.

"We need to unify people in seeking quality—that is the missing ingredient," Mr. Parker says. "We still don't have a definition of what quality is. We're off on a quest without knowing what we're looking for."

SIGNING UP THE PUBLIC

By Mark Walsh

In this chapter, we examine the critical need to make the public a full partner in the drive to improve the nation's schools.

FLINT, MICH.—Some 100 residents of this Rust Belt city have been invited to a college auditorium for a 90-minute "town meeting" on education reform and workforce competitiveness. The televised session will kick off a six-week campaign sponsored by many of Flint's business, community, and media leaders to improve public understanding of the need to restructure the schools.

If the decade-old message about the need to revamp the nation's schools were getting through, then this community should be the perfect place to look for a citizenry demanding change.

Few cities have felt the United States' declining economic competitiveness more than Flint, the birthplace of General Motors and its largest company town. As G.M.'s fortunes have plummeted, so have Flint's. More than 33,000 jobs have been lost here, contributing to an unemployment rate of more than 20 percent in this community of 140,000.

Despite the flagging economy, the average Flint resident has been slow to make the connection between the loss of well-paying blue-collar jobs and the need to improve education.

To help make that tie-in, civic leaders here brought in the Public Agenda Foundation to try to jolt residents into an awareness that Flint's future is linked to raising the academic performance of its students.

At the televised town meeting, three moderators roam with wireless microphones, à la the "Donahue" show. The discussion, though, seems less

Residents of Flint, Mich., gather for a "town meeting" on school reform and workforce competitiveness. In Flint and elsewhere, advocates of education reform— governors, educators, and businesspeople—are recognizing that they must find ways to build a deep and broad constituency among the public if they are to succeed in bringing about school change.

than spontaneous. One person after another touts an educational program or innovation that he or she believes is making progress here and in surrounding Genesee County.

Finally, Roy E. Peterson, the president of the local children's health center and a prominent civic activist, takes a turn at the mike and declares an end to the back-patting. "This sounds like a love-in," Mr. Peterson tells one of the moderators. "There are some big problems out there that we haven't heard [about] yet."

The Challenge: Bringing the Problem Home

The complacency evident in Flint is symptomatic of broader public attitudes toward the schools. Most communities, it seems, are hesitant, perhaps ill-equipped, to enter into a frank discussion of the hard issues that surround serious school reform.

Repeated warnings about poor student achievement and a growing concern about the nation's ability to compete in the world economy have penetrated on one level: National polls have consistently found that Americans believe our schools are in trouble.

But those same polls have found that many people believe those bad schools are in someone else's neighborhood, certainly not the schools that their own children attend.

"That is obviously a tremendous barrier to change," says Gov. Evan Bayh of Indiana, the chairman of the Education Commission of the States and a member of the National Education Goals Panel. "People think we need to change, but 'I'm O.K.' "

As a result, advocates of education reform—governors, educators, and businesspeople—face a monumental task. They must find ways to dramatize the problem that go beyond slick public relations in an effort to build a deep and broad constituency for reform.

That means reaching, with a sense of urgency, the majority of Americans without children in school. And it requires being clear about just what steps reformers want the public to take to support school change.

So far, it has proved exceedingly difficult to communicate to the public a vision of education that is far different from the rote learning that most Americans experienced when they were in school.

"Although experts tend to stress the kinds of skills required for the 21st-century world of work," a 1991 report by the Public Agenda Foundation states, "much of the public seems to yearn for the little red schoolhouse of the 19th century, with its emphasis on basic skills and traditional values."

While findings from a number of polls indicate that people remain generally satisfied with the quality of their local schools, they also provide evidence that Americans think the nation's education system as a whole must be overhauled to meet the economic challenges of the 1990's.

Two polls conducted by Louis Harris and Associates for the magazines *Agenda* and *Business Week* found that more than three-quarters of the respondents would be willing to pay more in taxes if there were a guarantee that the money would go to education reform.

Employers and college officials are especially concerned with the need to improve schools. A 1991 Harris survey for the Committee for Economic Development found that these groups have dramatically different views of how the schools are faring than do students and their parents.

Only 33 percent of employers and 41 percent of higher educators reported positively on recent high school students' ability to read. By contrast, 78 percent of high school students who got jobs and 86 percent who enrolled in college gave themselves positive grades in reading. Their parents had similarly positive opinions.

A harshly worded analysis of the findings charged that parents and students were "deluding themselves," and needed to be informed about "what employers and higher education expect."

But business and higher education have not rushed to make the changes in their employment and admissions standards that would bring that message home to students. Many people have argued that, without such changes, students will have little incentive to work hard in school and reform efforts will fail.

To many analysts, these polling data are evidence of a "reality gap." While politicians, policy experts, and the "consumers" of the public schools—business and higher education—are convinced that current schools are inadequate and must be improved, the public neither sees the need for radical change nor understands the enormity of the reforms being advocated.

The gap between public perception and reformers' admonishments for change has led to a number of high-profile efforts in recent years to enlist the citizenry in the cause of school improvement. Most of these, like the work here of the Public Agenda Foundation, have concentrated on public-relations campaigns.

The Public Agenda Foundation, founded in 1975 by the public-opinion analyst Daniel Yankelovich and former Secretary of State Cyrus Vance, is bent on linking educational improvement to economic competitiveness.

The foundation's "Help Wanted: Crisis in the Work Force" citizens'-

education campaign involves an intensive period of media coverage of economic and education issues to help the public understand the link between inadequate education and training, declining competitiveness, and a lower standard of living.

Scott Swenson, who oversees the Help Wanted project for the foundation, says campaigns in Hartford, Conn.; Indianapolis; Nashville; Phoenix; Seattle; Austin, Tex.; and other cities have significantly increased public understanding of education issues.

"The problem is that leaders have been talking about these issues for years and years," Mr. Swenson says. "But they have all this jargon—T.Q.M. (total quality management), site-based management, and so forth. The public has to understand the very basic issues."

The Help Wanted campaign is not designed to push one educational solution over another, he adds, but to get the public "up to speed."

The campaigns in Hartford, Indianapolis, and Phoenix increased support for extending the school year and giving tax breaks to businesses that upgrade worker skills, according to an evaluation of those campaigns. They also appeared to be effective in persuading members of minority groups that inadequate schools were an economic threat.

But they largely failed to shake middle-class complacency about the local schools. "Despite intensive media coverage of educational shortcomings," the evaluation found, "large numbers of residents in each campaign city continued to rate their local schools very highly."

Permitting Decisions 'To Move Forward'

It only makes sense that a business-oriented approach to education reform would appeal to Flint leaders. This city, after all, is still stinging from the filmmaker Michael Moore's darkly comic "Roger & Me," which explored G.M.'s role in the decline of his native city. The film, which lampooned the city's bungling economic-development efforts, still evokes strong reaction among Flint boosters.

"We felt done in" by the movie, says Mr. Peterson of the Mott Children's Health Center. "But in its anger, the community didn't see the truths that were there."

Determined to remedy Flint's plight, a civic partnership made up of *The Flint Journal*, WJRT-TV, the Charles Stewart Mott Foundation, the Genesee Area Focus Council, and the Flint Roundtable invited the Public Agenda Foundation to wage a campaign here.

To precede the effort, the Mott foundation surveyed Genesee County residents and found that most people remain pessimistic about the area's hopes for improvement, economic or otherwise. Asked what they believed to be the best things happening today in the county and in Flint, for example, more than two-thirds of the county residents said "nothing" or "don't know." Asked about the state of the public schools in the past three to five years, 17 percent of the respondents said they had improved, 44 percent said they were about the same, and 29 percent said they had gotten worse.

But the survey also showed that the public is not monolithic. Nearly half the minority-group members surveyed in Flint said the public schools had gotten worse in recent years.

Mr. Swenson says such signs of an appetite for change provide an opportunity for frank dialogue. "If the public is given the opportunity to talk about it," he says, "then they will come to the conclusions that will permit political decisions to move forward."

The key here, civic leaders believe, is to give residents a reason to support some of the good things under way by making stronger connections between education and the economy. The Flint school district, for example, has embraced a number of reforms—including outcome-based education and site-based management—and local industries are working with districts on school-to-work transition programs.

"We don't have any money, so we are forced to think and be creative," says Nathel Burtley, the superintendent. "We have asked, 'What should a community school system look like in a community that is downsizing?'"

John Austin, the executive director of the Flint Roundtable, an organization of business and community leaders dedicated to improving the Genesee County public schools, says the public remains "way behind," with "an outdated set of perceptions about the global economy."

In order for reforms to succeed, adds Mr. Peterson, who is also the leader of a children's-advocacy organization called Priority 90s, the public at large must be engaged.

"This community has a history of dependence," he says. "We depended on G.M. The workers depended on the [United Auto Workers union]. We have to take it upon ourselves to do more. As Flint goes, so can another 100 communities in this country."

But some key players here were less than overwhelmed with the Help Wanted campaign. Brian C. Veenhuis, the executive director of United Teachers of Flint, calls the effort "much ado about nothing."

"I don't think there's been that free and open discussion about the issues," he complains. "I think it has been very guided and very controlled by the Public Agenda Foundation."

As the Help Wanted campaign unfolded, it included dozens of coffee klatsches, civic meetings, newspaper articles, television reports, and citizen surveys. The ensuing debates highlighted some of the skepticism that greets the push for better schools.

At a meeting in a U.A.W. union hall, one activist sums up a concern that many residents here have when they discuss the need for increased skills.

"If they've got problems with the way the American workforce is educated, then why are the industries looking to move to Mexico?" he asks. "I can't believe the people there are better educated. That's cheaper labor, though."

Before the campaign ended early in 1993, thousands of residents of the Flint area filled out "ballots" asking whether they favored such proposals as lengthening the school year or requiring math and science during all grades for all students.

A sampling of reader comments published in *The Flint Journal* showed a range of opinion. One wrote, "We should move faster on improving our schools. The year 2000 is not soon enough." But another was doubting: "No society will ever educate its society to the level these so-called experts expect."

Communicating the Message 'in Human Terms'

There's no doubt that public-relations campaigns do have their limits in moving people to embrace needed educational reforms. Some educators have expressed resentment, for example, at the economic orientation of these efforts, arguing that there are compelling intellectual, social, and moral reasons to improve the schools.

Nonetheless, such campaigns remain a popular strategy in trying to mold public attitudes. One reason is that educators see them as a way to spread their message quickly and broadly. Another is that business groups have the high profiles and the money to mount such efforts.

For example, the Business Roundtable—an organization of chief executive officers of some 200 large national corporations that has made a 10-year commitment to systemic education reform—has spearheaded the development of a major five-year public-service advertising campaign devoted to the issue.

The "Keep the Promise" campaign, unveiled in 1992, involves free ads on television and in newspapers evoking the theme that the nation has promised each child a future and schools must improve to follow through on that obligation.

Margaret Mark, the executive vice president for research at Young & Rubicam, says the advertising agency was at first skeptical that a public-service ad campaign could shift attitudes on an issue such as school reform. "We concluded it would be very hard to get the majority of Americans to care about education reform," she says. "But it would not be hard to get them to care about children. We had to humanize the issue."

The first television spot focuses on Baby Jessica, the young girl whose rescue from a well in Texas captivated the nation. "No country comes to the aid of a child the way we do," says the spot. "Imagine if the same effort that went into saving that little child in Texas went into keeping the promise that every child in America gets the best education."

Another high-profile effort—President Bush's America 2000 strategy—is still alive in a number of cities and states. Even with the change in administrations, the new Secretary of Education, Richard W. Riley, is encouraging communities to keep up their efforts. In fact, Mr. Riley, who has given the effort the name Goals 2000, has himself participated in several satellite "town meetings" on school reform.

"America 2000 was a very important forum to get people involved," Mr. Riley has said. "We are going to take that and try not to miss a beat."

Members of the National Education Goals Panel are also well aware of the need to educate more of the general public about the six education goals whose progress it is monitoring. The problem, says Gov. Roy Romer of Colorado, a member of the goals panel, is that it is difficult for the average person to understand the concept of educational standards—a key point, since new performance standards are at the heart of the goals and the education reform process.

When Mr. Romer was attempting to explain what a standard was to a group of legislators in his home state, he made copies of an exercise from a book, *Measuring Up*, that demonstrated what math a 4th grader should be able to do. When they were done, the Governor says, "Every legislator took it and put it in his pocket because it is a concrete example."

Education-reform advocates, he charges, have failed to discuss such concepts in terms that the average parent can understand. "We have been too generic and too general about the language we use," he says. "We are not communicating it in human terms."

Providing New Images of 'Learning by Doing'

The best way to get the message about improved student learning across, some educators suggest, is to show people what that learning looks like and to make them feel welcome in the schools.

Doug Tuthill, the president of the Pinellas Classroom Teachers Association and a member of a Florida school-reform panel, uses a 15-minute videotape that shows students "learning by doing." He has shown the tape to people all over Pinellas County, including women in their 70's who belong to the local League of Women Voters.

Watching students doing meaningful work, he says, leads naturally into more abstract discussions of world-class standards and making learning relevant. "If you start with student learning," he says, "the pieces fit in."

The real challenge, he maintains, is not in convincing people that children should be well educated, but in helping them to see how they can become meaningfully involved in insuring that happens.

In Florida, where there are site-based management committees and spinoff subcommittees in each school, there are plenty of ways that the public can help out.

In Pinellas County, schools that are serious about involving local citizens have come up with a variety of common-sense strategies to make that possible: paying taxi fare for people who don't drive, providing on-site child care, meeting in local churches. "It's not glamorous," Mr. Tuthill says. "It's grunt work. But that's the kind of thing that people who are committed to [public involvement] are doing."

In Vermont, residents are invited to "school report nights"—like town meetings focused on student performance—to see what children have been doing in school. These kinds of meetings are easier to have in Vermont, because students in the 4th and 8th grades are collecting their work in portfolios.

Farmers fresh from milking their cows tromp through school gymnasiums in their muddy boots and ponder the student work that is plastered on the walls. Confronted with evidence that their children are capable of creative, complex work, people can more easily support reforms to enable that kind of learning, says Richard P. Mills, the state education commissioner.

"They are wild," he says. "You go into a gymnasium, and it's jammed with people, and you see student portfolios everywhere."

In Kentucky, the sweeping reform of the entire state education system has redefined the public's relationship to the schools.

The 1990 Kentucky Education Reform Act, known as KERA, mandated that parents be included on site-based management councils that are being phased in to every public school in the state. Schools currently forming such councils are trying to overcome low election turnout.

"Implementing this reform is not something the schools can do themselves," says Robert F. Sexton, the executive director of the Prichard Committee for Academic Excellence. "The bottom line is getting the individual parent and businessperson engaged. We are really talking about a civic movement, not just an education movement."

His group is helping to organize citizens' committees in every school district and is building awareness about the law through conferences and publications. Working with a statewide radio network, the committee has begun producing regular one-minute updates on school reform called "Today in Education."

A number of the state's leading businesses that have committed themselves to the successful implementation of the law are also focusing on involving their employees in schools.

Ashland Oil Inc., for example, sponsored KERA fairs at its facilities, stuffed information about the law in paycheck envelopes, and touted the reforms on its company electronic-mail system.

Many educators are becoming convinced, in fact, that finding ways to reach people where they live and work is an essential first step to deeper involvement in school reform.

To invite the public to participate in the development of curriculum frameworks, South Carolina officials printed thousands of copies of draft frameworks for math, foreign languages, and the visual and performing arts. Barbara S. Nielsen, the state superintendent of education, "insisted we send copies to every church, every neighborhood association, every beauty salon in the state," explains Dennis Bartels, a special assistant to the superintendent.

"The superintendent said, 'We are going to market these things,'" he adds. "We actually got responses back from hair salons."

A review panel is now incorporating the more than 3,400 responses to the frameworks into the final product. "This made me realize you really do have to market reform," Mr. Bartels says. "Just as a business creates a demand for its products, you have to create a demand for change."

Regaining Credibility With the Public

While it is true that educators and policymakers must become more adept at communicating their ideas, they must also become better listeners if they truly expect the public to be a positive partner for change.

Crises of confidence in the public schools are not uncommon. In many communities, members of the public have become vocal in their beliefs that districts are poorly managed, inefficient, and unable to respond to their concerns.

In Minneapolis, outraged constituents forced the school board to suspend the superintendent in February 1993 after an audit alleged several financial missteps. In making their decision, the board members cited an "erosion of public confidence" in the district's administration.

Certainly, many school officials learn to be better listeners after voters reject tax increases they don't believe are needed.

In Cincinnati, disgruntled taxpayers who complained that the public schools were performing poorly and were too top heavy with administrators forced the district into bankruptcy in 1990 by refusing to approve a tax-levy increase.

After the district promised to go along with the recommendations of a high-powered business group on streamlining the administration, the tide turned. Voters approved a levy, and, in return, the district slashed its administration by $16 million. J. Michael Brandt, the Cincinnati super-intendent, said at the time that the district had "lost credibility with the public." Now, Cincinnati educators hope that they have restored a measure of faith and will be able to turn to questions of improving students' performance.

Governor Romer has also heard the public's discontent, loud and clear. Last year, he unsuccessfully backed a ballot initiative that would have raised the state sales tax by one penny, with the funds committed to education. Voters rejected the initiative and, at the same time, approved Amendment 1, a tax-limitation measure that has forced districts across the state to slash their budgets.

Realizing that they had better pay closer attention to voters' ideas, state officials have set up interactive computers at several shopping malls, where residents can give their opinions on a survey about state budget priorities. The survey asks Coloradans, for example, whether they would support eliminating kindergarten or charging fees for foreign languages or sports.

"With the passage of Amendment 1 in November, the people of the state made it clear they want to be more involved in government decisionmaking," Governor Romer tells participants in an introduction to the computerized budget survey.

When things get bad enough, public uprisings can shake the foundations of a system.

In Chicago, parents, taxpayers, business leaders, and education advocates fed up with years of labor strife and abysmal test scores persuaded the Illinois legislature to restructure the Chicago public schools. The public is now running the city's 540 schools—hiring and firing principals and tending to the leaking roofs and chronic supply shortages that the bureaucracy was unable to fix.

The Chicago example is an extreme form of public involvement, but many educators who are trying to build bridges to their communities note that what they are doing is trying to create a political constituency for change.

"This is really old-fashioned, grassroots organizing," Mr. Tuthill says.

Jonathan Kozol, the author of the influential book *Savage Inequalities*, points out that parents and other citizens have to be empowered politically to develop their own lists of educational goals.

"I don't think we need to organize parents around a list of goals we have created," he says. "We have to educate parents in the political skills of making change. That is a very dangerous thing, because they might decide to get rid of us."

As Theodore R. Sizer, the chairman of the Coalition of Essential Schools, notes, parents and the public often have more prosaic but valid concerns than do reform-minded educators. Parents, he says, want to know that their children are safe at school and have caring, competent teachers. Without addressing these basic issues, he warns, schools are unlikely to be able to sign up the public for more ambitious reforms.

Indeed, advocates of public education have increasingly become concerned simply with keeping the public as a client.

An organization called Parents for Public Schools, which began in Jackson, Miss., has had some success at reversing the "white flight" that accompanied desegregation in that city.

The group has spawned a number of chapters across Mississippi and the nation. They try to spread the word that public schools have good things to offer and that children need to learn in integrated classrooms to prepare for the workplace.

Potholes and Protests: The Risks of Reform

The price a district ends up paying for not signing up the public can be even costlier when an ambitious reform agenda is on the line. When a community or school starts down the road to restructuring, it inevitably encounters potholes. The current system, after all, has vocal constituents who are satisfied with things as they are.

When a school starts changing such practices as ability grouping, grading systems, schedules, and teaching methods, it can run into heavy public resistance.

In many locales, parents of children served by gifted and talented programs have protested efforts to mix children of all abilities in classrooms, arguing that their children would lose out.

While many educators say they welcome public involvement, once the debate over reform begins, it can create unexpected pressure to produce immediate results.

In Rochester, N.Y., a series of high-profile reforms that dramatically boosted teachers' salaries have created a public backlash, with many residents arguing that teachers are not accountable. The backdrop to these discussions, as in many urban areas, is the poor academic performance of many minority students.

For the past several years, the public has loudly demanded proof that the higher salaries and reforms, like career ladders and site-based management, are working.

One local newspaper columnist summed up the mood this way: "The city school district does not exist to give well-paying jobs to ... teachers. And neither is its purpose to be a test lab for school-reform theorists. The good people of Rochester pay school taxes so their kids will get an education. And right now, that just isn't happening for enough students."

Even in Princeton, N.J., a wealthy suburb known for its high-quality public schools, a parents' coalition has demanded that the district close the achievement gap for minority students by, among other things, including them in more advanced classes. The parents also have fielded several school board candidates.

The nature of the reforms that are being advocated—teaching children to think critically, de-emphasizing the teacher as the font of all knowledge, and meshing schools with social services—also can offend deeply held beliefs.

One of the major goals of the Odyssey Project in Gaston County, N.C., was to increase parent and community involvement in schools. But the project, which received a coveted $2.1 million grant from the New American Schools Development Corporation, has instead stirred significant opposition from conservative community members who say the program subverts their religious beliefs.

Educators in the blue-collar, textile community say they never anticipated such protests, and concede that they may have added to the confusion by using educational jargon rather than explaining their goals in more common language. A major point of contention was the project's focus on student outcomes, which some community members charge was an attempt to teach values at the expense of core academic subjects.

The National Alliance for Restructuring Education, a partnership of states and school districts that won another of the sought-after grants, is well aware of the risks in significantly changing education. The group, says Andy Plattner of the National Center on Education and the Economy, one of the alliance partners, has identified securing public support as a key element in its success.

Many of the alliance's efforts over the past two years have been threatened, he says, because "the public was not on board."

The public often does not understand what a school district is trying to accomplish by restructuring, he explains, or doesn't feel "invited in" to the process.

For its project, the alliance will attempt two public-support initiatives. It is negotiating to have the Public Agenda Foundation lead a Help Wanted campaign in Vermont, Kentucky, and Rochester. It has also asked Ernesto Cortes Jr., a Texas-based community organizer, to develop a handbook for the participating sites.

Mr. Cortes and the Texas Interfaith Education Fund have developed a well-regarded model for helping low-income parents become involved with schools. Their project, now in some 55 schools in Texas and Arizona, uses trained coordinators who canvass the community, visiting parents at home to encourage them to visit the schools and to participate in sessions in which they learn about reform strategies.

"The focus is on developing a constituency for reform, and teaching parents and leaders that they have a stake in it," says Mr. Cortes, the director of the Texas Interfaith Education Fund.

"It is basically just a matter of teaching parents to understand the budget process and the bureaucratic process," he explains. "We try to get parents to understand the collaborative role they can play."

In 1992, the Texas Education Agency formed a partnership with the organization to help 32 schools develop educational plans.

The Texas Interfaith Education Fund's philosophies and practices were developed in Fort Worth, in conjunction with a local organization called Allied Communities of Tarrant. In 1986, the local group established a pilot parent-involvement project at Morningside Middle School, where the police were called to settle disturbances two or three times a day. Despite the problems, a meeting called to talk about solutions drew only two parents.

After the project began, test scores improved, violence decreased, and a core group of about 25 to 30 parents became involved in every major aspect of the school. Parents started attending workshops on standardized testing and on how to help their children continue learning during the summer.

"We are seeing the difference," says Morningside's principal, Odessa Ravin.

The Media and the 'Twilight-Zone Beat'

In trying to get across sophisticated new ideas about teaching, learning, and the nature of schooling for the 21st century, educators and their partners have not had much help from the media.

Although media coverage of education issues has improved in recent years—and newspapers in Chicago and Kentucky contributed to the momentum for reform—covering schools still remains the "twilight-zone beat," says a 1991 study in the *Gannett Center Journal.*

Bill Blakemore, an education correspondent for ABC News, reports on reform issues and on promising programs in "American Agenda" segments. By focusing on solutions, he notes, he is forced to do a better job of reporting what is wrong with schools. But generally, Mr. Blakemore says, "the broadcast media have missed the boat."

Part of the problem is that education is not perceived as important by assignment editors—because they, in turn, don't think the public is interested.

"Ten years into the reform era, the reporter who covers the schools has what is still considered one of the lesser assignments on a typical family newspaper or TV station," writes George R. Kaplan, a longtime observer of the media's coverage of education. "Editors believe, with some justification, that their readers and viewers are not poised breathlessly to receive the latest word on how the 6th graders of William Howard Taft Middle School made out on their reading tests."

The cynicism of the press notwithstanding, however, many have concluded that the public may now be willing and able to take on the serious challenge of improving the nation's schools for all children.

For starters, the public's anti-tax mood and desire to have a new role in government decisionmaking appear to provide a receptive climate for the open back-and-forth discussions that must occur.

The nation's governors, stung by a series of defeats of tax increases and reform packages, are particularly aware of the need to reach out to the public. "We are in an era when the public is hesitant to put dollars forward for reform unless it can be shown to have a clear effect," says Paul Goren, a senior policy analyst with the National Governors' Association.

Besides the Colorado defeat, a tax-and-reform package pushed by Gov. John Ashcroft of Missouri, a fiscally conservative Republican, was soundly defeated in 1991. But that same year, voters in Oklahoma rejected a proposed repeal of a sweeping education reform law that included additional taxes.

After their experience with ballot initiatives, Mr. Goren says, officials from states where voters rejected their proposals recommended pursuing legislation, rather than taking issues directly to the people.

Now, the governors' association is preparing a manual for state officials on how to attract and sustain public support for the national educational goals and state reform initiatives. Such political leadership, starting at the top with President Clinton, will be a key ingredient if the American public is to be mobilized to support real improvement in education.

But no amount of inspiration and exhortation from the top will be sufficient to get the massive job done. It's a task that requires the support, involvement, and commitment of all Americans.

"The power to make these changes," Mr. Mills, the Vermont commissioner, says, "is in the hands of millions of people."

PART THREE

OFF AND RUNNING

By Lynn Olson

HENDERSON, KY.—It's 8:30 A.M. and 45 children, ages 5 to 7, gather in a bright open space at South Heights Elementary School to begin their day with calendar exercises. "Five-year-olds, let's count together," a teacher commands, and the youngest members tally up the days of the month thus far. An older child digs through a packet of cards and selects one with "Wednesday" written on it in large block type.

"Let's spell it together," the teacher says. And the whole class chants in chorus. Over the next hour, the students sing songs about the days of the week, identify colors and patterns tied to the calendar activities, and chat about Dr. Seuss, the "author of the month," with a second teacher also working with the cluster of 45 youngsters.

Down the hall, nine educators—five teachers, two student teachers, and two aides—convene to plan next week's activities for another group of 5- to 9-year-olds. In the school's conference room, three teachers spend a day away from their classes to score the 4th-grade writing portfolios required by the state.

The building also houses a preschool for disadvantaged children; an extended-day program that provides after-school tutoring to students who need extra help; and a family-resource center that provides short-term counseling, parenting workshops, and social-service referrals to more than 400 neighborhood families.

Overseeing the entire program is a school council composed of three teachers, two parents, the principal, and the head custodian (on an ex-officio basis).

Welcome to Kentucky, where schools like South Heights Elementary are struggling to implement what many describe as the most comprehensive and integrated piece of school-reform legislation in the country.

At South Heights Elementary School in Henderson, Ky., Brooke Frazer plots a graph of her scores on daily activities for her math portfolio. After three years of lawsuits, continued debate, and foot-dragging, the Kentucky Education Reform Act has been most successful in bringing about changes in the state's primary classrooms.

The Kentucky Education Reform Act, or KERA, was signed into law in April 1990, after the state supreme court ruled that the entire system of public education in Kentucky was unconstitutional and ordered lawmakers to start over. The act weaves together changes in school governance, finance, curriculum, assessment, and teacher licensure to support strong, new learning outcomes for students. It also takes aim at pre-school and out-of-school factors that affect achievement. Financed with a $1.4 billion tax increase in its first two years, KERA is the most ambitious effort in the nation to use a comprehensive approach to state policy to bring about radical change in individual schools.

"Whether you agree or disagree with its underlying philosophy, it is a major attempt to change a very big system," observes Jane L. David, one of the dozens of researchers scrutinizing the progress of the Bluegrass State. "And, whatever happens, there's a tremendous amount to be learned from it."

But as the law completes the third year of a six-year phase-in, its policies are colliding with the hard realities of life in school, earning it such unflattering acronyms as the "Kentucky Early Retirement Act" and "Keeping Everyone Running Around."

"Will Rogers summed it up best when he said, 'Liberty doesn't work as well in practice as it does in speeches,' " jokes Marnel Moorman, the president of the powerful Kentucky Education Association. "We're finding that KERA doesn't work as well in our classrooms as it did in the law."

Today, Kentuckians are grappling with problems common to school reform everywhere: How rapidly and in what order should changes that will take years to complete be phased in? How should the capacity and leadership for reform be built into the system? How should the state education department shift from its traditionally bureaucratic role to one based more on being supportive? And how soon before students, parents, and policymakers can expect that true changes in the classroom will no longer be the exception to the rule?

Since the act was passed, more than 10 court cases have been filed challenging various portions of it. The attorney general has issued nearly 50 opinions directly related to education reform. And the legislature's Office of Education Accountability, created as the watchdog of reform, has logged approximately 3,500 phone calls.

Slumping revenues threaten the law's continued funding. And a growing chorus of teachers and administrators is demanding that the legislation be modified, despite staunch opposition from its creators.

Yet, as Pam Coe, the principal investigator for a study of the reforms by the

Appalachia Regional Laboratory, points out, "Kera is having more of an impact than anyone would have anticipated at this stage."

Despite resistance, changes are visible in some districts and schools. The public and educators generally back the direction of the reforms. And a much-feared backlash to the large tax increase that was passed to pay for the reforms has not materialized. Instead, much of the grumbling may indicate that the reforms have struck home.

'Second-Greatest Revolution' in American Education

The Kentucky legislation is based on two simple assumptions: All children can learn at high levels, and schools are the locus for change. It follows naturally, then, the measure's architects and supporters say, that schools should be given the necessary resources to help students succeed and that they be held accountable for the results.

Thomas C. Boysen, Kentucky's commissioner of education, describes the law as the "second-greatest revolution in American public education." In the early part of this century, the common-schools movement gave every child the right to attend school. "Kera," Mr. Boysen says, "has the intention of giving every child the right to succeed in school."

The law specifies six learning goals that all Kentucky students must meet. (Since the law's passage, those goals have been elaborated into 75 "valued outcomes.") It then orders the state to develop a new system of portfolios, performance assessments, and paper-and-pencil tests to measure children's progress. Schools are to be held accountable for how students do on such tests, as well as for attendance, retention, and graduation rates; students' health; and their postgraduation success.

If schools do well, they are rewarded. If they do poorly—and their proportion of successful students decreases by 5 percent or more—they are punished. For example, parents may be given the option of transferring their children to another school, and teachers and other school employees may be placed on probation and possibly dismissed.

In exchange, the law creates an equitable funding formula for schools in the state. It also creates school-based decisionmaking councils to give schools substantial control over how they operate.

In addition, the law mandates some instructional strategies and support services to help educators succeed with students. It requires that nongraded-primary programs be established in every elementary school by the fall of 1993; that high-quality preschool programs be provided for all 4-year-olds at risk of educational failure; that a network of family-resource and youth-service centers be created at or near schools in which at least 20 percent of students are eligible for free or subsidized school meals; and that extended-school services, such as before- and after-school tutoring, be provided for youngsters in need of extra help.

The state also anticipates spending $200 million to bring technology into the schools, and it has substantially increased its commitment to professional development and training.

Such changes would be radical anywhere, but no more so than in Kentucky. According to the 1990 Census, only Mississippi had a lower percentage of adults who had finished high school. Nineteen percent of the state's residents lived in poverty in 1989; the poverty rate among children was 25 percent.

That same year, no district in Kentucky—including the wealthiest—spent at least the national per-student average on its schools.

"What Kentucky supplied to the Rust Belt for years was a highly committed, hard-working, uneducated group of laborers," one observer says. "Detroit, Michigan, was designed for dropouts from Kentucky schools."

Henderson, home to South Heights Elementary School, sits in western Kentucky on the south bank of the Ohio River, overlooking the neighboring city of Evansville, Ind. An old river town surrounded by flat agricultural fields, its Victorian mansions still house tunnels used to help slaves escape to freedom.

The 7,800-student Henderson County district, which serves outlying communities as well as the city, is the 14th-largest district in the state. In 1990-91, the school year after the reform act was passed, Henderson received more than a 13 percent increase in state funding.

Measured by traditional criteria, Henderson County does pretty well. More than 60 percent of its graduates go on to college. Its dropout rate hovers at 2 percent. And the community is generally supportive of its schools. "We did a good job with the upper half of our kids," Gayle W. Ecton, the superintendent of schools, explains. "And yet, those of us who had looked at it knew there was a whole group of kids with whom we weren't doing very well."

Several years before KERA passed, Henderson began pushing a school-reform agenda of its own: promoting participatory decisionmaking throughout the district, investing in leadership training for its principals, and shifting greater control over resources to the schools. It has also formed a partnership with the Center for Leadership in School Reform in Louisville to help it navigate the change process.

As a result, school officials here were ready to commit themselves to the law, despite some reservations. "We've never agreed 100 percent with KERA," David McKechnie, the chairman of the Henderson County board of education, says, "but basically our attitude is, 'It's the law. Let's make it work.'"

Today, traces of the reform act's passage are everywhere, both in Henderson and beyond:

- From July 1990 to July 1992, state and local funding of precollegiate education in Kentucky each increased by almost 25 percent. The gap between the state's richest and poorest districts was reduced by one-third.

- All elementary schools, including those in Henderson, have already or are preparing to make the shift to ungraded-primary classrooms.

- More than one-third of Kentucky's schools, and all 16 of those in Henderson County, have school-based decisionmaking teams.

- Major progress has been made in developing the first stage of the state's new assessment and accountability system. Earlier this year, every school received a baseline score indicating how far it must improve to qualify for rewards or avoid penalties.

- For the first time, extra educational and social services are available at the school site for large numbers of children and their families.

- The Kentucky Department of Education has undergone a wrenching reorganization in which all of its employees were forced to reapply for their jobs.

Law's Comprehensiveness Is Taking Its Toll

To many politicians and educators, KERA's strength lies in its comprehensive and interconnected nature. "We've learned ... that, if you work on one problem at a time—piecemeal—you never get it done," Superintendent Ecton says.

But the sheer pace and number of reforms have left many schoolpeople overwhelmed and unable to focus on the larger picture. "Our teachers are exhausted, to be quite frank," says Jim Young, the superintendent of the Russellville Independent School District in southwestern Kentucky. "And I think this is a statewide phenomenon. They are just worn out."

Principals and teachers complain that it's impossible to keep up with all of the paperwork and reading materials generated by the law. Phyllis Becker, an English and Latin teacher at Henderson County High School, says, "I've been taken out of my classroom so much for meetings and committees and workshops that I don't feel I'm doing as good a job as I have done in the past." And Steve Garner, a 4th-grade teacher at South Heights Elementary, says: "We need the reform. But they want to see a lot of results so fast that it's putting too much pressure on us to get things done."

The biggest debate centers on whether the state's time lines are realistic. Most lawmakers argue that the tight deadlines keep everyone motivated and focused on the task at hand. But schoolpeople complain about doing too much at once—and not always in the right order.

Political wrangling at the state level, for example, has held up money to buy new technology. And educators are scurrying to revamp their instructional content and methods even before the state's new assessment system and draft curriculum frameworks are in place. "There're a lot of people who argue a lot of our time lines were a little too aggressive," State Sen. David Karem of Louisville says. "I'd argue, if you don't make aggressive time lines, it isn't going to happen."

The pressure is greatest in the elementary schools, where teachers charge that it's impractical to demand that ungraded-primary classrooms be fully in place by the fall of 1993.

Even in schools that embraced the requirement ahead of schedule, researchers have found that educators vary considerably in both their support for the program and in their ability to teach in the desired ways. A study released in early 1993 by the National Governors' Association and the Prichard Committee for Academic Excellence, a citizens' group that has been a driving force behind the reforms, concludes that the deadline is not realistic for most schools.

"We've got teachers who've been teaching 20 or 25 years," Mr. Ecton, the Henderson superintendent, notes. "And then all of a sudden we say, 'Let's do cooperative learning, peer tutoring, and the whole-language approach and use developmentally appropriate materials.' It's overwhelming, and you get more resistance."

At Longfellow Elementary School in Mayfield, in the far western part of the state, Principal Elsie Jones has told her teachers to take it slowly, regardless of the state mandates. "We're going to do the best we can do for our students," says Ms. Jones, who has strong reservations about mixing kindergarten students in with older youngsters. "And we're not going to lie about it either."

Teachers who question the wisdom of including kindergartners in ungraded programs say they object to the approach on two grounds—both for developmental reasons and because of logistical problems posed by half-day kindergarten classes.

Some of the disgruntlement stems from a feeling among teachers that they were misled. The Kentucky Department of Education originally told schools that they would have until 1995-96 to fully implement the requirement. But lawmakers, who felt that schools were dragging their feet, returned to the issue two years after KERA was passed and clarified their intent to have an earlier deadline.

On the other hand, educators acknowledge that many schoolpeople feel pressured now because they did not begin to make changes soon after the reforms were first passed in 1990. Instead, they wasted two years hoping that the law would be repealed.

Similarly, because schools have until 1996 to form school-based management councils, many have held back.

In the Fayette County school district, which includes the city of Lexington, Superintendent Ronald E. Walton says a number of school faculties have voted several times to reject proposals for school-based management. "Teachers are saying, 'Look, we've got our plates full, and, if that's not something we have to do right now, we're just not interested in taking on another assignment,' " he explains.

"We all know that there are those people who would never move short of a keg of dynamite," Mr. Ecton says. The time lines "were our keg of dynamite."

Student-Assessment Results Spur Host of New Questions

But if the time lines were the dynamite, the burning fuse that has sent educators scurrying is the state assessment results, released in the fall of 1992, and the "threshold" scores assigned to schools earlier this year. The scores specify how much each school will have to improve over the next two years to avoid state penalties.

Although Kentucky is still in the process of developing a full-blown assessment system, interim measures in reading, writing, math, science, and social studies were given to all students in grades 4, 8, and 12 last year. For the first time in the state's history, how pupils performed was compared not against each other but against absolute standards for what students should know and be able to do. The state determined how many students performed at the "novice," "apprentice," "proficient," and "distinguished" levels.

The results were startling. Roughly 90 percent of the state's students scored below the "proficient" level, including many who have traditionally done well on other measures of performance.

But it's not clear whether the gap between where students are and the state's high expectations for them will serve as a rallying point for reform.

Gerald Wischer, the president of the Ohio Valley National Bank in Henderson, says, "Those tests didn't come out nearly as well as the community thought they should."

"Maybe," he speculates, "we're not as good as we thought we were."

Other superintendents and principals say parents are not particularly upset about the results because they're not sure the tests are valid. "Quite honestly," Mr. Ecton says, "I think that with many of our staff and our community members, too, there's a good bit of denial that our kids aren't that bad." Nancy Graham, a parent and a member of the school council at Spottsville Elementary School in Henderson County, reflects the view of many parents when she says, "I don't know that I put a lot of value on the tests."

Far more threatening to educators are the baseline and threshold scores released for each school earlier this year. The baseline scores reflect a combination of how a school's students performed on the assessments, as well as such data as school-attendance and graduation rates. The scores are based on a scale of 0 to 100, with most schools scoring around 30. Although schools have 20 years to bring all students up to a "proficient" level, they are expected to improve by a certain percentage every two years, known as the threshold score.

Schools that exceed their threshold goal by 1 percentage point or more are eligible for significant monetary rewards. Those that miss the mark will be required to produce a school-improvement plan and be given state funds and technical assistance to do so.

Schools that decline by less than 5 percent will also be assigned a "distinguished Kentucky educator"—one of a number of experienced teachers and administrators on leave to the state education department—to help them shape up. And educators in schools whose scores decline by more than 5 percent will be put on probation, with the possibility of dismissal. Parents can also choose to bail out of such schools.

This strict accountability lies at the heart of Kentucky school reform, which relies on local educators and parents to restructure their schools so that all students can succeed.

Ed Reidy, the associate commissioner for curriculum, assessment, and accountability, says that release of the baseline scores and of the thresholds that schools must meet in 1994 have made school reform "real" to people.

The data reveal, for instance, that many schools in wealthier districts have as far to go in boosting their performance as their poorer neighbors.

"We called in all the school principals the day that we gave the results," recalls Ruie Murphy, Henderson's assistant superintendent for instruction and student performance. "It was like attending the funeral home when you walk in and there's been a sudden death. For the first time, I think, the real sobering effect of all this hit the administrators."

But others question whether most schools will be able to reach their thresholds in 1994, and particularly in subsequent years, as the gains rely more and more on pulling all youngsters up to a high standard.

And they note that most teachers, rather than being motivated by the possibility of a reward, are now motivated by fear. The state has set aside $34 million in a trust fund to pay for the rewards in the years to come. But teachers still remember a pledge by former Gov. Martha Layne Collins to pay them a $300 bonus that never materialized. "I've heard more people worry about being sanctioned than I've heard talk about being rewarded," says Mike Haile, the president of the Henderson County Education Association.

Whether such fear will prove to be a potent motivator in a system where successes are rarely recognized and failures are often overlooked is hard to forecast. "You don't assume that when people resist, it's because they're unwilling to change," argues Phillip C. Schlechty, the president of the Center for Leadership in School Reform in Louisville. "I think there's been too much made of [rewards and sanctions] and not enough made of the support."

"People in the schools that we've been observing know what skills kids are going to be required to have," Ms. Coe of the Appalachia Regional Laboratory says, "but they haven't a clue as to how to impart those skills. The people who are running scaredest are the people who have the least idea about how to achieve the changes."

Educators also complain that the law includes no consequences for individual students based on how well they perform on the assessments and that youngsters, therefore, have no incentive to achieve. "Students feel no responsibility," Michael Bussiere, the coordinator of health and physical education at Henderson County High School, asserts. "We're expecting students to go in and perform to the best of their ability on these tests, and I think that's unrealistic."

Trading Old Regulations for Even More New Ones?

Theoretically, the tradeoff for such strict accountability was a substantial amount of freedom for schools.

Indeed, since 1990, some of the state's most onerous requirements for schools have been dropped. For example, the state no longer tells teachers how many minutes to spend on reading or math each day. And it has thrown out an accreditation process that once held schools accountable for the number of books in their libraries and the number of guidance counselors on their payrolls.

The department of education has also tried to couch much of its advice to schools in the form of advisories and suggestions, not mandates.

But many charge that the system is still too bureaucratically driven. "Very frankly, we are finding even more regulations and more restrictive regulations than we were before KERA," says David Keller, the executive director of the Kentucky School Boards Association.

"Local educators are so used to being told exactly what to do, and state officials are so used to telling them," observes Robert F. Sexton, the executive director of the Prichard Committee, the citizens' advocacy group, "that changing those cultures is very slow and difficult. Every time the state department says anything, it's taken by many school districts as a regulation—which to me demonstrates that they want those regulations."

But KERA has also generated a lot of paperwork. Under the law, school boards are required to direct every school to develop a school-improvement plan. In order to receive new computers and technology from the state, schools must submit a technology plan. Each school must have a professional-development plan. And every elementary school must have an ungraded-primary plan as well as a plan for purchasing textbooks and manipulative materials.

Lawmakers have also asked the state department of education to monitor how schools spend their funds for extended-school services. "I think that accounts for the feeling that this is a lot of monitoring for a deregulated situation," Commissioner Boysen says.

"We are thinking as hard as we can about how to simplify the planning and process requirements," he adds. "I don't think we've got the right mix now." But, he cautions: "This is a planned decentralization. It's not a planned loss of control."

Educators, blaming Mr. Boysen's reported tendency to micromanage in part, also fault the department for distributing inconsistent information and disseminating it in an untimely fashion. At South Heights Elementary, for instance, teachers who needed to score portfolio assessments on a Wednesday complained that they first received the forms that Monday.

And at the high school, Ms. Becker says: "We don't feel that the instructions we get from the state are adequate. It's almost like, 'Do it, and then we'll tell you what we wanted you to do.' "

Since December 1992, at least six top officials at the department have moved on—some voluntarily, some not, and several to higher-paying jobs outside the state. Mr. Boysen describes it as "trying to manage the fit in jobs that themselves are evolving," and claims, "Morale is good."

"The number of people who have left or indicated that they're leaving is not unexpected," agrees Joseph W. Kelly, the chairman of the state board of education. "This is an extremely high-visibility, high-pressure, stressful environment that the department operates in."

Many maintain that, under the circumstances, Mr. Boysen has performed admirably.

But communication with the field is clearly a problem. "My personal feeling," Ms. Coe says, "is that it may have been a mistake to reorganize the state department so thoroughly at the same time the districts were being required to restructure."

The law also contains some built-in tensions between top-down and bottom-up reform. For instance, it requires schools to create decisionmaking councils that are designed to give local educators greater control over the reforms. But then it specifies who can sit on such councils: one principal, two teachers, and two parents.

Although schools can appeal to the state board of education to create councils with a different composition, some educators complain that their proposals have been rejected.

In the Jefferson County school district in Louisville, nearly 130 of the district's 150 schools engage in some form of shared decisionmaking, most pre-dating KERA. But only three schools have voted to adopt school-based decisionmaking councils, as defined by the law. And two of those use alternative models that were approved by the state board.

In Henderson, many school councils include teachers' aides and other noncertified employees—who make up more than 40 percent of the district's workers—on an ex-officio basis. "But it's still not the same," says Superintendent Ecton, who worries that such employees have been sent a message that they're not important.

'It Can Be Different, and It Can Be Right'

Despite such strains, KERA has begun to spark flickers of change in the classroom—though they have yet to ignite into a full-scale explosion. The most visible glimmers are in the elementary schools.

At Spottsville Elementary School in Henderson County, a teacher leads a mixed-age group of 7- and 8-year-olds through an integrated unit of social-studies and math activities. The lesson begins with a game: Thirty-four children sit in a circle on the floor and pass a red balloon to the beat of music. When the record stops, the child holding the balloon must describe a time when there was "scarcity" in his life—only one bicycle and two children, three ice-cream cones and four friends.

The teacher, Janey Couch, then groups the students in teams of four, each of which is given a paper with some drawings on it. Working cooperatively, the children are to look at the pictures and place an "X" next to those that depict a shortage. "You've got to work together," she warns them. "Everybody in the group has got to decide and agree."

After 15 minutes or so, the class reconvenes, and the teams defend their findings. One picture shows three people and four cookies. Some students identify a shortage, since there are not enough cookies for each child to receive two. Others, noting that each youngster could eat a cookie with one left over, disagree. The teacher accepts both arguments, as long as they are reasoned clearly.

Then she asks the teams to get back together and create math problems that depict each drawing. When the whole class gathers again, students have come up with an impressive array of mathematical equations that encompass addition, subtraction, multiplication, and division.

Although Ms. Couch forces each group to think through its response, her basic message is this: "It can be different, and it can be right, because we asked you to make mathematical problems with these pictures. I didn't tell you what type."

Throughout the exercises, a second teacher acts as coach and guide to individual teams struggling to reach a solution.

This is precisely the kind of problem-solving, hands-on activity that KERA is meant to generate.

But from school to school and even from classroom to classroom in Henderson and throughout the state, such breakthroughs are fitful and uneven. "Some schools have made significant and dramatic progress," one interim research report observes, "and for others, the progress was barely discernible."

Moreover, as a visitor works up through the education system—from elementary school to middle school to high school—the changes become more sporadic and less pronounced.

In the earliest grades, fewer desks have been aligned in rows. Room arrangements are more flexible, and hands-on activities and scads of laminated books, written by students, are evident everywhere. More and more activities also span the disciplines, such as when children at South Heights construct a time line of Dr. Seuss' life after reading several of his books.

In the 4th grade, where the state has required students to keep writing portfolios of their work—and now math portfolios as well—teachers report more writing going on. And there is a greater emphasis on cooperative learning and teamwork. Particularly in schools where their colleagues have embraced ungraded-primary classrooms, teachers in grades 4, 5, and 6 are beginning to look over their shoulders at what's coming.

At the junior high level, at least in Henderson, teachers are also beginning to explore cooperative learning and mixed-ability grouping.

But most acknowledge that the tough nut to crack is the high schools. With the exception of being asked to do more writing projects, because of the portfolio requirements, Henderson students report little or no difference in their classrooms. The final recommendations of a statewide task force on high school restructuring are expected in the fall of 1993.

A casual walk through Henderson County High School—a large comprehensive school in a sprawling building—reveals both rays of hope and signs of ennui. In one English class, special-education and regular students work side by side with a team of two teachers who enthusiastically describe their use of investigative projects and cooperative learning. But in another room down the hall, the teacher marches sophomores through workbook exercises on normative-case pronouns, and several students slump at their desks. One student mutters that timeless complaint: "This class is sooo boring."

Asked about the changes under KERA, Ms. Becker, an English teacher at the school, says: "I don't know if you could tell just by looking. I don't think it would be that obvious."

Building a Culture To Sustain Reform

The uneven nature of the changes in schools and classrooms underscores the biggest hurdle that KERA faces—how to build the capacity and leadership for reform. "If we don't build a culture that's going to sustain and support and nurture the changes that we've put in place," Mr. Ecton warns, "they're not going to live. I think there's maybe a lack of appreciation for that at the state level."

Under KERA, the state allocates funds to districts for ongoing training based on their student enrollment. The money amounted to $17 per student this year. In addition, lawmakers have permitted local boards to use up to five instructional days for staff development.

Across the state, teachers say they are getting more and better training than ever before. And in districts that have made the investment, educators report feeling more confident about their ability to implement the law. Henderson, for example, has more than tripled the amount of professional development offered to its employees in the past two years.

"We put more training money into this than we've ever had before," Mr. Sexton of the Prichard Committee says. "Over all, a remarkable amount. But it's still not enough. The scale and scope of this thing is so huge that there's almost a bottomless pit of need."

Although the law created eight regional training centers to assist teachers and administrators, they are staffed at a ratio of one employee for every 1,000 teachers. Many districts have not used the available instructional days for training. And researchers question whether educators are getting the right kind of support and guidance.

Compared with the amount of professional development offered to teachers, there is even less training available to superintendents, board members, principals, and union leaders on how to manage reform. "The legislature is at fault," Senator Karem concedes. "We did not provide enough assistance for training and for professional development at all in this situation." But, he adds, "They're hard dollars to provide."

Moreover, many teachers feel they are already getting more training than they can absorb. The real problem, they say, is not information but time. Sharon Stalls, a teacher at South Heights Elementary, says some of her colleagues "have reached their saturation point. We really need to go back to the classroom and implement what we've seen."

Henderson County's experience also highlights how much district leaders can promote reform. But while KERA is clear about what school boards and superintendents should not do, it is less clear about what they should.

In response to charges of cronyism, nepotism, and abuse throughout the state, lawmakers in 1990 banned school boards from hiring anyone below the level of superintendent, required that they institute competitive-bidding and other commonly accepted business practices, and made it easier for the state to remove administrators for malfeasance or failure to comply with the law.

The act simultaneously strengthened the hand of individual schools. As a result, many board members and their chief executive officers perceive

KERA as a distinct loss in power. Forty-three of the state's 176 superintendents left their jobs last year; and another 35 to 40 are expected to do so this year. About one-third of school board members in the state have been elected since 1990.

"School boards have yet to find their niche," Mr. Sexton notes. "They have a lot to do, but many of them are still saying they don't have anything to do. What that really means is that they don't hire."

The biggest battles have come in poverty-stricken eastern Kentucky, where state officials are engaged in a showdown with local residents over their right to intervene in districts where corruption has very nearly been accepted as a fact of life.

While reform activists want stronger state action, opponents complain that the state has muscled its way into local affairs without understanding how things work.

In Floyd County, in one of the state's coal-mining regions, an investigation by the Office of Education Accountability led to the ouster of the local superintendent. The removal of a school board member is still pending. But local residents and school administrators have fought back. An anonymous letter mailed from district headquarters and tracked back to administrators there urges an all-out fight against the law's changes.

Mr. Boysen exacerbated the situation when he personally intervened in the search for a new superintendent and reduced the available candidates to one administrator from central Kentucky, who had served on an advisory panel with him. Since then, observers have questioned whether the new superintendent is executing the improvement plan developed by the state.

Tom Gish, the publisher of *The Mountain Eagle* newspaper in neighboring Letcher County for 35 years and a first-term member of the state board of education, says Mr. Boysen "was slow to grasp the depth and the pervasiveness of the problems in eastern Kentucky, where it's been a matter of using the school system primarily ... as a vehicle for hiring one's friends and relatives—and if a kid got an education out of it, it was more or less accidental."

In nearby Harlan County, the state has ousted three of five board members and forced the superintendent's resignation on charges of corruption. And it has issued a lengthy improvement plan calling for a host of changes in the district, whose policies it labeled "outdated, incomplete, and inadequate." In November 1992, about 100 people gathered at a local high school to applaud speakers demanding that the state "get out."

Roger Noe, a Harlan County resident and the former chairman of the

House education committee, lost his bid for re-election in part because of the board upheaval. Nonetheless, he argues that, as districts like Harlan County are brought to task, other school systems "will take a good hard look at themselves ... and move in a more positive direction."

But such changes will not come overnight. And it remains to be seen whether state-level intervention can inspire and help those who aren't committed to reform in the first place.

After three years of battling the system, Regina Sizemore, a parent in Letcher County who served on a school council and ran unsuccessfully for the local school board, finally withdrew her children from the public schools and began educating them at home.

"I'm not sure that people want things to change," she says. "KERA is good as far as it's written down, but it's going to take more than just a law. The reason that most people in this community are reacting toward KERA is because it's a law—not because fundamentally they think our education system is bad."

The Need To Create a 'Commitment to Change'

Yet, most agree that if the reform law is to work, it must ultimately win the hearts and minds of not only the state's educators, but of parents and citizens who don't have children in the schools. "We're still concentrating on overcoming resistance to change," Mr. Schlechty of the Center for Leadership in School Reform in Louisville argues. "Creating commitment to change is what it's about."

Until now, the reform act has had some powerful friends, including two successive governors. The Prichard Committee, a nonpartisan group with an 11-year track record of promoting educational improvement, has organized some 60 community committees in local districts to support the reforms. And it has served as a tireless watchdog and critic, hiring out-of-state consultants to monitor the implementation process.

Business support has also "packed a major wallop," in the words of one observer. The Kentucky Business Roundtable—led by Ashland Oil, Humana, and United Parcel Service—has made a 10-year commitment to help implement the reforms.

Its support led to the formation of the Partnership for Kentucky School Reform, a nonpartisan coalition of more than 60 public and private leaders from the state's business, civic, government, and education communities. The partnership has sponsored a $1.5 million public-relations campaign to sustain support for KERA. And it has encouraged companies to set up their own programs to involve their employees in the schools.

"We've been doing all we can on trying to educate Kentuckians on the importance of seeing this through," says Kent C. (Oz) Nelson, the chairman of the board of U.P.S. and a founder of the partnership. "We can't go tell the teachers how to teach, and we can't go tell the kids how to study. But one thing we can do is generate support for the right kinds of improvements in education."

In contrast, many observers fault the higher-education community for failing to rally behind the reforms, change their admissions or teacher-education requirements to reflect the new standards, or provide sufficient technical assistance.

And despite such efforts, public understanding of the reform act and why it is needed remains disappointing. A 1993 Bluegrass State Poll shows that 55 percent of Kentuckians have not heard or read anything about the changes brought by KERA since its passage in 1990. Moreover, few people—including educators—see the law as an interconnected whole. Those familiar with the act tend to know only one piece, such as the ungraded-primary program or the family-resource centers.

"I'm not sure how important it is that the person on the street understand how all the pieces fit together," says Ms. David, the researcher who authored the N.G.A. report. "It's much more important that educators and the public have a clearer image of what challenging curriculum and instruction look like." But that image, she maintains, "is missing for a lot of educators, as well as for students, the parents, and the public."

The state education department has taken steps to alleviate the problem. It published 55,000 "truth in testing" sheets that provide citizens with examples of open-ended assessment questions, a scoring guide, and samples of student work at different levels of proficiency.

It has also involved some 300 teachers from across the state on "content committees" that are developing the assessments in particular subject areas. Another 250 teachers who have volunteered to become "KERA performance-assessment fellows" have given 20 days of their time to learn about the assessments and their implications for instruction.

But many of these efforts have yet to reach local communities. In Henderson, George Warren, the executive director of the Henderson Area Chamber of Commerce, admits that businesspeople have been minimally involved in implementing KERA "because they really haven't been asked."

And while parents are more aware of the individual pieces of KERA, they are by no means comfortable with it. Many parents, for example, would prefer letter grades to the more descriptive transcripts of student performance that are now required for primary school students. Some miss the worksheets that their children brought home every night. And others worry that students are being tested too much.

Turnout to elect the parent members of school-based decisionmaking councils in Henderson and throughout the state has been low. And at one school, Jefferson Elementary in the city of Henderson, a small contingent of parents formed a protest group after their children were placed in an ungraded classroom of 6- to 8-year-olds.

Mr. Bussiere of Henderson County High School says: "We have to change student attitudes. Probably more than that, we have to change parent attitudes. If it's a community where parents don't value education, no legislation is going to change that."

For KERA, the bumpiest roads lie ahead. Most of the reform act's funding has materialized until now, despite cutbacks in other state services. But times are tough. For this year and next, state funding for education is virtually flat.

Mr. Boysen estimates that it will cost about $225 million in new monies in 1994-95, or a 10 percent increase, to keep the reforms on track. At the same time, Gov. Brereton C. Jones is pushing a health-care-reform package that would require $50 million in new revenues.

Meanwhile, there still isn't a district in Kentucky that spends at least as much as the national per-pupil average on its schools. But as the huge influxes in funding that accompanied KERA's early years begin to fade, all districts will have to learn how to meet higher expectations with existing resources.

And, because of the equalization formula, the state's property-rich districts are likely to feel the pinch first.

"We're just going to do the best we can," Mr. Karem, the majority leader in the Senate, says. "We're going to try to be as aggressive as we know how. ... But God knows if we'll ever make it where it needs to be."

Against this backdrop, pressure to open KERA up for debate and mid-course corrections is mounting. But legislators remain tremendously reluctant to tinker with the law—based on a fear that picking away at individual threads will eventually unravel the whole cloth. "I doubt if I would be in favor of changing anything," Sen. John (Eck) Rose, one of its architects, says.

Certainly, for many teachers, KERA is not perfect. But as Carolin Abbott, a teacher at South Heights Elementary School notes, "I really think it is the best thing they've done in Kentucky."

"Finally," she says, "Kentucky is really beginning to do some things that are right for kids."

ROAD MAP TO REFORM

By Lynn Olson and Robert Rothman

Without a doubt, the last decade has been one of the richest and most exciting in American education, both in the number of new initiatives launched and in the sustained focus on reform.

Dozens of networks of reform-oriented schools and teachers have sprung up since *A Nation at Risk* was published in 1983. There are groups working on national standards and assessment systems for what teachers and students should know and be able to do. There are organizations focused on creating a stronger school-to-work transition for the non-college-bound, and those advocating universal access to preschool for disadvantaged youngsters. At the state level, policymakers have passed successive waves of reform legislation.

But while the high level of activity has been unprecedented, the reforms themselves remain fragmented and chaotic. Connections among the myriad reform efforts are still rare and, where they exist, are usually informal.

Ernest L. Boyer, the president of the Carnegie Foundation for the Advancement of Teaching, says: "You could draw a 'Keystone Cops' image here of people charging off in different directions and bumping into each other and, in some instances, having a conflict with one another. There's no overall sense of where the problem is and how we should work together to get there."

Such diversity of approach is particularly problematic for teachers, who feel buffeted by one reform after another, many of which conflict.

"I'm sometimes dismayed and frustrated by the endless confusion and cacophony of voices," adds Mr. Boyer, who fears that, as a result, reform efforts end up being dissipated. "I guess one would have to say, 'Welcome to America.'"

Now, some are suggesting the need for a more coherent national game plan

At a crude level, reform strategists can be divided into two camps: those who believe that schools must change from the ground up, one building at a time; and those who believe that federal and state policies should provide the stimulus and the conditions for building-level change.

in an effort to increase the pace of reform and the chances for success.

"We've got a national problem," argues Robert B. Schwartz, the director of educational programs for the Pew Charitable Trusts. "We need a national strategy." He envisions a forum of educators, business leaders, and politicians "where broad agreements could be struck about who should do what to advance the scale of reform."

But others worry that attempting to orchestrate the reform process from on high is the wrong way to go. Calcifying the changes now under way could prove disastrous down the road, they argue.

Even some of those who support a stronger national role—through the creation of standards and assessments for students, for instance—worry about taking too many steps too quickly.

"It would be a great irony at this moment if we centralized the school system into a single national system," contends Lauren B. Resnick, the director of the Learning Research and Development Center at the University of Pittsburgh. "We are coming to understand that you can't run the system with top-down rule-making. The actual coordination has to be closest to kids."

One Approach: Making the Effort School by School

At a crude level, reform strategists can be divided into two camps: those who believe that schools must change from the ground up, one building at a time; and those who believe that federal and state policies should provide the stimulus and the conditions for building-level change.

Notable examples of the school-by-school approach include the Coalition of Essential Schools, founded by Theodore R. Sizer of Brown University; the Accelerated Schools Network, founded by Henry M. Levin of Stanford University; the Success for All program, founded by Robert E. Slavin of Johns Hopkins University; and the School Development Program, founded by Dr. James P. Comer of Yale University.

"My personal belief is that there's no other way to make change," Mr. Slavin explains in defending the strategy of school-by-school reform. "The only thing that really matters in reform is what happens between teachers and kids. ... Anything that takes place too far from the level of the classroom and the school doesn't make a difference."

In addition to the school-by-school consortia that have blossomed over the past decade, a number of foundation-funded networks have been created to link teachers and scholars based on their subject-matter orientation or their instructional approach.

These include such groups as the Foxfire Teacher Outreach Network, the Urban Mathematics Collaborative, the Collaboratives for Humanities and Arts Teaching, and the National Writing Project—all designed to support richer teaching and learning in the classroom. A growing number of school-university partnerships, such as the Puget Sound Educational Consortium, have also joined the reform movement.

Such networks have inspired a fierce loyalty among those involved. And they have proved to be particularly effective both in sustaining reform and in providing meaningful professional development.

In a summary of a five-year study, Milbrey W. McLaughlin, a professor of education at Stanford University, found that teachers who are part of a "learning community" that extends beyond their individual classrooms are much more likely than isolated teachers to adapt to changes in the student population and to alter their practices.

In some cases, school-by-school reformers have joined together to build on their efforts. In 1992, a design team known as the ATLAS Project—which consists of the Coalition of Essential Schools, the School Development Program, the Education Development Center in Newton, Mass., and Project Zero at Harvard University—received a contract from the New American Schools Development Corporation, a private, nonprofit foundation, to create a group of "break the mold" schools that mesh their views.

In a separate development, the National Center for Restructuring Education, Schools, and Teaching at Teachers College, Columbia University, has brought together members of the existing networks to focus on common problems, such as the development of performance assessments for students.

But the list of lighthouse schools that have floundered or gone under is long. Some leave the ranks of the exemplary after a dynamic leader has left the scene or in the wake of steep budget cuts. Others fall victim after a run-in with an inhospitable public.

The repeated rise and fall of innovative programs highlights one of the central shortcomings of the school-by-school approach.

"You can't change one piece of the system without reforming other pieces," argues Phillip C. Schlechty, the president of the Center for Leadership in School Reform in Louisville, Ky. "So you reform a schoolhouse. The kids leave the schoolhouse, and they go to another schoolhouse within that same district. The very notion that we have high schools, elementary schools, and middle schools precludes certain kinds of reform if you start reform at the building level."

Mr. Schlechty also charges that both school-by-school reformers and those who favor a more comprehensive, statewide approach have largely ignored the role of school boards and district-level officials in providing leadership for reform efforts.

"We've got to talk about inventing district-level capacity to support and sustain building-level reform," asserts Mr. Schlechty, whose organization seeks to provide that support. "People talk about systemic change, but they don't approach it systematically. In the U.S.A. right now, for the most part, the most significant financial, political, and economic unit is that unit which represents the voters through boards of education."

Recognizing the importance of state and district policy in sustaining school change, some school-by-school mavericks have begun to focus on the modifications needed in the larger system to support their efforts.

Mr. Comer of Yale University, whose network includes more than 250 schools nationwide, says he now sees the need to influence district policies that have obstructed the spread of his ideas. "We know that you can't just continue to go school by school," he says. "You've got to have a systemwide effort that will involve more schools more quickly in building-level changes."

Similarly, in 1988, Mr. Sizer and the Coalition of Essential Schools formed an alliance with the Education Commission of the States to create Re:Learning, which is designed to link the school-reform agenda with state-level policy. Re:Learning now encompasses schools in 10 states, and its membership is growing. "What's good for kids," Mr. Sizer explains, "should drive the system."

Even so, the slow pace of school-by-school reform has frustrated some policymakers. Worried that they will be long gone from the reform scene before a significant number of schools are revamped to their liking, they are calling for the creation of a statewide framework that would provide a more powerful lever for moving the reform agenda forward.

A Second Approach: Changing the Rules of the Game

This second group of reformers is focusing on what has come to be known as "systemic" change: the careful alignment of state policies—particularly those regarding curriculum, assessment, textbooks, and teacher licensure—with high and ambitious standards for student learning.

Like the school-by-school advocates, these systemic reformers acknowledge that the existing policy structure inhibits innovation. But they contend that a more positive framework could be created that would both encourage and support deep changes in teaching and learning.

"You can change a school, but you haven't changed the superstructure," Frank Newman, the president of the E.C.S., says. "You haven't changed the rules of the game."

Other national organizations that endorse this view include the Business Roundtable, the Council of Chief State School Officers, and the National Governors' Association. In addition, a growing number of states, such as Kentucky and South Carolina, are pursuing systemic-reform initiatives. And the Clinton Administration has come down firmly behind this tactic.

The current effort to create national standards and a national system of assessments for students also falls roughly in this camp.

Among those engaged in systemic change, as well as in the work on national standards and assessments, an increasing amount of cross-fertilization is occurring, both formally and informally. The National Board for Professional Teaching Standards, which is developing a series of performance assessments and certificates to recognize outstanding teachers, is working closely, for example, with those who are developing curriculum standards for students.

"There's a lot of independence," says James A. Kelly, the president of the national board. "It's a messy system. But it is more coherent than it is at a casual glance."

Nonetheless, many educators harbor strong doubts about the wisdom of pursuing the kind of tightly aligned strategy advocated by the systemic reformers.

"Ultimately, it is important for us to be connecting the right ideas to make the environment more coherent for schoolpeople, so they are not subject to contradictory policies, as they are now," says Linda Darling-Hammond, the co-director of the center for restructuring education at Teachers College. "But," she adds, "the quality and nature of what is in the system is extremely important. In a rush to get things lined up, there is always the danger we will do something not very thoughtful."

Critics of systemic reform also worry that attempts to increase the number of "reformed" schools too quickly will lead to changes that are broad but shallow. Instead of a handful of truly transformed schools, the nation could end up with thousands of schools that supposedly have restructured but really haven't changed much at all.

"The emphasis across the country right now on trying to create large-scale systems turns a lot of people off," admits Gordon M. Ambach, the executive director of the Council of Chief State School Officers, "because they think it's never going to have an impact on the classroom."

"That's wrong, in my judgment," he adds. "No sustained, effective activities at the school level are going to occur unless there is a genuinely supportive and nurturing environment that is provided by the district or by the state or even nationwide."

Wedding the Top-Down and Bottom-Up Approaches

At least some now advocate a marriage between what have frequently been referred to as "top down" and "bottom up" reform. But courtships across this great divide are relatively rare and difficult.

"Just trying to keep the conversation alive between people who work at the school level and people working at the systemic-reform level is essential, but it's hard," Mr. Slavin says. "There're a lot of folks who work at the systemic-change level who don't think school-by-school change is possible ... and vice versa."

"I'm not opposed to systemic changes in accountability and funding and so on," he adds, "but those have to be accompanied by school-by-school kinds of reform, if it's actually going to make a difference for children."

Members of the National Alliance for Restructuring Education—which now includes five states and four school districts—portray their partnership as an effort to wed the two strategies. While the alliance is working with its state- and district-level partners to pursue broad changes in policy, it is also signing up teachers at individual schools to alter curriculum and instruction within their buildings. And it is providing them with the technical assistance to do so.

Some states—California, Kentucky, and Maryland among them—are also relying on teachers to help develop, as well as use, their statewide assessment systems based on the belief that the measures must be useful in individual classrooms as well as at the policy level.

But the most widely praised effort at bringing the two camps together is the "gurus" meetings—a series of three discussions to date between small groups of leading education reformers that has been co-sponsored by the Rockefeller Foundation, the Pew Charitable Trusts, Atlantic Philanthropic Services, and the John D. and Catherine T. MacArthur Foundation.

"What we wanted to do was simply provide a forum for people who have been toiling in the vineyards on very serious school reform for a number of years to talk to one another and to learn from each other's experiences," explains Marla Ucelli, a senior program adviser for the Rockefeller Foundation. "Their energies are so devoted to their own efforts that they never have an opportunity to really share."

The first meeting, in November 1990, involved about a dozen reformers and foundation officials. The school-by-school strategy was represented by such advocates as Messrs. Comer, Levin, Sizer, and Slavin. Representing the systemic-change approach were such leading spokesmen as Marc S. Tucker, the president of the National Center on Education and the Economy, and David W. Hornbeck, the co-director of the National Alliance for Restructuring Education and one of the architects of both the Kentucky Education Reform Act and the Business Roundtable agenda.

Several working relationships have emerged from the get-togethers, including what became the ATLAS project. A second meeting, in June 1992, included, in addition to the national players, a handful of principals and superintendents. And a third meeting took place in December 1992. All of the gatherings have been kept small and informal to encourage the serious interchange of ideas.

In a similar vein, the Pew Charitable Trusts has created the Pew Forum on School Reform, which brings together about 25 of the nation's leading educators and policymakers to try to make intellectual sense of the various strands of the reform movement and to discuss strategies needed to achieve reform goals.

But Jane L. David, the director of the Bay Area Research Group, notes that Americans lack models for thinking productively about how to wed top-down and bottom-up change. "We tend to think of it as if there's an answer—a perfect balance—rather than that there's an ongoing tension, and the balance is constantly shifting," she says. "It's our general inability to live with the same kind of ambiguity and complexity at the level of policy that we expect teachers to handle in classrooms."

A 'War Room' Devoted to Reform?

In trying to make more sense of the current cacophony of proposals and protestations, some have called for a national focus similar to what has recently been bestowed on health care.

Gov. Roy Romer of Colorado, the chairman of the N.G.A., argues: "We've got to get this thing going faster. We need more leadership. We need more strategy. I'm ready to buy a federal role in setting priorities in education. Just give it to me in a way that is not prescriptive."

"The 'war room' is a bad analogy," the Democratic Governor continues, "but it's the one I think about. It's kind of like having charts on the wall as to who has what assignment, who can push what button."

Others favor the current loose configuration of reform efforts and urge that connections and partnerships be allowed to develop naturally. They doubt that any one group—however high-profile—could ultimately be successful in advocating a single plan for rescuing the schools. Some even trumpet the merits of heterodoxy.

"One of the central failings of the status quo is being too wired by interconnecting obligations and relationships," says Chester E. Finn Jr., a founding partner of the Edison Project, which is developing a national network of for-profit schools. "It's like Gulliver tied down by so many strings."

"In a system as vast as K-12 American education that is in need of so much change, with as little clarity as to which changes work best," he continues, "I think a degree of diversity and unplanned occurrence is probably a virtue rather than a vice."

Perhaps the single biggest concern of entrusting the reform effort to a "war room" is that such an approach could ossify change efforts prematurely or homogenize everything down to the lowest common denominator.

"It matters a lot to have Kentucky doing something very different from what Vermont is doing," says Richard P. Mills, Vermont's commissioner of education. "We're all intensely collaborative, but we're also intensely competitive. We want to borrow ideas that have been developed someplace else. Let's keep that spirit alive and not let this thing get rigid."

Indeed, some suggest that, given what we know about the way change occurs in the real world, any kind of logical, highly rational approach to school reform will ultimately fail.

Ted Kolderie, a senior fellow at the Center for Policy Studies in Minnesota, argues that real change in complex systems occurs through a combination of trial and error and pressure from the outside, not as a result of centralized planning. "Did we have a central mechanism, a national commission, a czar when we decided we couldn't use horse-drawn carriages in cities anymore?" he asks.

This notion of introducing an external change agent into the reform mix is already evident in the school-reform arena. It drives proposals that would enable parents to choose from among private and public schools at taxpayer expense, and those that would allow individuals and organizations outside the education establishment to create and run public schools.

Picking Up the Pace With a Stronger National Role

Those who advocate a national push to accelerate the pace of reform have proposed a variety of scenarios. Some suggest that the federal government take the lead, both through legislation and by capitalizing on its use of the bully pulpit.

"A lot of people would disagree with me on the federal folks getting too involved in education," says Roger Noe, the former chairman of the House Education Committee in Kentucky. "But I think they could take a stronger stand in helping coordinate these efforts on a state-by-state basis."

In the spring of 1993, the Administration was negotiating with Congress on a bill with four components: a section codifying the national education goals, provisions establishing a federal role in developing national education standards and assessments, the creation of a national board to help set skills standards for various industries, and a grant program to help states and districts develop plans for "systemic reform." Marshall S. Smith, who has been named to be the undersecretary of education, says the bill "doesn't orchestrate [state reform]. But it provides incentives."

Next year's reauthorization of the Elementary and Secondary Education Act, which contains the vast majority of federal elementary and secondary education programs, could also provide a vehicle for relating federal dollars to the reform agenda.

A major report issued in December 1992 by the independent Commission on Chapter 1 advocates using remedial-education funding to leverage change throughout the system, not just for students who qualify for the categorical aid. It would also hold youngsters who benefit from the program to the same high standards as other children and use rich new performance assessments to evaluate their progress.

In some ways, notes Gregory R. Anrig, the president of the Educational Testing Service, the federal government has already taken the lead in coordinating the reform effort through its support of national standards. The standards, he suggests, provide a "core around which various reform efforts can coalesce."

Others argue that U.S. Secretary of Education Richard W. Riley and President Clinton could convene some type of national forum on education. "This is a wonderful opportunity for the federal department, not to direct or to search for an overall system," Mr. Sizer says, "but to press the agenda and pour the coffee."

Furthermore, a stronger national role does not necessarily mean a federal one. An independent commission could be created in an effort to bring cohesion to various reform efforts. Howard Gardner, a professor of psychology at Harvard University, envisions a kind of "educational supreme court"—a permanent, ruminative body of educators, researchers, politicians, and business leaders—that could develop a long-range vision for moving education forward. Mr. Boyer of the Carnegie Foundation suggests that Congress create an independent "national council of education advisers," parallel to the President's Council of Economic Advisers, that would periodically report on educational progress and help sort out priorities.

Others propose forming national task forces around specific issues—such as how to meet one of the national education goals.

"I don't think all the wisdom in education is centered in Washington, D.C.," Rep. Dale E. Kildee, D-Mich., says. "We want to galvanize the wisdom in states and school districts."

A less centralized option would be to increase the frequency and level of conversation among the various reform groups, individual schools, and teachers by creating a computer network dedicated to educational change.

In addition, both the federal and state governments could do more to support the existing networks of reform-oriented schools and teachers.

But while many see the advantages of creating a stronger national presence, they worry about who would be in charge of such an endeavor and who would get to choose such a select group. "The skittishness some have about a national coordinating strategy is, Who is doing the deciding?" Ms. Darling-Hammond says. "How do decisions about what we are told to do get informed by a wide array of viewpoints and voices?"

'Too Much Noise in the System'

Whatever their differences, most see a pressing need to help schools sift through the maze of reform initiatives so that they can forge a coherent plan for change.

"At the local level," says Christopher T. Cross, the executive director for the education initiative of the Business Roundtable, "there's too much information and there's too much noise in the system ... for people to really be able to ascertain what's valuable and what's not. That's the place where I think the federal government could provide some help, as well as some of the professional associations."

Some districts and states are attempting to do just that. The Dade County, Fla., school system has held a districtwide fair to present teams of educators and community representatives from individual schools with information about national and local education networks and research. The hope is that each school will use the information to develop a specific theme or focus. The district will provide the support and resources to do so.

Similarly, South Carolina officials have created a "systemic-innovation network" to provide schools with information on projects from around the state and nation as well as research from the federally sponsored regional laboratories. In Vermont, Mr. Mills notes, state officials regularly sit down to review how the various reforms that they are pursuing interconnect.

Such guidance is particularly needed in the development of state and national curriculum standards. Without a better way of thinking through such efforts, observers note, they could conflict or overwhelm schoolpeople.

"My concern is that, if you take each of the standards and aggregate them," Mr. Cross says, "the net effect would be that children would have to go to school 18 hours a day, 365 days a year probably. There has to be some rationalization of all this."

One group that is attempting to do that is the Alliance for Curriculum Reform. "We can help [schools] find their way through the thickets of the many reforms and facilitate how they can put them together in ways that make sense," Judith Rényi, the director of CHART and the co-founder of the alliance, says.

But Mr. Boyer cautions that the very notion of developing content standards based on traditional academic disciplines may be counterproductive. What is needed, he suggests, is a series of seminars to explore alternative models that are more interdisciplinary in nature.

Missing Pieces, Missing Players

Reformers also speak as one voice about some of the areas that must be addressed for reform to succeed—including the failure of the public to buy into education reform, the unwillingness of higher education to embrace the reform agenda, and the ineffective job of the mass media. Most notably, they point to the lack of deep and sustained professional development for teachers and others in the system.

"You don't have to spend very many days in real schools," argues Kati Haycock, the director of the school/college trust at the American Association for Higher Education, "to become deeply worried about how we could possibly get kids to standards teachers don't meet."

David K. Cohen, a professor of education and social policy at Michigan State University, suggests stipulating that no state agency or subject-matter group be allowed to make a proposal unless it contains a "fully developed agenda for professional education. That would give reformers the same requirements for managing reforms that reformers now delegate to teachers."

Experts also agree that the public must buy into the reform agenda if it is to succeed, and that that is far from happening. "We have failed to engage the general public in conveying the notion that this is something that touches everybody," Mr. Finn of the Edison Project argues. "Education reform is a tempest at the surface of a very deep, very calm body of water. That calm worries me a whole lot."

Higher education has also been glaringly absent from the reform debate. In addition to training the next generation of educators, colleges and universities could play an important role in defining curricular content and in setting expectations for students. Currently, however, Mr. Gardner says, institutions of higher education "don't see [reform] as their problem, and the kinds of signals that are therefore sent by admissions officers ... are very antithetical to the deep problems that we see in American schools and in society."

Still others argue that reforms must reach beyond the education community to address the influence of the mass media and other societal institutions. Mr. Sizer points out that children spend more time in rooms in which televisions are on than they do in classrooms. "In the discussion of school reform," he says, "we have forgotten that we're talking about education reform. One of the most important educators is the mass media. They are not at the table at all."

Whatever the strategy, transforming schools and crafting policies that promote and sustain building-level reforms is a relatively new endeavor. And we are not very good at it—yet.

After a decade of effort, most reforms are still identified with a handful of prominent individuals and have not become common currency within the education community as a whole.

Moreover, the vast majority of schools are not connected with any network and are doing very little to change. "With all the talk that's going on," Mr. Slavin says, "I still think that we're nibbling at the margins. I think that there's a lot more talk about reform than reform that actually takes place."

"If you were blindfolded and put in a school that says it's engaged in reform," he asserts, "you still wouldn't know it after the blindfold was off."

Participants in *Education Week*'s Roundtable

SAMUEL R. BILLUPS
is an assistant professor of education at Delaware State College and the state's co-ordinator for Re:Learning, a joint effort of the Education Commission of the States and the Coalition of Essential Schools.

MICHELLE FINE
is a professor of psychology at the graduate center of the City University of New York and a senior consultant to the Philadelphia Schools Collaborative, a project to redesign that city's comprehensive high schools.

PATRICIA ALBJERG GRAHAM
is the president of the Spencer Foundation and a professor of the history of American education and a former dean at the Harvard University graduate school of education.

DAVID W. HORNBECK
is the co-director of the National Alliance for Restructuring Education, a joint effort involving five states and four school districts, and a senior adviser to the Business Roundtable. He was also a key architect of the Kentucky Education Reform Act.

ROBERT S. PETERKIN
is the director of the Urban Superintendents' Program at the Harvard University graduate school of education and a former superintendent of schools in Milwaukee and Cambridge, Mass.

ROBERT F. SEXTON
is the executive director of the Prichard Committee for Academic Excellence, a citizens' advocacy organization dedicated to improving Kentucky's schools.

CHRISTOPHER T. CROSS
is the executive director of the education initiative for the Business Roundtable and was the assistant U.S. secretary of education for educational research and improvement in the Bush Administration.

SUSAN H. FUHRMAN
is a professor of educational theory, policy, and administration at Rutgers University and the director of the Consortium for Policy Research in Education, a federally funded research center. She is the editor of *Designing Coherent Education Policy*, a new book on systemic reform in education.

KATI HAYCOCK
is the director of the school/college trust at the American Association for Higher Education and was a member of the Commission on Chapter 1.

RICHARD P. MILLS
is the commissioner of education in Vermont and the chairman of the coordinating council for the National Alliance for Restructuring Education.

GOV. ROY ROMER
of Colorado is the chairman of the National Governors' Association and a member and a former chairman of the National Education Goals Panel. He served as a co-chairman of the National Council on Education Standards and Testing.

THE ROUNDTABLE

Education Week has conducted a number of roundtables over the years. But none has attempted to tackle so ambitious a topic as the one that follows.

In March 1993, we convened 11 of the nation's leading education reformers to spend a day considering new directions for the school-reform movement. David W. Hornbeck, the co-director of the National Alliance for Restructuring Education and a senior adviser to the Business Roundtable, moderated the session. Our hope was that we could begin to rough out an action plan or implementation strategy for the next phase of school reform.

Easier said than done.

While the participants agreed in principle that America's schools must be changed in substantial ways and that incremental change will not suffice, they diverged on the specifics of how best to accomplish that transformation.

Echoing the opinions expressed in the preceding chapter, some thought a stronger national, or at least state, role is needed; others were more inclined to stake the future on the diversity of locally initiated change.

Following is an edited transcript of the *Education Week* roundtable on school-reform strategies for change. It is divided into eight sections that reflect key points of discussion.

In addition to highlighting some of the most important developments in the school-reform movement, the transcript has been organized to focus on key roles to be played at the federal, district, and school levels. Because the role and responsibility of states wove throughout this conversation, we did not attempt to isolate it as a separate topic.

At stake, of course, is the next generation of students and schools. Gov. Roy Romer of Colorado, one of our roundtable participants, summed it up when he said: "We need a national movement that says, 'If we don't do this one right, and if we don't do it quickly, we're in real trouble.' "

'To Get Change, You Need Pressure and Support'

EDUCATION WEEK: After more than a decade of school-reform efforts, there is no shortage of ideas about what needs to be done to fix the nation's educational system. But there is no clear idea of how to actually do it.

One school of thought is that there needs to be some kind of national strategy that includes a role for the federal government, for states, for school districts, and schools—in other words, a coherent plan for who does what and when to get from where we are to where we want to be.

Another school of thought is that reform can only be done on a school-by-school basis, and that federal and state governments should provide the resources and get out of the way. Let the schools do what they think is best.

Whatever position one takes, the how-to question is still the tough one. How do we actually bring about change in a vast, complex system that is notorious for resisting change?

MR. MILLS: We haven't helped administrators and teachers become masters of change, and we haven't become masters of change ourselves.

We propose changes, but we really don't know how to help people through them. There are some among us who are experts at this, but we almost never invite them in.

Michael Fullan is an example. He's a Canadian scholar, and he's very painstakingly assembled the research on what's known about teachers and principals and superintendents and what's known about change. He points out some things we've all experienced. There's a performance dip when you try to do something different. Things tend to get worse before they get better.

In educational communities, as soon as things start getting worse, the change is dropped. That's the behavior of an amateur in any other field, but that is what we do all the time in education. We try something, it runs into problems, and so we drop it, and we try something new.

We do it with people, too. A kid has a problem learning something, and we conclude the kid's not going to make it. The principal's been in the job for four years, and things are going a little ragged, so let's get somebody else. We just don't know how to persist through the difficult times.

Fullan also says to get change, you need the right mixture of pressure and support. We've got the pressure, but we don't provide the support.

MR. PETERKIN: The superintendent from Louisville [Ky.] and the superintendent from Hartford [Conn.] came to talk to my class about how their communities are involved in trying to restructure schools. Both are very thoughtful people and have given a lot of thought to the process of change. Both are supportive of change—one supports the Kentucky Education Reform Act, and the other supports the equitable treatment of kids in Hartford. And yet both, I would argue, feel somewhat blind-sided by these changes.

In the process of change that their communities have been going through— that they helped design and lead—it seems like some external force has suddenly come in and superimposed another change, which may or may not be beneficial. We don't have a mechanism to support the people who are taking the risks in the process of change that's been ongoing.

In addition, many people who are burned out on the changes of the 1980's are finding it hard to accept the responsibility for change in the 1990's. They got behind all the basic-skills stuff and standardized testing and high graduation rates and the like, and now find themselves almost vilified as we go through the next developmental stage of reform.

We never were very explicit until about two years ago that we had changed the rules of the game. I mean, school systems never had a chance to celebrate the shift from basic skills to advanced skills.

EW: Some people argue that the great majority of teachers, administrators, and school board members have not really bought into standards and performance-based education yet. If you are going to try to change the minds of the public, you may have to start by changing the minds of the education establishment.

MR. MILLS: It must be very frightening for teachers reading about all the reform activity and imagining more and more and more being layered on. We need to bring a lot more people into the design of these things. Partly so that we have their ideas, but partly so that they can say, "Wait. We need to throw out something if we're going to add more on."

The deputy commissioner of my state was always talking about planned abandonment. It's not for a commissioner of education or secretary of education to say some of these things need to be cut away. Local school communities need to be in a position to make those decisions.

The system feels clogged now. Schools are trying to do everything we said they should do in the last half generation, and we are now giving them more to do.

MS. FINE: For us, this latest stage of reform is a new set of ideas. We have abandoned the 80's. But teachers haven't. They are still having to do all of that other stuff, and then we add 16 more layers.

It's not just adding standards and performance-based assessments, either. It's that the conditions of teachers' work lives haven't changed, that they haven't really gotten control over the time and resources.

MR. BILLUPS: We've got to convince a lot of people that change is necessary. Too many school-based people don't see a need for change. We try to solve a lot of the problems of the schools by initiating new projects, when what we really need is systemic change. I don't think enough people in education see the need for real change.

MS. HAYCOCK: We shouldn't skip the education community, but I'm not sure the established organizations are the best way to reach them. I think networks ...

MS. GRAHAM: I agree with networks.

MS. HAYCOCK: That is a very powerful way. We have to learn from that.

MS. GRAHAM: I think they ought to be part of the conversation.

MR. CROSS: And then there is the problem we have within the system of getting people to accept and to acknowledge what works and to make use of what works.

MR. BILLUPS: If we could put some of these programs into policy form, and institutionalize them on a large scale, we might begin to get to the point we want to get to.

EW: There are structures in place that could play a central role in that process, such as the National School Boards Association, the secondary school principals, the elementary school principals, and the American Association of School Administrators. These groups have affiliates in every state. They are spending time and money and energy informing their members. They hold national and state conferences. Their members occupy key positions in schools and districts.

GOVERNOR ROMER: These organizations representing various educational interests rise up and represent their members in Washington. Somebody ought to be thinking about how you get them on board for these changes. It's kind of like putting an army together. It's like in the Revolutionary War. They called the militia out on the green, and they had to organize themselves in platoons, and decide, here's the leader. But somebody has to get the battle plan, and say, "This is the strategy, this is the battle plan, you've all got a role to play. Now go train yourself to do that role."

I don't think that we are looking at the whole picture well enough.

MS. GRAHAM: The way to influence teachers and administrators and some school board members is not directly but indirectly. People whom they look up to as being powerful can help them see how things are changing for them and get them to participate in the conversation about why changes are necessary.

But a frontal-assault method is not likely to be as effective for schoolpeople. Traditionally, they have changed things as a result of public pressure.

GOVERNOR ROMER: One problem with changing the system is that it doesn't have a "clean-out mechanism." In the private sector, there's a very convenient thing called bankruptcy that cleans out those companies that are not successful. We need a mechanism for the bankruptcy of public institutions. We live with them too long when they don't work.

How do we get a serious conversation about these issues going throughout America? How can we get governors, state school officers, superintendents, all these folks in America to take the need for real change seriously? Because, if we don't have an ongoing serious discussion, we're going to cobble it up.

What discourages me is that we had a kind of boomlet a few years ago when we said we're going to go for the goals. Remember, the President of the United States and 50 governors had a summit, then we had the [national education] goals panel, and, for a while, we had great stuff on C-SPAN. We began to educate a lot of America through that. Then, zip! It just sort of slowed down.

I'm worried that we're not going to get to the hearts and minds of the leadership of this country on this issue.

We need a national movement that says, If we don't do this one right, and if we don't do it quickly, we're in real trouble.

'A Premise of Reform: All Children Can Learn'

MR. HORNBECK: One of the biggest changes we have to persuade schools to accept is the conviction that all children can learn to a significantly higher level and that we know how to be successful with all children—at least we know enough so that a lack of knowledge shouldn't be considered a barrier. That is a fundamental premise of systemic reform.

MS. GRAHAM: The schools are very good at figuring out what society really wants them to do, and it is a dramatic new departure for schools to have to start educating all their children to a high level of academic achievement. Americans have not cared about learning for two-thirds or more of our population in the past, and we are now changing that.

MS. FINE: There is even a disbelief in public education in the possibility of improved outcomes. In fact, many people don't believe it's possible.

In urban areas, when we generate positive outcomes, people—even school district administrators—accuse us of cheating. It is hard to imagine that we are working in systems that disbelieve their own efficacy and, therefore, generate a set of rationales about those kids, those mothers, those communities.

That's what happens when some of our charter schools, which are absolutely committed to being heterogeneous, start to generate positive student outcomes. They get trashed by their colleagues and by administrators.

People say, "Well, you've got the good kids, right?" So, we do all these analyses showing that in the 8th grade our kids wore their hats backward, and didn't come to school. And guess what: A good school can make a poor kid look middle class.

MR. PETERKIN: We need to create a sense of connection between schools and communities. We've got to connect people with all schools, the schools in their community, the schools in their state, the schools in the nation. You could say, "Well, isn't that too big a job?" But we should at least start by trying to get individual communities interested in all the kids in those communities.

We're still suspending our belief that certain groups of kids can succeed. We're hoping that we can make the pool of successful kids somewhat larger. But many people don't believe the pool can include 100 percent of the children.

We will never get the commitment to all children by public support alone. It will take a firm connection and ownership and investment—emotionally, financially, and statutorily.

MS. GRAHAM: One has to broaden the conversation so that it's other people's children that you're worried about, not just your own.

We keep talking about the parents, who, of course, should be interested in their children's education. But we haven't been able to broaden the discourse to talk about how the nonparent community needs to be interested in children's education.

A very important element in trying to get educational reform going is in moving away from the exclusive focus on parents as the only adults interested in children's education and broadening our effort to the larger society so that they will support it with votes.

MR. PETERKIN: There is a potential, at least, for the reform effort to increase the gap between minorities themselves—between poor minorities and affluent minorities.

We need an inclusionary statement, a standard that has some strength to it, that recognizes the diversity of this country and our need to make sure that the issues of race, class, and sex are addressed.

MR. SEXTON: It may not be too hard to get general agreement on the broad concept that all children can learn. But as you get into particulars—like, what does this really mean for my child?—you have problems with your community and your parents.

It's a given in an outcomes-based system that a community has to have all children learn. That's absolutely imperative. However, as the assessment results and the so-called thresholds—the so-called goals for the schools— hit the streets, it brings to the surface something that is very, very troubling: that is the view that if all children learn, my children learn less. In other words, a lot of parents think somebody has to lose if their kids are to win.

We want the whole community to be responsible for all the kids, but there's still this lingering fear among some that it might not be the best thing for my kid.

What we're really trying to get across is a concept of the greater community. That's a totally different kind of discussion than we've traditionally had about school. It's hard to make the argument in Hazard, Kentucky, that schools should change because it's important to the health of the national economy. It's hard to make those big arguments in a small town—or really in any place. The discussion has to get to where people are.

MR. HORNBECK: The commitment to all kids must certainly come from passion and outrage. And it needs to come from the engagement of parents and the public. But I would argue that there must also be an incentive system actually built around a belief that all kids are going to learn.

The experience in Kentucky makes the point. That law was built with a fairly significant reward and penalty system in it. School staffs can earn as much as 40 percent of their annual salaries as a financial bonus. But they can also lose their tenure and be subject to dismissal based on student performance.

You can't apply that kind of system only to advantaged children. The disadvantaged child must also succeed in order for teachers to be rewarded.

I would go so far as to say that, if we believe all kids can learn at high levels, and if we think there's enough known about how to do that, then it follows that if a kid doesn't learn, it means he hasn't had an adequate opportunity to learn.

That's a big leap, but I'm prepared to have that proposition embedded in the heart of federal, state, and local policy. It can't be just a rhetorical flourish; it has to be at the heart of the actual mechanisms that make the system work.

'Standards Must Reflect Challenging Outcomes'

MR. HORNBECK: Have we gone far enough in the discussion over the last two or three years to agree that we need national standards and assessments?

I sense a general agreement that the educational system must be outcome-based, driven by standards for what students need to know and be able to do. And that we need to provide curriculum frameworks and technology for instruction—all geared to the content standards.

These high-level standards should arise out of the professional community, like the standards formulated by the National Council of Teachers of Mathematics. They should be run through a whole variety of inclusionary processes, involving people outside of the profession, and they should be voluntary.

We also need assessment strategies as rich as the standards, strategies that no longer rely on norm-referenced, standardized, multiple-choice tests, but actually assess student performance.

Three years ago, there would have been deep, deep arguments about that proposal. But my sense today is that most people now agree on these issues.

MR. MILLS: I think we agree around tables like this. Beyond tables like this, I don't think we are yet seeing the consequences of our acts. For example, the three sets of national standards that I have seen all seem to assume that their particular subject area will have 40 percent or more of the child's education. No one has added them all up to see how much of the curriculum and the schedule they would occupy.

And those are just content standards. We also will have performance standards and school-delivery standards.

The point is that, if we don't simplify this thing, it's going to be very complex and very rigid. There's about two years of simplification and integration that has to go on.

MR. CROSS: And rationalization.

MR. MILLS: And rationalization. How does it feel locally when you are in a classroom and you are trying to get 20 kids excited about Shakespeare and you wonder if you're on the standards?

You might pull out a wallet-sized card once in a while to look at standards, but you wouldn't pull out a long booklet. Yet, it's the booklets that we are producing.

It's like in an individual life. You can make list after list after list of things you need to do and just become a slave to your Daytimer. Or you can figure out what your life is about.

What we need to do is ask what the school is about, not what is on the list.

MS. FUHRMAN: It is essential that standards reflect the kind of challenging and ambitious outcomes that we want to see for children.

We all know of outcome-based systems or standards-based systems that have focused at a very low level and have been built around basic skills. In fact, many of the reforms of the early 80's had this flavor.

As we think about changing the system, we need to stress the richness and sophistication that we're now aiming for based on our new understandings about how children learn.

We don't just want curriculum frameworks. We want a process of developing them that engages the profession and the public so that everyone aims higher for education.

MS. GRAHAM: Take it even a little further than that. Think about how a youngster should be educated, and what the important but limited role of the school in educating that kid is. We talk as if standards for schools and for kids would translate into an educated kid.

Eighty percent of the students in grades 10 to 12 in New Hampshire work during the school year, and 4 to 5 percent of them work more than 20 hours a week. What happens to standards in schools when kids are engaged like that?

To focus solely on the question of curriculum and performance standards for kids in school and to miss the broader context in which these children live is to miss the most basic point: School is a rather weak treatment in the life of kids, when you compare it with employment, with poverty, and even with that old bugbear, television.

We need to think more comprehensively about the issues for children and not get into quite as excruciating detail about the issues of standards per se. We need to think about bolder steps to define how the child will be educated. The standards of the school are important, but mainly as a segment of a broader problem.

MR. HORNBECK: That's right. But standards still have a relationship to academic disciplines. They shouldn't be done piecemeal. A whole should emerge from this in some manner.

And if we're going to get such standards, I believe they should be set at the national level involving input from many sources. But their implementation is a decisive first-line responsibility of the state.

MR. SEXTON: Are you talking about specific outcomes or are you talking about high standards that a nation should expect to achieve in the preparation of its children?

MR. HORNBECK: I am talking about something as specific as the N.C.T.M. standards translated into measurable terms.

MR. SEXTON: That is political dynamite.

MR. HORNBECK: Do you mean to have them set at the national level?

MR. SEXTON: Yes.

MR. HORNBECK: You think these standards should be set at the state level?

MR. SEXTON: Yes. Delicately done.

MR. CROSS: Are you distinguishing between federal and national?

MR. SEXTON: I don't know anymore. The opponents of outcome-based education, like those in Pennsylvania, make no distinction between federal and national. Their cast of villains ranges from the federal government to the Carnegie Foundation to the corporations to anybody in Washington to the Business Roundtable to the Trilateral Commission.

MR. HORNBECK: But you could have standards come from a national effort that was entirely nonfederal. If the New Standards Project, for example, had 46 percent more of the kids in the United States in it, and 31 more states in it, it would be national—because 54 percent of the kids and 19 of the states are now in it. It's not federal.

MR. BILLUPS: The first thing we must do is decide what we want students to be able to do by 4th grade, 8th grade, at the end of high school. Then we have to figure out what it takes to get there. We have to do what I call "planning backward."

MR. MILLS: Yes, but we can't just work on standards and get that done right, and then turn to the next piece and get that right. We need to approximate the whole system, and make the approximation better and better and better as we go along.

MR. BILLUPS: Even before we get to the standards, we need to know what we are looking for. That would help guide us in our thinking about the standards and, of course, in our thinking about how we want to get there. We will get there in different ways as far as the individual schools are concerned.

When we talk about national standards, we have to remember that schools are different and communities are different. If there is some way we can build that into the idea of national standards, then we should come out with something that is workable.

EW: We have been talking about national standards. What is the role of the state in setting and implementing standards?

MR. HORNBECK: I still think that one of the roles that belongs decisively to states is the definition of the standards/outcomes for kids, and the formulation of assessment strategies that will determine whether or when the kids have achieved them.

Schools should certainly be able to add, to interpret, to implement, and all that, but the basic responsibility is the state's.

GOVERNOR ROMER: As Governor, I've got to get some enforcement mechanisms. I've got to go to my higher-educational institutions and ask them what in the hell they are doing about these standards in teacher training. Are they using these standards? And I need to go to the school districts that I help finance—and lose a whole lot of political skin trying to raise revenue for—and ask them if they are using these standards?

I recently had a conference in southeastern Colorado with math and science teachers, and I asked what percent of the teachers in Colorado are dealing with the content of the N.C.T.M. standards? Is it 20 percent? They answered, "Noooo, you're a little high."

Don't laugh. That's what those math teachers replied. I'm faced with that, and I'm trying to say that we've got to get this thing going faster. We have to have more leadership, we have to have a strategy.

I have been a very strong advocate of national goals, but I don't think we have set them yet. That's why I am interested in standards. I don't think we will really have goals until I can walk into a parent's home and say specifically, "This is what we are after."

One of the greatest problems we have in reforming education in America is we do not yet know what it is we are reaching for. We've got some general rhetoric that has no content yet. When you get content, then you've got some goals.

MR. MILLS: The state has a vital role here, and it fails if it doesn't bring thousands of people into the discussion.

MR. HORNBECK: I agree. But in Vermont, for example, you included like mad, and, in the final analysis, the state board, or you, or somebody, decided the four goals.

MR. MILLS: That's right. In the end, the state board said it had heard enough. And the board members were very careful to point out how many thousands had been heard. They were able to point to ideas and phrases that came from different places.

It's up to the state to say, "We need this conversation." It's up to the state to see that it takes place. It's up to the state to listen and then say, "O.K., we've heard, now it's time to act."

MS. FINE: This relationship between leadership and participation is very important.

In public school systems, it seems we have either leadership or we have participation. There is this funny splitting—people have ideas, and they ram them down folks' throats, or they do this participatory stuff that ends up being pretty weak at the knees. The idea of bringing people together around a particular agenda and then taking some tough stands yourself seems to me to be worthwhile. It's important to understand that because you have inclusion and broad participation doesn't mean leaders can't take some tough stands.

That raises the question: Is the state the right place for the tough stands? I find the state pretty appealing as a place to do some hard work. But Pennsylvania provides an example of the opposite. The Pennsylvania state learning outcomes got eaten by the fundamentalist right, because they were the only ones who were organized. They took out whole language and higher-order thinking and anything connected to what they were calling diversity. So you got this very shutdown conversation about learning.

Where is the safe place to do some of that hard stuff—the place that has the courage to make the hard decisions? I want to think it is the state, and then I go back to Pennsylvania and I think, "Who are you kidding?"

MR. HORNBECK: In some ways, you only need one example to say that it's possible. I would still come out at the end saying the conversation needs to take place, and it needs to be inclusionary. It at least needs to be inclusionary for political purposes, to get public support, even if you don't care about the substance that comes out of it.

But in the final analysis, there is a buck-stopping-here aspect. There is a significant—perhaps even dominant—state role.

'Concrete Consequences Must Be Set for Schools, Professionals'

MR. HORNBECK: A central premise of the national standards and assessments movement is that consequences both for students and schools should be attached to the achievement or non-achievement of the outcomes. But high-stakes consequences should not be applied until all students are guaranteed an opportunity to learn.

GOVERNOR ROMER: I'm reluctant to get into strict accountability until we get a better way to measure, and until we get a better definition of what it is we want somebody to accomplish.

We haven't defined clearly enough what it is that we're after or how to measure accomplishment to punish or reward performance very strictly.

If we demand too strict accountability at this point, people are going to teach to the test, to respond to the rewards and punishments. That would stifle the kind of experimentation and innovation that needs to occur.

We need to figure out how to make the transition from where we are to where we want to be without lessening the motivation for all the in-service and pre-service training that has to occur.

MR. HORNBECK: That's the reason we ought to be about the business of identifying the standards and the new assessment practices.

But for the sake of discussion, let's assume for a moment that we have those. Then what would go into an accountability system? Or, on the other hand, what do you do about accountability in the meantime while you're developing new standards and assessments?

GOVERNOR ROMER: In Colorado, I would like to have us all be born again in terms of our interest in standards. I would like us to begin to understand what they are. I would like us to work with other states to develop some testing methods and a resource barrel of tasks that we can share.

I would like us to have a great professional-development program for teachers and to involve all of the teachers in helping us deal with the assessments. And I would like the state to provide the funds to encourage and nurture these things.

The English Inspectorate has been mentioned. I would like to have such an inspectorate that would go around to schools and say: "Hey, we are not going to measure students; we don't know enough yet to do that. But we are going to make judgments about your effort."

And maybe we suspend the accreditation process as we know it for five years, so we can free up money and people to do this. And have at least a continual dialogue with schools in which we make judgments about inputs and outcomes as they are occurring.

Simultaneously, I would set in motion a process to develop statewide testing. It may take three years or longer, but we make sure that testing is aligned with the goals we want to accomplish.

Clearly, there is a transition period. To require rigid, strict accountability based on present tests would defeat the motivation of the system to change.

MR. MILLS: That sounds good to me. People involved in the New Standards Project and the Vermont portfolio effort are not trying to beat the test. What they are trying to do is think through each of the standards and what would constitute a really engaging task for student assessment.

They are arguing with one another about instructional practices that work. If we suddenly pull down the curtain and say, "O.K., now this is on the test," the game would change very rapidly. The innovation would stop.

GOVERNOR ROMER: I want to know how schools are performing. I am skeptical about the present method of assessments, but I will use them until I have something better. They have validity, but they have limits.

MS. GRAHAM: But you are going to use the old assessments until you get your new set. And that's the crux of the policy dilemma we are in right now. Most of us don't like the old assessments. But we think there has to be some measure, and we can't decide whether we should use those old, inferior, inadequate assessments for real accountability, or whether to continue to treat them as we always have, as if they had no consequence.

MR. PETERKIN: I remember a school board meeting where my teachers gave me and the board the number of days we spent testing. Not minutes, not hours, but the number of days that we spent using tests that the board and I didn't like to use. And the state was giving us some more.

There is a growing frustration among teachers who are being asked to deal with more content while this proliferation of tests is taking more time away from instruction.

Nothing that anybody has said so far makes me believe that kids aren't going to be caught at the 4th, 8th, and 11th grades, sitting in a classroom, taking and retaking some test, whether we are talking about the new standards or the old standards.

MR. HORNBECK: There is no reason in the world why we can't abandon nationally normed standardized tests right now—except political reasons and parents who resist.

MS. FUHRMAN: This need not be an either/or. There are a number of states that have sort of second-generation standardized tests. There are a variety of ways to go about it.

MS. HAYCOCK: Once there is agreement on content standards at the state level, and assessment mechanisms are developed, there ought to be substantial, concrete consequences, both rewards and sanctions for schools and the professionals within them.

MR. SEXTON: I favor real consequences, too. The obvious problem is that some schools don't need those consequences and others do. In the ideal world, we would identify those schools that need consequences, and we would have a different set of expectations and requirements for them.

The thing that now concerns me as those consequences are closer to reality in Kentucky is that the teachers were hit by the negative side. On top of fatigue and stress, there's fear. And I am truly and genuinely surprised at the misunderstanding of the whole concept of sanctions, and the fear that is out there. I just didn't realize where teachers' heads are, especially elementary teachers.

We have no consequences for children in Kentucky at this point. I don't see how we can go along without having incentives and consequences, at least for high school students, as a way of encouraging older kids to want to do better in school. This society doesn't provide those incentives now.

The incentives and consequences don't have to be driven so much by testing. I look first at the community consequences: job incentives, for example. How can you get employers to make high school important? How do you get parents to make it important?

MR. HORNBECK: The only serious disagreement over national standards and assessments is over two issues. One, whether there should be high stakes for teachers and administrators; and two, whether there should be high stakes for kids.

And the main concern about kids is not whether there should be high stakes, but what conditions need to be in place before the high stakes are applied.

GOVERNOR ROMER: You mean delivery standards?

MR. HORNBECK: Yes. At the federal level, for example, the House won't let a bill go through without addressing delivery standards. And I think the advocacy community, joined by some other people, will say you just simply cannot deny kids promotion, graduation, jobs, and college without some mechanism that first levels the playing field for them.

GOVERNOR ROMER: It's the chicken-and-the-egg situation. You say we can't attach high stakes until all kids have the "opportunity to learn." In my state, an awful lot of districts are not going to be moved to provide that opportunity to learn until they see the challenge of what it is kids need to know and be able to do. It is a circular thing.

What bothers me about the House's position is that it will require micromanagement on what delivery standards are. They didn't understand the interactions between content standards, assessment methods, and teaching methods.

We ought not cede to the House of Representatives the right to dictate educational policy in America. If we cannot come to terms with that, we ought to say, "Bye-bye, we'll go do it another way."

MS. FUHRMAN: We make a mistake when we think about delivery standards as a federal issue, because, whatever the House of Representatives does, the states are going to have to face the opportunity-to-learn questions. Isn't guaranteeing equal opportunity what states and the federal government have always been about? Or should have always been about?

This is a very complicated issue. It encompasses a broad range of policy, financing, teacher certification, as well as a set of resource standards. It's an issue the states are going to have to face, whatever happens in Congress.

MR. PETERKIN: I really don't think we are that far apart on this whole issue of incentives and rewards. Governor Romer framed the issue as a chicken-or-egg situation. Well, for once, I would like to see the egg come before the chicken.

I would like to see the onus placed on adults long before it's placed on children. When people tell me that we have to continue to codify our children and to fail some of them while we try to fix this flawed system, I am going to fight it.

If you tell me, however, that adults are going to work to build capacity, are going to be involved in reaching conclusions—not just discussion for discussion's sake—and that institutions are, therefore, going to be powerful enough to move the lives of children in concert with the community, then I'm all for it. I'm all for rewarding them until the cows come home.

But if kids continue to fail, and the institution isn't doing anything about it, then I want that institution to pay the price long, long before their kids pay yet another price.

MR. HORNBECK: There is no disagreement that every child deserves an opportunity to learn. The issue is whether there should be a direct connection between the use of standards and assessments—either developed with federal money or implying federal imprimatur—and the denying of graduation, promotion, jobs, or college based on those tests.

I believe that there needs to be that linkage. I can't bring myself to the point of saying we can use that test to deny college or a job by official state action, even though we haven't provided the kids an opportunity to learn.

But that connection will require us to fashion a set of features that would be standard in that area—what have been called delivery standards. Most of the time when people talk about that, they begin to talk about narrowly drawn, prescriptive kinds of things.

I heard somebody yesterday say: "What do you want? Do you want to specify the number of globes in the geography classroom?" Some people have even talked about teacher-student ratios as one standard.

I'm talking about much broader standards; for example, whether we ought to deny a kid graduation if his teachers are unable to pass the exam that the kid is expected to pass in order to graduate.

This is a very fundamental question about the values of this country and the federal role. It is going to be a matter of heated debate in the months ahead.

GOVERNOR ROMER: Let me start from where the real world is. I'm embarrassed to use my airplane example, but here goes: You ought not be allowed to fly a plane unless you know how to fly the plane.

Therefore, when I run a flight school, are you saying that the Federal Aviation Administration shouldn't let me have a standard with consequences, which is a flight test, unless I can also prove that everybody had an opportunity to learn down here?

MR. HORNBECK: No. I'm saying that the person we put in the classroom has to know how to fly, or the person ought not to be flying, and we ought not to be sending kids up in an airplane with people who are going to kill them. That's the issue.

GOVERNOR ROMER: Let me go at it again, David. When we went to Congress with S 2 last year, we said this nation needs to adopt content standards for what a youngster ought to know and be able to do. Second, we need to find a way to measure how well they do it, because that's the way the real world is.

Therefore, we ask your assistance to put this panel in place, where it will just give a Good Housekeeping seal of approval. We also ask your assistance to get the Department of Education to start developing some research on proper assessments.

The House said, "No, not fair. You shouldn't ask students to meet high standards unless you can insure that they have the opportunity to learn."

I agree that good public policy says you've got to do them both simultaneously. But the Congress wants to prove you've got the opportunity to learn before we apply the standard.

Now, let me go back to my airplane analogy. We live in the real world, and people fly those airplanes. We are going to have more people flying every day. And we have got to continue to have a gate through which we don't let people go. The world really works that way.

Whether you apply for a job or apply for college, there is a gate, and they are going to have criteria for that gate no matter what we do with law. That's the real world.

In education, we're trying to prepare people for those gates of employment and professional certification. We ought to create learning atmospheres, experiences where all youngsters have an opportunity to hit those gates. That's for sure. That's a commitment I'm willing to make.

And I'm willing to sit with an "opportunity-to-learn commission" and say these are general descriptors as to what schools in America ought to include in order to make sure kids have the opportunity to learn. But I want to stop right there. I don't want to then say that, if you don't comply with those prescriptors, you don't get federal funds.

MR. HORNBECK: Now, just so I understand, let's say you've got most of the teachers in a state unable to pass the exam, just to use an example, that the kids in the state are expected to pass. Yet, you think the real world, as you describe it, should deny those kids the chance to pass through the gate?

GOVERNOR ROMER: No, no, I don't buy that. I'm not into exams with high stakes. I'm willing to bring a youngster through this K-12 system and give him any kind of a damn thing you want to give him. Say, "Thank you, glad you were here." That's O.K. by me—almost—as long as what happens within that system internally was really aimed at making him educated. I think we can do a lot better than "thank you, glad you're here."

But once they leave the K-12 system, they're going to get a job, fly an airplane, go to college, or whatever, and those are real gates. So we want to give that youngster guidelines as he goes through that K-12 experience that assure him he's going to be qualified to get through the next gate.

And the most honest thing you can tell a senior in high school is whether you have given him what he's going to need to live his life. That is what he wanted to come to school for. Now, if you lie to him, you've done the worst thing in the world.

If I go to the hospital for a CAT scan, don't lie to me about what it says. We should give the student an honest CAT scan of his educational achievement.

Measurement has meaning. What I'm worried about is when we get to the prescriptive nature of standards that relate to opportunity to learn, we really have got to be careful. It's helpful to say to people this is what a good school looks like, and this is what good teaching looks like. We give schools examples of what we think are good practices, then they go do their own thing. I don't want a federal law that says you do it the way we prescribe it or else, bang, you don't get the money.

MR. HORNBECK: I would, in fact, be prepared to say that if you don't succeed, then we will examine whether you meet some very parsimonious, stripped-down delivery standards. In fact, there are only three or four things that I would put on the list of opportunity-to-learn standards.

And I won't even prevent you from giving the exam, any of that kind of stuff, but you can't, by way of state action, deny ...

GOVERNOR ROMER: If you don't produce the result over a period of time that we think you ought to produce, we're going to come in and ask...

MR. HORNBECK: We're going to ask you if you're helping kids.

GOVERNOR ROMER: And you're going to take your charter away or your money away.

MR. HORNBECK: If it's used for high-stakes purposes, yes.

MR. CROSS: What's the incentive, then, David, for the system to do all that it needs to do to teach the kids, if they can continue to not have high-stakes requirements or high-stakes consequences?

MR. HORNBECK: I think the incentive to the system is to be one of the early states that can demonstrate clearly that they're producing a quality workplace. You get economic development; that's the reason we're in this business anyhow.

MR. CROSS: But as Rick has pointed out, they're out there now. I would turn it around and say that, until you have high stakes, you're not going to motivate the community to take it seriously.

MR. HORNBECK: Well, that is clearly a difference of opinion.

MR. MILLS: Should the accountability in the system be at the very, very top, or should there also be accountability at the bottom? In the business world, the accountability is right there at the cash register, and it is the customer who demands performance. We're envisioning a model here where it's way, way, way up someplace at the Securities and Exchange Commission level.

And I don't think that is where the levers for change ought to exist. I'm not starting to make an argument for choice. I'm just saying that the performance, the enforcement of the quality in this educational system, has to be much closer to where kids are and parents are.

EW: If enforcement of quality is where the kids and parents are, how do you deal with schools in East St. Louis, the schools Jonathan Kozol wrote about in *Savage Inequalities*? Who is going to take the steps necessary to change that situation? And how would they do it if there were opportunity-to-learn standards and sanctions for failing to meet them? Imagine the changes that would be required to provide an opportunity to learn in some of the dreadful schools described in Kozol's book.

MR. MILLS: We need to look at it at both ends. I think Kozol's argument is telling—maybe for a state to play in the game there have to be a few basic gauges. Not a detailed micromanaged plan, but a band of equity.

MR. HORNBECK: I would insist on a standard that assured that teachers have the capacity to teach what we expect kids to learn. I think it's insane to think that we ought to hold a kid responsible for knowing algebra or flying an airplane if we don't have teachers who know how to do that. And in Kentucky right now, 75 percent of the teachers would have a very difficult time with the examination.

MR. MILLS: Seventy-five percent?

MR. HORNBECK: That is what has come back in reaching the top standard.

MS. GRAHAM: That raises certain questions about whether the kids can reach that standard.

MR. HORNBECK: That's exactly my point.

The second opportunity-to-learn standard that I would have is to have an inspectorate of very highly professionally trained people who, on a sample basis, would go to a state that was seeking this federal imprimatur and examine the portfolio of curriculum, technology, and instructional activities that the school and the school district thought was the array of arrows in the quiver that was responsive to the standards.

And everybody doesn't have to do the same thing. There could be lots of different ones. Somebody might think that their kids need to go to a downtown library, and others might think the library has got to be in the school; some might use computers to access a variety of data bases.

The third standard would be a system of professional development that was reasonably calculated to maintain teacher competence vis-à-vis the content standards for students. It always comes back to the student standards.

And the fourth would be some form of system of consequences, and by that I mean both positive and negative, that are connected to the performance system.

Those would be the four things that would be the delivery standards for the system. If those four things were in place, I think you could reasonably say that you had provided an opportunity to learn.

And if you don't have teachers that know it, and you don't even have a science lab, for goodness' sake, or any evidence that there's any way to do that, and you don't have any system of professional development that any professional would think related to the standards, then you ought not to be able to deny kids stuff in the process.

GOVERNOR ROMER: I could probably buy your four standards. But in my gut, I'm worried that it wouldn't be limited to four once people start making lists.

When you start describing the delivery standards that Congress is going to police, you lose me. And that's what I sensed was happening the last time in Congress.

I believe Congress will probably create a "commission on learning." That is a healthy thing for two reasons. One, it helps Congress know somebody's going to pay attention to this, and it gets them out of the role of micromanaging. Second, they really can do some good work, like begin to describe what a good school looks like in its various forms and what good teaching is. They can't be prescriptive; it needs to be done with enough breadth and pluralism that we can invent some variations that fit in.

Maybe we could begin to get together on this issue of opportunity to learn.

'We Need To Be Thoughtful About the Federal Agenda'

EW: Last year, a bill called S 2 died in the U.S. Congress. It would have supported state and local reform efforts and authorized a federal role in the development of national education standards. The Clinton Administration is now negotiating with Congress about a new bill that some are calling "son of S 2."

Moreover, the Elementary and Secondary Education Act, which includes the majority of precollegiate programs funded by the federal government, is up for reauthorization next year. And pressure is building to change the act to align it more closely with the education goals and with the ideas of systemic reform.

Some see this as an opportunity for the federal government to expand its role in education, to provide the stimulus and seed money necessary to give added impetus and direction to systemic reform. They see an especially important role for President Clinton and Hillary Rodham Clinton, both of whom have been deeply involved in school reform.

What should the federal role be?

MR. SEXTON: I'm not enamored with the federal role. Kentucky's revenue projections for the next five years show a fairly modest growth rate—and so do the federal government's.

Most of the growth goes to health care, some goes to education, and none goes to anything else. I agree that there are things that we must get on the federal agenda—including leadership. But unless the Administration and the Congress concentrate on health care, on getting the economy moving, on reducing the deficit, on restoring some confidence in the political processes that are driving things locally, then a major federal effort related to education may be wasted.

If the federal government will concentrate on those key issues that will affect whether the states can do this job, maybe the states can do the job. There are things in education the federal government can do, but I don't think they're the key elements that have to drive the reform agenda across the nation.

GOVERNOR ROMER: That thought drove the National Governors' Association's agenda for this year. Unless you get control of the economic factors and the health-care costs, we are going to be unable to govern at the state level. And even though I had education as my highest level of interest, as the chairman of the N.G.A., I put it third on the priority list, because I thought those two preceded it on the federal agenda.

But we need to be very thoughtful about the federal agenda. We need a national strategy for education reform. I do not think that we are going to get there without utilizing the leadership at the federal level, in addition to the leadership at the state and local levels.

MS. FUHRMAN: I certainly agree with the need to address health care and the basic economic issues, but I would disagree that the states can get systemic reform on their own—not only because of the importance of federal leadership and the efforts that the federal government can exert in areas of collaboration and support for people trying to do this job, but because I also believe that the federal categorical programs pose challenges to the reform agenda.

I think that if we don't deal with having these programs interact with what the states are trying to do, then the reform will be neither systemic nor real, because we will leave out children who are served largely by these categorical programs and whose entire education is driven by remedial pull-out programs. There is a major agenda for the federal government.

GOVERNOR ROMER: Let me give you a federal strategy that might curl your hair. Just imagine a law that would pass Congress that says we're going to develop a 10-year national strategy, and we're going to ask the Secretary of Education to provide the leadership.

Under this strategy, each state will be asked to develop a 10-year plan for systemic reform, including standards and assessments and all of the things that most reformers agree on. The states would have a whole lot of latitude the first year to go out and do their thing. But for the second through the 10th years, a state's continued funding would depend on the progress they make on their systemic-reform plans.

This law would give the Secretary of Education the opportunity to waive every federal regulation that now exists on all the present acts, and give the states permission to take those and fold them into their own strategies as they develop them.

Now, that is a way to play the game that we haven't been using. It does put a great deal of confidence into a federal establishment, and we may not want to do that. I'm not sure we want to federalize the leadership that much. That traditionally worries me.

But I'm willing to consider an approach like this with some degree of openness because we are doing so poorly in really getting this reform going. And I think that we've got to work both from the top down and the bottom up if we're going to succeed. We've just got to find the right balance.

We are in a real economic crunch and will be for some time. If we don't get at some of the tough problems pretty soon, our hills are going to be too steep to climb. So we've got to give up some of this classic notion that the states are the laboratories of democracy. Hey, we don't have time for all that experimentation on problems like the deficit and health care and education.

I'm more willing to give more leadership, responsibility, and authority to the federal government, so long as we have the right kind of controls and constraints on it.

MR. MILLS: I strongly disagree, even though that is probably the way things will go. It's very likely that the nation will agree on a list of things that we need to do, and they could be written into federal law.

We would probably get something like we've had for 27 years with Chapter 1—a checklist, a monitoring approach, a very rigid "cap analysis." We'd probably get a law that specifies what you're supposed to have in reform, looks at what you have, and says it's not good enough so we're going to cut off the money.

The federal government is a very late player in this game. It would be unseemly for the feds to come in and say, "This is how you have to be inventive. Let's look down the list and see what have you done about the passion thing."

There are a lot of people who want to do it that way.

GOVERNOR ROMER: I understand the danger in this, Rick, but do we need to take it to the extreme and not even try?

Take the standards. We have not done very well at all with national math standards. How long have they been out there, five years or so? They haven't penetrated the mind set of America.

We've got a whole lot of things in Chapter 1, and the structure is wrong. Is it inappropriate for somebody who's doling out federal money to say let's do a less-wrong thing? To really start pushing standards-based education as one of the criteria, but allow considerable flexibility in how it's done?

MR. MILLS: Let's do it the way you've been doing it—walking around with a copy of the standards in hand, putting them into the professional-development programs, putting the spotlight on the teachers who are actually teaching them, and wrapping them around the state-level assessment.

It matters a lot to have Kentucky doing something very different from what Vermont is doing. We're all intensely collaborative, but we're also intensely competitive. We want to borrow ideas that have been developed someplace else. Let's keep that spirit alive and not let this thing get rigid.

I think one of the dangers is that the reform effort could have an orthodoxy, and we could exclude contrarian views. We need the contrarian view. We don't need a federal approach that discourages it. Kentucky might invent something next year that's the key, but, if it were inconsistent with the federal guidelines, it wouldn't get off the ground. I want to bet on Kentucky.

MR. HORNBECK: Isn't it possible to hold both of those things together?

When we were working on the National Council on Educational Standards and Testing, we envisioned national, not federal, standards. Those standards would drive a federal law like S 2, but they would still be national, not federal. They would also be voluntary.

Vermont could come to the agency created by S 2 and present its portfolios and ask, "Does this assessment strategy measure up to the anchor standards and assessments?" Kentucky could do the same thing with its education-reform act.

MR. MILLS: That makes sense.

MR. HORNBECK: If one does that, you can hold together at one time the national/federal leadership.

When we get around to discussing things like opportunity-to-learn standards or delivery standards, we can talk about the conditions under which the federal/national imprimatur is placed on Vermont's successful system. But it seems to me you can hold together the two propositions that Rick and Roy have put on the table.

MS. FUHRMAN: I think Rick's concern about rigidity and people going into a compliance mode suggests that there's a mindlessness about the kind of checklists, or ways of judging what states are doing or what localities are doing.

When we talk about capacity, we need it at all levels; we don't need it just in the school. As important as that is and as much as we need professional development, we also need it at the district, at the state, and at the federal-government levels, and in national efforts.

So when this agency says, "What you're doing seems to fit the spirit of this piece of legislation, that it is done with intelligence," that's a kind of negotiation, and it's not a checklist. If we're talking about national efforts to encourage states, we need to talk about a national capacity to think about these issues, and we need to think about that at each level of the system.

MS. GRAHAM: Resources at the moment at the federal level are very limited. Therefore, to expect a very elaborate role and performance from the federal government is very worrisome. I would prefer to see a federal role that is big on inspiring goals and not so big on making judgments about state progress.

There is no one clear way to get educational reform in this country. The federal government traditionally has had a lot of difficulty thinking of multiple avenues toward a single goal. It tends to think of a single way to get to a goal. There isn't any single route to getting all kids to learn at high levels. The danger of having a federal guideline is that the federal government will try to say there is only the Vermont way or the Kentucky way or the Maryland way.

I would argue for dramatic images at the federal level, dramatic statements of goals, dramatic statements on how important it is to our country, but not prescriptive measures.

MR. HORNBECK: Does your wariness include high voluntary national standards?

MS. GRAHAM: I'm much bigger on talking about dramatic presentations of goals than I am talking about standards, because standards, in my book, while highly desirable, translate very quickly into a mechanistic mode of application that I, frankly, fear from the federal government.

GOVERNOR ROMER: I think that we're too polarized. There is middle ground. S 2 called for a state-by-state plan. I think "son of S 2" will include the elements of the hypothetical federal law I sketched out earlier.

The federal government is probably going to funnel money to states, and it might be more rational to do so in a way other than the highly prescriptive way they do it now under Chapter 1. I would like to believe in a federal establishment, Education Department, and President who would have the wisdom not to do it prescriptively. We can get them to help us be strategic without being prescriptive.

The standards of the National Council of Teachers of Mathematics are not part of a federal program; they're national. That's a model we ought to emulate and duplicate as we develop other standards. Colorado should not redo the N.C.T.M. standards. We don't have the capacity to do it, and we're not going to get it done. But we could adopt them in Colorado.

MS. GRAHAM: In this sense, we're on the same goal. The question is, How are we going to get there? To what extent do we believe that strengthening, or making more explicit, certain federal activities is going to be helpful, and, if so, which activities? I don't think we're disagreeing about the end; I think we're disagreeing about what the mechanism is at the federal level to enhance the education of kids.

What is the mechanism at the federal level to get communities and states to be more effective in serving children? When Title I was adopted in 1965, the idea was that the states and the locals weren't doing a damn thing for poor kids, and particularly minority poor kids. Those regulations were intended to force states and locals into doing something that states and locals didn't want to do.

We're not at that point now. We should be figuring out what can be enhanced at the state and local levels to get the job done.

MR. HORNBECK: The situation in 1993 is not all that much different from 1965 when it comes to high levels of performance by kids in our cities. The states have not stepped up to the plate and even begun to take on the challenge of meeting the educational and social needs of those kids.

Surely, developmentally appropriate pre-kindergarten programs of high quality would make a contribution to the education of the disadvantaged. In fact, such programs are important enough that you would expect the 50 states to have guaranteed them at least for their poor kids. But only about five states have. That's hardly stepping up to the plate.

And it gets worse with initiatives that haven't yet been shown to work. So the challenges of the 1960's haven't all been met.

But at least we've moved to the point that advantaged kids are about to take off, because the society has figured out we've got to do that. And that raises the historical federal role regarding access and equity, because we don't want to have the gap between advantaged and disadvantaged kids get wider.

But neither do we want to make the mistake that we've historically made of only targeting poor kids. We need at least voluntary across-the-board standards for both poor kids and rich kids.

MS. FUHRMAN: The challenge today is just as great as it was in the 1960's. But the substance of the challenge is different and requires different mechanisms. It's not simply a problem of access that can be solved by targeting where the kids get the services. It's a question of quality that can be influenced by carefully constructed federal policy. Voluntary national standards are a good way to go, and anchoring a number of existing federal programs to those standards and asking states to carry them out is a good way to go.

GOVERNOR ROMER: The Americans With Disabilities Act offers an analogy. Do you realize what the A.D.A. has done to us? I'm out there spending money on the A.D.A., whether I like it or not, folks. And it comes first. It's absolutely the highest priority in my budget.

Or take the environment. I'm out there spending money on the Clean Water Act, because that is what everybody said was the first and foremost thing.

I care deeply about clean water. I care deeply about people with disabilities. But I care even more about the ability of a child to mature and to think and to have great values.

I'm just about at the point of saying: "Folks, if I'm going to be ordered to do A.D.A. and be ordered to do Clean Water, then I'll buy a federal role in setting priorities in education and providing leadership. Just give it to me in a way that is not prescriptive."

MS. GRAHAM: But can you get it in a way that is not prescriptive? That is the issue: Can you give quality in a way that is not prescriptive?

MR. HORNBECK: I think you can.

MR. PETERKIN: I'm not as strong as the Governor is on being ordered to do things. But there are some ways to enforce the kinds of reforms that we're talking about and still let them be played out at the local level with a kind of richness and variety.

Schools are ready to meet some standards, but they want some dialogue about what those standards are, and how they pertain to kids, and how they're carried out. And if we attempt to prescribe all that, we will be battling over the checklist. And it won't be because the General Accounting Office says we've done something inappropriate. It will be over whether we have every single one of these specified components in that school system that will make it look exactly in Kentucky as it does in Vermont.

MR. HORNBECK: What, then, are the implications for a federal/national initiative that is appropriately reflected in federal law?

MR. MILLS: The federal regulations, the federal statutes have to be consistent with what states have done. Any mismatches there need to be found and eliminated.

Second, there hasn't been sufficient federal investment in a lot of the national reform structures that have been invented, like the New Standards Project, for example. The state-by-state National Assessment of Educational Progress hasn't been reauthorized, hasn't been funded. Those are major mistakes on the part of the federal government.

MS. HAYCOCK: The House is the only side that's gotten started on the education agenda. They've had hearings on state systemic reform, one on assessment, and one on Chapter 1.

One of the tensions here is that, while a lot of states are moving pretty aggressively on systemic reform, a lot of them are not. And the appropriate federal role, given those circumstances, is a little more complex than just getting out of the way and providing some resources.

What ought to be done for states that aren't moving aggressively on the reform issues? Should the feds push them on things like setting standards?

MR. MILLS: The feds don't know how to do that. The hearing that I attended was wonderful. Congressmen were genuinely asking questions and listening. But I would be appalled to have the pioneering experiences of states codified by the federal government and then rammed right back at the pioneers.

I don't see how a federal agency could have compelled Kentucky to do the right thing. If the federal government tried to tell us how to do reform in Vermont, the Green Mountain Boys would rise up again. What we need is not to be told how to do things. We need the other partners to do the things that only they can do.

MR. SEXTON: That takes us back to the leadership role. If you don't want to codify, you can at least lead. For example, I have been quite surprised in the past few years at the ability of the White House to go to the business leadership and send a message.

I would like to see the President talking from his bully pulpit to people in communities and saying, "Why don't you folks get together and figure out how to take care of the children in your community? And why don't you business leaders think about ways of encouraging older youngsters to want to do well in school?"

Maybe the President ought to reach out to the students, too, especially the older ones. Maybe one of the incentives in this system—or one of the messages that the whole culture sends to young people—is that education and hard work don't matter. What matters is consumption and watching television and whatever else.

GOVERNOR ROMER: What if this President had not chosen to get into health-care reform as the major new thrust of his Administration, but had started off saying the greatest crisis in America is our ability to compete in the global marketplace 25 years from now, and our ability to have communities that function, and a society that is increasing its values, rather than diminishing them.

And, therefore, we, in 100 days, led by Mrs. Clinton, are going to come up with a strategy for changing our schools. Now, some people would say the federal government can't do that because education is so local.

But they're now doing it on the most personal thing in this country, and that is who your doctor is and how he treats you and how you're going to pay him and how long you're going to be hooked up to the machine and when are they going to pull the plug on you.

We buy into that. Think about it a moment. Now, if we buy into that, why are we so worried about the federal role in education? I just finished a conference call of about 25 states on the health-care issue. Why? Because they know their futures are going to be radically affected by what is done on health care.

I agree with this President picking health care and the deficit as his top priorities. But I use this as an analogy, because we have a sacred-cow attitude about education as a strictly local issue. It is a state and local issue, but the federal government has a role. There ought to be a way they can put the 100-day sense of urgency on it without prescribing, without micromanaging.

Our challenge is how to put together an effort similar to the massive reform of health care, set some time lines, and make some assignments. Sure, we have to do it in partnership—make the proper delegation of authority to the school itself, to the district, to the state, to the national level, and have the President hold everybody whom he employs accountable for their role in this effort.

It is so massive, the power that the federal government has. It has never been focused on education; that is not "the agenda."

MS. FINE: But if it were, what would be helpful to you? What would the Administration or Congress be doing that would strengthen your arm in doing the work you need to do in Colorado?

GOVERNOR ROMER: First of all, the standards themselves are very slow in coming. We need the standards.

Then we need the iterative process, going back and forth several times until we have what we want and everybody has a sense of ownership. It wasn't dictated from the top down.

Then they help us move quickly into R&D, and we begin to develop the assessments, the methodology, the tools we need. And they help us with the professional development as we go.

The President of the United States could call in every textbook publisher, because the standards of America are being driven by the textbook publishers and the test publishers of America. Workbooks are driving the content of the curriculum and also a lot of the teaching methodology. He would let them know that we're going to have pluralism in approach here. We're not going to dictate from the top down. We want the free-market system to work.

That's what we're doing in health, isn't it? We're going to vertically integrate health care in America practically overnight. Why don't we call in these publishers?

I could go on and on.

For example, we could say that all federal funds that come to Colorado in any way, shape, or form in education have got to help further standards of education. Anybody who applies for any grant has to include a page on their form showing how their program would further our education goals. We do this all the time in other programs. We just don't have a mental image of the power that we have.

So the federal government could do these things and leave it to the proper kind of decision being made at the school building—which is essentially what is American about this.

MS. FUHRMAN: I think the process that you're talking about is going to happen with regard to standards. Unless huge formula fights kill proposed changes in these categorical programs, it's quite likely to happen in E.S.E.A., too, and more broadly.

But that iterative process has to be an intelligent discussion between states and the federal government, not just pro forma. And that's where the capacity of the federal level is just as important as the capacity of the state and local levels to have a good discussion about whether the state system is a meaningful system with accountability and standards and opportunity to learn, so that you would want federal dollars to flow through that system.

MR. MILLS: The power to make these changes is in the hands of millions of people. The President needs to do powerful things, like help the public understand what it could look like if we all worked together, to hold up the standards as they appear and ask people if their community is educating its children to these standards.

And then do it again and do it again and do it again with each new set of standards as they come out. The President could take the microphone and talk about the National Assessment of Educational Progress results rather than have that come out as it does. When the panel produces the report on the condition of education, let the President go on television and say: "You ought to read this; I just read it, and I'm appalled. You probably have condition-of-education reports in your town. If you don't, you ought to ask why you don't."

Let the President visit schools and show you how you visit a school and find out what's really going on. Show parents how they can do this. Those are the kinds of powerful gestures that would energize millions of people.

Behind that, there is all kinds of intensely technical interagency, intersector work that has to be done. But that can't all be controlled; it has to be inspired.

MR. CROSS: We need to distinguish between setting a national policy and the federal role. Many of the tasks we've set out for the President are about creating national policy. Then the federal government has a role, such as enacting a law and carrying it out.

There is a good deal that can be done in terms of the federal role—of convening and driving the message home, and really being sure that things happen, and using federal resources to help do that, but not be the entire carrier of the message.

Because, if we rely totally on the federal government, we would be letting the states off the hook. We'd let the local districts off the hook. We'd let everybody off the hook on the assumption that the feds have taken care of everything.

MS. GRAHAM: I agree with the power of symbols. I have a quite low approach to all of this. The President has a limited amount of time, and education invariably is not going to be his first or second priority. Education is likely to be, at best, the third priority.

And so, while it is very important to use the President whenever the President can be used for that, we need to have a strategy as well that does not rely on Presidential stump speeches.

If there's one thing the American people are interested in at the moment, it's a little honesty in all of this. And that means not just a federal initiative that promises a lot and then collapses.

GOVERNOR ROMER: We've got this new President, we've got this new Education Secretary. And we've got this new bill and money that are probably going to come out of Congress.

So let's take advantage of that. Let's get going on curriculum frameworks, for example. We don't need to do it in 50 states. Let's get clusters of four or five states to do it. And get some R&D money out to clusters of states to develop assessment strategies. Let's get five really good varieties of 4th-grade math assessments, for instance. The New Standards Project could play a leadership role. If we work together on this, we can accelerate the process by several years.

'Why Don't We Take the Role of School, Community Seriously?'

EW: The constitutional responsibility for education rests with the states. They have delegated substantial authority to local school boards, and that has made the school district the dominant entity in the governance of American education.

One of the most powerful ideas of systemic reform is that the historic delegation of authority should continue downward—that decisions affecting instruction should be made at the school level. Individual schools should control budget, personnel, instructional practices, scheduling, and student/teacher assignments. This is not an idea that finds universal favor with district-level administrators.

MS. FINE: I wonder what would happen if we really took that idea seriously.

We should probably amend it to be school and community, which then makes us think about such issues as desegregation, magnet schools, and choice. If we were really serious about that, we would have to have a trust in teachers and the public that is relatively unprecedented.

MS. GRAHAM: Which we ain't got.

MS. FINE: Which we ain't got. We've all criticized the trickle-down theory when it's applied to the economy, but we're still willing to believe it would work with education. Why don't we take the role of school and community as seriously as we take the federal and state roles?

MR. HORNBECK: In emphasizing school and community, do you presume a set of outcome standards?

MS. FINE: The image that I have is that the public school, like private schools, is really the site of budgeting, decisionmaking, and accountability.

The state should have a very tight, diverse but tight, accountability framework with consequences.

GOVERNOR ROMER: On the content?

MS. FINE: On content, on student involvement, on engagement with the community. If you move all that responsibility and the resources to the local school, you absolutely need a very tight accountability framework at the state level. But it has got to be an accountability framework with consequence and an accountability framework that takes equity seriously.

Right now, we have the fantasy that local districts do equity and accountability, and I would argue they do not. They do nothing. What they do is reproduce a set of explanations for why they can't do equity and accountability.

We don't hold anybody accountable now. Principals aren't held accountable. Schools aren't held accountable. So, yes, there has to be firm accountability.

But if you're going to hold schools accountable, then you have to move the resources and the decisionmaking to the schools, and you have to provide as much capacity-building as you can for teachers and parents and community. You need to seek help from universities and business and labor.

I'd like us to try focusing on school and community because, unless you take the school as part of the community, you're going to lose the kind of equity questions that we all care about.

MR. BILLUPS: I can accept the idea of moving responsibility and accountability to the school level, but only if we provide teachers with the professional-development support they need to do the job, and only if we start preparing new teachers for their new roles.

MS. FUHRMAN: That's a very productive way to talk about how we get systemic reform. Let's assume that the school is the site of decisionmaking and accountability and that the state really enforces and supports that notion. Then let's imagine what the school and the people in it and the state would want of the federal government.

We would want support for collaboratives, for professional development in a way that is flexible and constructive. We would want the federal government, in its programs for special needs, to be compatible with what we're trying to do as a state and local system.

There are ways to think about the federal role that are very supportive of the idea of school and community as central.

MR. PETERKIN: You talk about federal, state, and local. When we think about local, we think about schools. We have conversations about schools. What we don't have conversations about at all is the rest of the actors in the school systems.

Take school boards. I'm not arguing that they are the most important people in the system, but, if we don't include them, we're going to think we worked out a good system and then later realize that school boards are still in the way of getting from here to where we want to be. Likewise for state departments and chief state school officers and the federal government.

Between the schools and the federal government are others who have roles to play, and, if not recognized, they will gum up the works because they're not finding a role. They won't just go away.

MR. HORNBECK: Let's talk a bit about how we might build a system of successful education from the school level up.

A law has been proposed in Washington State that sets out to do that in a way. It would give the power for selecting all personnel to the school. It would give the school the power to determine how all the money is used, with the school board deciding its allocation to the school and raising its share of the money. After the allocation is made, the school would have full authority to make the decisions.

In short, the law would give the school complete power over curriculum and instructional activities and the scheduling of the school day within specified opening and closing hours. The kid would get assigned from the outside. Once the kid's in the school, then assignment of kids and teachers—during the day, during the year, and across multiple years—would rest with the school.

The proposed law mandates that all state laws and regulations affecting education that do not govern health, safety, and civil rights, and that are not re-enacted by a specified future date, are voided. Laws or regulations that should be re-enacted can be.

Instead of waiving specific regulations, this proposal does the opposite. Its premise is that there are no regulations. When you get to an accountability system, the consequence or the penalty for a school not measuring up is to be re-regulated. In effect, a school is penalized if it is not doing what it ought to do, instead of being rewarded with a waiver if it does well.

If you were to have schools with those powers, what would be the implications for the central districts? What is left for them to do? What about the other players Bob Peterkin mentioned?

MR. MILLS: Is the name of this game to make sure that everybody now in the system has important work to do? Or is the name of this game to make sure that every kid grows up to be a healthy, competent person?

MR. PETERKIN: The question is what people think their jobs are now. If there is not something in that statute that prevents school boards, for instance, from re-enacting all the regulations the state dropped, then you have not gained very much.

If there is not a role in a restructured system for people in the present system, then they should be let go. If there is a role, then it ought to be clearly defined to serve the purpose of the school. This is not about protecting roles.

MS. FUHRMAN: There are roles in between the school building and the state. If they did not exist, people would reinvent intermediate units of some sort.

I am not an apologist for school boards, but I think that articulation among levels of schooling and economies of scale require an intermediate unit to assist schools. We should not create a system in which schools are expected to fend entirely for themselves.

Moreover, the body that levies taxes and justifies schooling to the public is going to want to have a lot of say about values.

People have concerns for all their children, not just the one who is in elementary school, and so they want to see how the whole system fits together. Since we already have districts and school boards, perhaps we can think of how they can be encouraged to play their roles better.

MR. BILLUPS: Or have them think about what their roles should be.

MS. FINE: There is little evidence that people on school boards and in district hierarchies have the capacity, desire, or will to radically rethink what they do or how they do it. Those institutions are ironically still called public, but, in fact, are not very publicly accessible—or even breathing—institutions.

We would invent things between schools, but would we invent things that are deeply hierarchical, controlling, and relatively expensive?

Isolated schools do not do very well; schools do best when they are attached to something outside of themselves, whether that is a coalition or a writing network or a portfolio project. Attachment is important for the intellectual and emotional life of the school. But turning that into a hierarchical supervisory relationship kills the kind of intellectual and emotional support we need.

I also worry about those large districts creating safety nets for schools. Who in Chicago worries about the schools that are falling apart, for example? Someone called those schools "the de-institutionalized mentally ill of educational decentralization." I am a big fan of reform in Chicago, but I am not convinced that the current bureaucratic structure does anything to sustain the intellectual and emotional life of teachers, parents, and kids.

Unless we figure out how to reinvent central districts, if they continue to exist at all, then we may come up with state and federal efforts to fix education, but will have ignored the institutional stranglehold that central districts have on the schools.

MR. HORNBECK: This notion of a non-hierarchical connecting tissue among and between autonomous schools is an interesting one. If a school does not function well as an island unto itself, what does it need help with, at something short of the state level? How would we define that in functional terms, rather than hierarchical terms?

One clear area would be transporting and feeding students, and buying in bulk. A second area might be in the delivery of professional staff development—largely determined by the schools, but almost the professional side of bulk purchase. A third area—perhaps most important—is in building public understanding and support.

MS. GRAHAM: An example is the network of Sacred Heart schools that creates an architecture of attachment. It is a very useful model for professional development. The schools have established a common purpose for what they are up to and are able to talk to each other about what they are trying to do in their separate institutions.

That is the level of conversation that I think is missing in the public school system.

MR. CROSS: You seem to suggest that each of the schools has its own board.

MS. GRAHAM: That is exactly right.

MR. CROSS: What is also needed here is the vision of what we want the educational system to do. A culmination of the Sacred Heart schools is they all have an image, and they all have a common understanding of that.

In all this decentralization, we still have to have a vision of what the public education system is about. Several nations have systems that are functioning pretty well, but, ironically, every one of them is a centralized system. What does that tell us about the success, perhaps, of the provocative kind of decentralized system Michelle is proposing?

MR. HORNBECK: Perhaps that's a potential American contribution.

MR. CROSS: Right. And I am not arguing for centralization. I am just saying I think we have to keep it in mind.

MR. HORNBECK: Should the responsibilities for children's health and social services be lodged in this intermediate entity that we were talking about, this "connective tissue" that would link autonomous schools?

When one defines the outcomes we want in a system, they're not only academic outcomes, but "kid well-being" outcomes as well. If we then have an accountability system with incentives connected to outcomes, the teacher would be held accountable for how well the kid could read, but the health worker might be accountable in part for how healthy the kid is, and the social-services worker might be held partly accountable for how many fewer dysfunctional families there are in the community than the previous year.

Maybe, if we even have a board, it should be a board of children and families, not a board of education.

MR. MILLS: That's an intriguing idea that probably will come, but I would go at it indirectly.

In Vermont, we found it is important for educational services to literally sit down and rewrite the education visions and rewrite the services vision to get a combined vision. That's going to lead to changes in the goals, so we might end up with combined goals.

At a local level, it involves principals. One principal said: "We used to think we were in charge, and our job here at the school was to point out to the parents what they needed to do to help us. But, suddenly, I had an insight that really the parents are in charge, and what they were trying to do was raise their children. And, as a school person, I was supposed to help them. As soon as I started thinking of the world that way, everything became different."

It's working on the basic perception, and the basic vision at both ends of the system, that requires the work first. We have dysfunctional local boards now. Imagine what it would be like if we had two unintegrated, undigested systems pushed together where players were educated differently and had different jargon and a different legal structure, a different sense of purpose. It would be even more chaotic.

MS. HAYCOCK: David and I were at a meeting with health and social-service people to discuss this subject. One of the things they said to the educators quite clearly was that, if we have in mind a system where we eventually will all be held accountable for getting kids to certain outcomes, you damn well better either slow down your process or broaden it quickly to include things that we hold dear as well. You are so focused on geography and mathematics and science, and we don't necessarily think that is the be-all and end-all for kids.

You can move in the direction David is talking about when you have districts and counties that have coterminous boundaries. But we've got tons and tons of situations where you've got 27, 30 districts within a city, much less in a county. So rethinking the size of these intermediate units becomes a factor, assuming they continue to be geographical—which may not be the right assumption.

MS. FUHRMAN: If we are going to think about true school-site governments, then we have to think about working to finance the permanence of that. We might think about the financing by allowing tax check-offs, school by school.

Unless we do that, then we ought not be so quick to jettison the local elected authority that deals with taxing. I mean, if you are going to keep district financing even though you have school budgeting, then you ought to think about a structure to meld the two.

MS. HAYCOCK: We probably ought to acknowledge that we're not going to get where we want to go as a country so long as the financing structure continues to be dependent on local taxing efforts. Ultimately, we're going to have to address the question of whether there is a better way to finance education in order to get where we want to go.

MS. FUHRMAN: There is a lot more we can do to make the system more equitable.

But when we look at states that have virtually eliminated the local role—like California—the local funding share drastically goes down. There is a real value in local people deciding what kind of education they want to buy and investing themselves, therefore, because they have to pay for it. But there is also an advantage in having several players in school finance able to ante up a bit.

My second point has to do with the overall adequacy and the seriousness of dealing with the school-finance issue. Our research has shown really large increases, controlling for inflation, across the country in every state over the last 25 years—in some states, as much as 300 percent. Nationally, an average of at least 30 percent a decade. So there have been huge increases in what we spend, and yet enormous dissatisfaction with what we get.

There is no one—including my own state, where spending has gone up over 300 percent—who feels comfortable that that money is buying enough. There is no one who feels they have enough.

There are a lot of reasons. Some of the money is going just for the keeping up; we want teachers' salaries to keep up with general salaries. That doesn't mean we are necessarily buying more services that you can see.

Some of it is because we don't know very well where the money is going, and can't express it. We ought to be able to tell people how much of it is going into health care, for example, and not into the classroom. Our accounting categories are so bad that we can't even do that.

The third problem is a really serious one. In the absence of the kind of national standards and state standards being proposed, we don't have direction for the system. We don't know where we should be going. So, if we say we don't have enough money, what is the basis on which we say "enough"? We don't have a way to think about what money buys and what direction we want to go in.

That's why I think these reforms are that much more important.

MR. MILLS: I think we do know where the system is supposed to go. That is what state and local and national goals are all about.

But, by and large, the education-reform effort is disconnected from finance. We have a finance system virtually everywhere that invests in the status quo enthusiastically. And we have a reform effort that questions the status quo.

We have to connect dollars to performance, not in a crude way, but in a way that says, "To get the money, you've got to be in the performance game. And if you are not playing the performance game, that's O.K., too. But no money."

MR. SEXTON: The autonomous school approach that Michelle describes may work fine in an urban environment, but in most rural districts, the question is where to get the talent, the skills, the resources to do all the things we are talking about.

There is another thing that is really important and requires some pretty hard-nosed political thinking. A huge part of the function of local districts is the management of employment programs, which is at the heart of the political structure of the community. It is old-fashioned local-jobs, community-based politics. And in many places, the school district is by far the biggest employer in the area. About 10 percent of all the jobs in our state and in other similar states are within the school.

So, if you remove that function from the district, and if boards are limited to setting visions and evaluating standards and building community as opposed to managing schools, what do you do with that political function that is so central to the whole political structure of most states and localities?

Is there some other place for that function? If not, the only alternative I know of is that your political culture in your community has to change.

MR. MILLS: If we were to spell out the powers that are reserved to the school community, we should come up with a very clear and powerful list of things that schools can do. If we spell out those reserved to the state, the list should be much shorter. It should include the responsibility to define goals and to define a framework of curriculum, but not the curriculum itself; states ought to have the responsibility to measure results and to audit those results.

We should have a still smaller list of things that the feds do.

'I Am Concerned How the Grownups Can Do a Better Job'

EW: It is certainly true that national standards and assessments won't be effective unless they are adopted by states and implemented by schools. And they won't be applied in the classroom unless teachers accept them and understand how to put them into practice.

That means we've got to provide opportunities for professional development along with the time and financial resources needed for teachers to take advantage of them.

That also means we must reshape teacher education programs so that they are aligned with new standards, assessments, pedagogies, technology, and restructured schools.

MS. FINE: We can't just up the standards without paying attention to the teachers and professional development. It's an absurdity to imagine that.

MS. GRAHAM: I am still concerned about the grownups in schools and how they can do a better job, because I really believe that the deep problem is with the grownups in the schools.

Remember that experiment where Toyota, I think it was, took these "inadequate" General Motors workers and retrained them? All of a sudden, these workers who were no good at all for General Motors were doing a good job.

If we believe that all children can learn, we also ought to believe that all teachers can learn. And we ought to be figuring out how to link up a system of retraining existing teachers and preparing new teachers in a better way.

This is where I would hold the colleges and universities responsible. The leverage to do that is with the states, who fund public higher-education institutions, which have no standards in their schools of education worth mentioning.

I would let the market system work in deciding which universities get the contracts for the retraining and professional development. That would force colleges and universities to develop programs that would be effective for experienced teachers and administrators, to help them meet the new standards that are being expected of them.

We can also consider what needs to be done about those naughty prestigious private institutions that drop their schools of education and ignore their responsibilities for training teachers.

Governor Romer, I would guess that a very high fraction of teachers in Colorado have graduated from a public institution in Colorado, and that the leverage point for you may be in manipulating the funds to the higher-education system in ways that stimulate the higher-education system to put more of its energies into working both with beginning teachers and with experienced teachers and administrators.

GOVERNOR ROMER: That's dead right. We don't have our teaching colleges really wired into this, and they get an awful lot of largess out of the government. If you had an orchestrated strategy, you could bring a lot of motivation to change in higher education.

Of course, everybody's going to say, "Wait a minute, you're getting heavy-handed." We'd be accused of micromanaging. But we should use the leverage we have at the state level to motivate these institutions. When you give out money, you motivate one way or the other. We just need to get smarter about how we do it.

MR. HORNBECK: There is a growing belief that there should be widely accepted standards for what entry-level and non-exceptional teachers need to know and be able to do. Would you make it mandatory for a state's schools of education to incorporate them in their programs?

MS. GRAHAM: By non-exceptional, you mean ...?

MR. HORNBECK: They would not aspire to be board certified. It seems to me that somebody ought to be going about the business of identifying what those teachers need to know and be able to do, and developing assessments that will measure that. Those standards and assessments need to be parallel to the standards and assessments that are getting developed for students by the subject-matter groups and for advanced teachers by the National Board for Professional Teaching Standards.

MS. GRAHAM: I would be enthusiastic about having those kinds of activities preceding the imposition of high-stakes consequences for students. I think a student who has never been exposed to a teacher who is competent is paying a very high price for the teacher's incompetence.

We really need to take a hard look at what's going on with teachers. There are many wonderful, gifted teachers in America, but there are also many who are not at this moment performing as wonderful, gifted teachers.

What we need to figure out is a system that could improve the performance of the many teachers whose performance could be improved.

MR. HORNBECK: If the efforts to determine what teachers should know and be able to do came to fruition, wouldn't one then get rid of all of the certification requirements that currently exist that have anything to do with accumulating courses and credits? And wouldn't that fundamentally alter the relationship between higher education and elementary and secondary schools?

MS. GRAHAM: It would be a dramatic change for colleges and universities if they could not rely on state certification requirements as a justification for their education programs, both for teachers and for administrators.

Public education institutions get their money on a head-count basis, and departments of education exist so that the history department can have a few good students, and the place can keep afloat financially by putting its weak students in education and physical education. And that's not good.

GOVERNOR ROMER: I haven't gotten around to putting the leverage on higher education about standards, but I can tell you I ought to. Somebody ought to stuff that in my face and say: "Romer, if you really believe in improving education, why don't you go for where the money is, or where the real power is?" And then help me identify those points.

I'm afraid we're not getting our hands on the levers of power.

MS. HAYCOCK: We need a carefully coordinated, very aggressive strategy to deal with the problem, because most of higher education is completely asleep.

The deeper we get into K-12 reform, the clearer it becomes that we are not going to be able to bring about substantial change in K-12 without substantially reforming higher education. Not just teacher education, but the way kids are admitted and what happens in undergraduate education.

MR. MILLS: In Vermont there is tremendous pressure on schools for performance.

To get relicensed, teachers have to convince a board of their peers that they have grown as professionals. So in the midst of all this pressure, they are putting together their own individual professional-development plans that get approved by this relicensing board of their peers.

That creates a very different kind of market. Instead of each individual coming to the college, as I did when I was a teacher, and being told by the college what I had to do, higher education is now being told what it is expected to provide. The whole region of the state and the whole profession in the state constitutes an organized market that says, "This is what we want in higher education. Either you deliver it, or private providers will spring up and deliver it."

And there has been a dramatic change in where people go for their continuing professional education.

MS. HAYCOCK: If you only move to an outcome system for teacher certification, you are still missing probably three-quarters of the problem that higher education causes for K through 12 reform.

What we really need to think about is if this logic we have articulated for K through 12—i.e., that we need clearer goals in order to improve the system—applies to higher education, too.

And we ought to be thinking about outcome standards at least in some core things that all B.A. recipients ought to be able to do. And we need a National Assessment of Educational Progress test for college graduates to illustrate to people why this is important.

MR. PETERKIN: We have given little shrift to how we move the standards that we all covet to teaching and learning in classrooms. Four or five years after the math standards were developed, few people have helped teachers at the local level really make the transition from a standard to a practice.

'Raising Public Awareness About the Need for Change'

MR. HORNBECK: Public-opinion surveys consistently show that Americans may not be satisfied with schools in general, but they tend to think their own schools are doing pretty well. That is viewed as a major barrier to getting systemic reform.

The kinds of changes being proposed in this country are pretty dramatic. In some places, like Pennsylvania recently, they have generated considerable controversy. How important is it that the public support systemic reform, and how can we win that support?

MR. MILLS: We're trying to sell systemic reform to a lot of people who aren't buying. If we just asked people, including students, for their opinions, they would give us a systemic-reform agenda that is not crazy. I'm trying to learn how to listen to those people and how to harness their passion for change. It's powerful stuff.

MS. GRAHAM: If we're going to get significant change—and my heart and mind belong to change—we have to enlist passion in this effort.

We need a clear, or at least a more compelling, statement of why this change is important or what this change is about. It's very hard to get people to sign up for an agenda that is lacking the dynamism of passion.

MR. CROSS: It is essential that we reach parents, as a defined, discrete, and targeted part of the broader public.

MS. HAYCOCK: Change will occur only when there's both a policy structure that encourages it and permits it, and when individual educators, parents, and others see the change as theirs.

That only occurs around small tables, and the process of creating ownership ought to get at least as much attention from strategists as the process of creating a rational policy structure.

We spend 99 percent of our time at meetings like this on policy structure, and that is important. But I think we're pretty close to agreement on policy issues, and now we need to begin to figure out the very much more complicated task of getting thousands of communities across the country to take ownership of these ideas.

MS. FINE: One problem is that we lack images of what good schooling might look like. Does a good school have to be small, does it have to be community-based, does it have to engage the community of teachers and parents and students?

Absent those images, especially for those of us struggling in urban communities, the only images out there are of deadly, violent, awful schools. We know what makes a good school. I feel like the public is owed that.

MR. MILLS: Governor Dean of Vermont once asked me what really needed to be done about education in our state. I started to list things very quickly for about two minutes. He listened intently, and, when I finished, he asked: "But what really needs to be done?"

I escaped by saying, "Let me tell you what I saw in a classroom of a 3rd-grade teacher." And I described what went on in that classroom. And he said, "That's right; that's what I want for every kid."

We're not conveying these images. We're not yet giving the public the keys to the reform process. It is as if we don't quite trust them.

We didn't really ask the public what the goals of education should be. We got a lot of smart, powerful people together to write the goals. But we didn't ask the public, "What do you want for your children? What are you willing to give up to get it?"

These groups working on the standards, that are very powerful and very effective, have not asked the public in any systematic way: "What do you think every child should know and be able to do?" When you do that in a small community, you get a very lofty vision. People do not generally say, "We just want basic skills."

The public can be trusted an awful lot more, and if we were willing to design this educational system we want in a much messier way, we would get much more lasting change, and we would harness the passion that is right there.

MR. CROSS: We talk about public support for high performance. But we need public support for high performance and reform, because there's a lot more that people believe needs to be done than just high performance. There are a number of other elements that the public is concerned about, including the whole question of decentralization.

MS. FINE: We bypass parents and communities as both serious critics and constituents of public education. How do we educate the public, engage them in public critique and engagement with the schools?

MR. MILLS: I'm very intrigued with the British Inspectorate system.

These inspectors have almost no power except the power to go and see schools and talk about what they see. They don't check for compliance, they just go into a school and look at teaching and learning. Then they write about it, and their reports don't read anything at all like a state or a federal report. They are very literate discussions of what the children know and can do in relation to a set of national standards.

The reports go first to the school and then to the community, so there is this continual argument and discussion about what's important and what's being delivered. We ought to invent something like that.

In Vermont, we have "school report nights" that work for us. There are other things that work in other places, but there is not an awful lot of good information to fuel a sensible conversation in a community about schools. Lacking that, we talk about things that are not very important. We form our opinions and base our policy on that marginal information.

MS. FUHRMAN: Those of us in this room may have no problem with the systemic-reform agenda, but my feeling is that it is not widely shared or known about at all.

A major concern is the media, the fact that education reporting in general—quality aside—is very focused on individual schools. That's great and important, but there is very little sense of these kinds of system issues that comes across in the press.

When you talk about higher-order thinking or more authentic assessments, the press makes that sound as if that is less hard-nosed than multiple-choice exams. The media are just not well informed about these complex issues.

Maybe our *Education Week* colleagues can tell us why this is so. Is it just that education reporters have the most junior beat?

EW: Perhaps you are aware of the inadequate coverage in education because you are an expert in education. If you were an expert on foreign affairs, you would probably feel the same way about the way the media reports on the

Serbian-Bosnian conflict. Mass media don't do well with complex issues in any field; coverage tends to be a mile wide and an inch deep.

MS. HAYCOCK: And educators don't explain these issues clearly to anybody.

MR. SEXTON: I think it's a state role to provide that explanation. I find it interesting in Kentucky that many people believe that, as a result of the reforms there and because they take the outcomes as the ultimate signal of state control, the system is more centralized. The truth is that the reforms have resulted in a decentralized system, pushing responsibility to local levels.

In some cases, it gets right back into the secular-humanism argument that there are forces out there trying to control the minds of our children. Then they turn that into the political argument, that the state is controlling.

The other interesting thing has been that in opinion polling in Kentucky, we saw that the most popular element of the reform was local school-based decisionmaking and "accountability," as the polling firms phrased it.

The least popular thing, of course, was assessment and testing. Talk about not understanding. Here's a public that has been demanding more accountability for years, but puts assessment and testing at the bottom of the list. I guess neither of those things should surprise us. It makes the state's job even harder.

MR. HORNBECK: It also reflects our totally inadequate ability to have people understand. I mean, for accountability to come out highest and testing to come out the lowest ...

EW: The dilemma may be that, in order to get public support for the genuinely radical change that is being called for, you have to convince the American people that schools are so bad we almost have to start over again. Confronted with such bad news, is there a danger that people will become so discouraged or defensive that they either give up or resist?

MS. GRAHAM: It is extremely important to point to success in unlikely places, and kids who are doing well in unlikely circumstances.

It's very important to say that schools have made big changes in their agendas before and that we are simply asking schools to make another big change. And that we believe that schools have the capacity and the flexibility to make the big change, but not to minimize that it is a big change.

MR. MILLS: We have real communication skills in this country, through advertising and through political campaigns. We can't go at the public through C-SPAN. The general public doesn't watch C-SPAN. The Presidential election was built on that recognition. It went through a completely different medium, and that is what we need to do.

MR. CROSS: The Business Roundtable has started a public-advertising campaign that is being sent to every TV and radio station and newspaper in the country. The objective is to raise public awareness about the need for change in education.

GOVERNOR ROMER: That's the campaign called "Keep The Promise," where people see these messages on television and are invited to call an 800 number. They're motivated. But there's no network to follow up on the 800-number calls. And, even if we did have a network, how do you connect that with everybody who's got a role to play? How do we divide the tasks? You know: "Here's your role, go play it."

The real challenge here is to take those standards developed by the National Council of Teachers of Mathematics and others like them, and begin to get them into the minds and hearts of parents in America. Tell them what they mean.

MR. MILLS: But, you see, with a political campaign, it comes to something that we want a person to do. You want them to vote. And with an advertising campaign, you want them to buy something. I don't think we're clear enough on what we want people to do with this information.

It's not enough to motivate people, you have to motivate them toward something.

MS. GRAHAM: They are supposed to teach their kids.

MR. MILLS: We need to say that clearly.

GOVERNOR ROMER: I keep looking for little levers that may be explosive. Let me give you one. How many kids in higher education do we have with student loans, how many millions?

MR. CROSS: Probably about six million.

GOVERNOR ROMER: What if we were so crass as to say that one of the requirements in order to get a student loan is to pass a 7th-grade math test, based on the new standards? Now, that's all you do, 7th grade. What would that do? It would force everybody in America to grab for the book. What the hell is this thing? Now, that's not too bad of a gate for people to go through.

You would certainly focus the minds of America. Do you realize what that would do? It would send shudders through the whole society. They would have cram courses. It would be a wonderful thing. There are magic buttons out there that would explode this thing in America. We're just not pushing the right ones.

MR. CROSS: In 1990, they couldn't even get a debate in Congress about having any standards for student aid. Nobody would even talk about it.

MS. GRAHAM: The kind of alternative that we might be looking for is something like the anti-smoking campaign—which was, after all, initiated out of [former Secretary of Health, Education, and Welfare] Joe Califano's son's displeasure with Joe Califano's smoking. That campaign certainly displayed a federal dimension in terms of federal leadership.

It was a campaign to mobilize—not the poor, which it did not mobilize—but at least the middle class and the affluent to change a habit that they very much liked.

And there's a sense in which I think what we're trying to do here is to change a habit relating to schooling that has been very comfortable for us. We are trying to get people to make a very unpleasant, to many, transition from something that's been pleasant to something that will be good for them and that they will learn to love.

We at least ought to see what, if anything, can be learned from the anti-smoking campaign, realizing that this time we can't ignore the poor.

MR. HORNBECK: Maybe we should hire James Carville [of the Clinton campaign]. If we were to approach this communication problem the way serious Presidential candidates approach winning an election, we would do it both on the street and on the airwaves simultaneously. We know how to do this as a people.

MS. GRAHAM: We've just never done it in education.

MR. SEXTON: We have talked to people about the general idea, and a huge number of people have bought the concept that schools need to get better. But we have not gone into that in enough detail so that, when you put the program out there and do it, people will support you.

As people come down to the particulars, they are no longer talking about concepts. They're talking about whether they want their kindergarten child mixed in with older children. They're talking about whether they want their athletic policy changed. And that is where it gets real for people. The fundamental questions are: Do you want the discussion? How far do you want the discussion to go?

In Kentucky, former Governor Bert T. Combs, who happened to be the attorney in our court case [challenging the state's school-finance system], argued again and again that the public does not necessarily want to agree to every particular. What you want to ask them is to acquiesce to spending more of their money, and to acquiesce to leadership's recommendations as to the particulars that have to get done. That, of course, is the heart of governing.

GOVERNOR ROMER: How could we entice other policymakers to sit through discussions like this so that they get a feel for what is possible, what is quality, and what it is that they could do about it?

Public policymakers are in the position of having to drink out of the fire hydrant. They can't handle it all; they've just got to get an in-depth experience.

We have a committee in Colorado in which the leadership of the legislature and I have been putting together a standards bill. And we had at least 10 sessions, and we went through all this stuff.

All those legislators are gung ho now. They're ready to go out and fight the war. But it is that kind of experience that policymakers need. There is a way to get inside people.

If standards are that important, this President could do a lot about standards. The first thing he could do is buy 25 copies of the N.C.T.M. booklet and just sit them on every chair in his sitting room. Anybody visiting him would have to move it to sit down. And they would wonder, Why is this here? The President of the United States wants me to look at it.

APPENDIX

A CHRONOLOGY

The Editors

Ten years ago, the National Commission on Excellence in Education concluded that we were "a nation at risk" because of the lackluster performance of our elementary and secondary schools. Although the effort to reform the schools predated the commission's report, the document quickened and intensified a period of self-examination and efforts at renewal among our schools that few in 1983 ever dreamed would have lasted to this day.

What follows is a chronology of the school-reform movement, from the formation of the excellence commission to the present, as reported in the pages of *Education Week*. Our intent was not to be definitive, but rather to chart the movement's major milestones and to try to convey the flavor of its myriad trends and crosscurrents.

The reform movement shifts into high gear in 1983 with Terrel H. Bell's release of A Nation at Risk, *a report that shocked the nation with its grim assessment of student achievement, its martial metaphors, and its dire warning of a "rising tide of mediocrity."*

1981

August

Secretary of Education Terrel H. Bell announces the establishment of the National Commission on Excellence in Education.

Secretary of Education Terrel H. Bell sends a memo to the White House recommending that the U.S. Education Department be downgraded to a sub-Cabinet-level foundation.

Eighty percent of Louisiana's teachers sign up for a state program that will give them extra pay for participating in classes and workshops aimed at improving their performance.

September

Education Week is launched as "the newspaper of record in American education" by the nonprofit Editorial Projects in Education, founder of *The Chronicle of Higher Education.*

Improving the teaching profession is the key to better schools, a poll of education policymakers by the Education Commission of the States reveals. Thirty-six percent predict schooling in their state will improve over the next two years; an equal proportion say it will not.

The Kansas state board of education raises academic standards for prospective teachers, joining several other states that have done likewise. California lawmakers adopt competency testing for would-be teachers.

The College Board announces Project EQuality—a 10-year effort to reverse the 14-year decline in Scholastic Aptitude Test scores. Average S.A.T. scores in 1981: verbal 424, mathematics 466, both unchanged from 1980.

To save money, Detroit jettisons its 11-year-old system of community school boards and districts, a pioneering effort in local control.

New York State's board of regents warns schools they may lose their state accreditation if they fail to lower their dropout rates.

October

The National Council for Accreditation of Teacher Education requires applicants for the first time to maintain specific student-teacher ratios and funding levels.

Education school deans from major state universities and land-grant colleges endorse tougher teacher training standards, including a move toward five- and six-year programs.

A task force formed by the Southern Regional Education Board issues a 25-point plan for upgrading education in the region. It calls on states to set minimum academic standards.

President Reagan promises Roman Catholic educators he will press Congress to pass a tuition-tax-credit bill.

November

American students do reasonably well on multiple-choice English tests, but stumble badly when asked to explain a story or poem in written prose, the National Assessment of Educational Progress reports.

The National Commission on Excellence in Education decides to narrow its focus to grades 7-12 and to pay particular attention to raising standards.

December

Stanford University announces a three-year study of the nation's schools that will focus on policy decisions, curriculum alternatives, and teacher preparation.

New York State's board of regents proposes elevating teaching to a legally recognized profession, in part through the creation of a state teacher-licensing board.

1982

January

A foundation-supported, 18-month study calls for a major overhaul of the National Assessment of Educational Progress.

The Texas Education Agency embarks on a thorough revision of the state's basic public school curriculum as mandated by the legislature.

Gov. William F. Winter of Mississippi asks state lawmakers to create a statewide kindergarten system and pass a tough compulsory-attendance law.

A committee of the Tennessee board of education recommends merit pay for school employees, financial rewards for high-achieving districts, and the abolition of teacher tenure.

February

President Reagan proposes cutting the Education Department budget by one-third, prompting howls of protest from the education community.

March

Precollegiate math and science must be improved if the United States is to remain economically competitive, a panel created by the National Governors' Association concludes.

The nationwide shortage of qualified math and science teachers has reached "critical" proportions, the National Science Teachers Association warns in a report.

April

The Reagan Administration's plan to transform the Education Department into a foundation grinds to a halt in Congress.

The Connecticut state board of education adopts a 25-point plan to improve teacher quality. Features include recruiting bright high school students into the profession and competency testing for education school graduates.

With funding from foundations, Pennsylvania announces a five-week program in science during the summer for high school juniors and seniors. Several other states have recently adopted similar programs.

The National Science Foundation creates the Commission on Precollege Education in Mathematics, Science, and Technology.

The quality of New England's colleges is slipping because of problems in the region's public schools, a study by the New England Board of Higher Education concludes.

May

Raising money for public education is the top concern of policy leaders in state government and education, a survey by the Education Commission of the States shows. Teacher quality ranks fourth on a list of 16 problem areas; quality of elementary and secondary education ranks ninth.

As many as two million students may graduate in 1990 lacking "high order" thinking skills, a study by the National Assessment of Educational Progress predicts.

National security will be weakened if problems in precollegiate math and science are not remedied, Secretary of Defense Caspar W. Weinberger warns at a meeting sponsored by the National Academy of Sciences.

Hearings are held in Washington on a joint House-Senate resolution urging each state to establish a commission on teacher excellence.

State boards of education in Texas and Delaware consider competency tests for prospective teachers; 19 states have adopted similar measures in recent years.

June

In an editorial in *Science*, the president of the National Academy of Sciences decries the state of precollegiate math and science education.

August

Alabama and Kentucky are among the first states to pass laws authorizing "forgivable loans" and

scholarships to encourage college students to become science and math teachers.

The Tennessee state board of education approves a two-tiered diploma system under which students who fail an exit examination will get a "certificate of attendance" instead of a diploma.

The North Carolina state board of education approves a statewide teacher- and principal-evaluation plan.

September

The Paideia Group, headed by the philosopher Mortimer J. Adler, issues *The Paideia Proposal*, an education-reform manifesto.

Wisconsin drops lifetime teacher certification.

Virtually all states have adopted reforms drawn from "effective schools" research, a 50-state survey by the Education Commission of the States shows.

Average scores on the Scholastic Aptitude Test in 1982: verbal 426, up 2 points; math 467, up 1 point. The College Board attributes the first rise in the scores in 19 years to gains by minority students. However, in releasing for the first time minority students' scores, the board reveals that whites outscore blacks on the math portion of the test by 121 points.

Business, education, and civic leaders announce the "Boston Compact," a four-year effort to boost the high school-completion rate in the city by promising jobs to graduates.

Decrying a "lamentable" lack of history in school curricula, a commission of the Council for Basic Education argues in a report that schools should provide an "irreducible minimum" of instruction in the subject.

November

Twenty-seven states have adopted or are in the process of adopting tougher standards for admission to college, the National Association of Secondary School Principals reports.

The school board of the Los Angeles Unified School District votes to require students to maintain a C average in order to participate in extracurricular activities, an increasingly popular policy.

December

The Mississippi legislature approves a $106 million reform package that includes mandatory statewide public kindergartens and a big pay raise for teachers.

Minimum-competency testing has contributed to the decline in critical reading and analytical skills, the National Council of Teachers of English charges.

The Education Commission of the States forms a task force composed of governors, business executives, and labor leaders to explore the connections between education and the economy.

California's state board of education and its new schools chief, Bill Honig, draft a tough "model" academic curriculum for the state's public high schools.

Twenty-five bills to improve math and science instruction were introduced in Congress this past session, all died. Tuition-tax-credit legislation died in the Senate.

1983

January

More than a third of the states face unfavorable prospects for maintaining an adequate level of financial support for schools, the U.S. Education Department reports.

The New Jersey state board of education dumps a statewide testing program criticized as being too easy, replacing it with a tougher test that students will have to pass to graduate from high school.

The American Association for the Advancement of Science kicks off Science Resources for Schools, a nationwide project to improve the quality of science instruction.

The National Collegiate Athletic Association adopts Proposition 48, a set of tough academic standards for freshmen athletes beginning in 1986.

States face budget deficits that could swell to well over $2 billion by the end of the year, the National Governors' Association reports.

California joins the growing lists of states that have begun to use tests to screen candidates for the teaching profession.

Gov. Lamar Alexander of Tennessee proposes a $210 million school-reform plan that includes merit pay for teachers; mandatory kindergarten; "Basic Skills First," an elementary school curriculum; and tougher math and science requirements for graduation.

February

Although the "back to basics" movement of the 1970's led to gains among low achievers, it also led to low achievement in math and science among top students, the National Assessment of Educational Progress reports.

The South Carolina state board of education, along with the Kentucky state board of education, join a growing list of states strengthening high school graduation requirements.

The number of top-scoring students on the Scholastic Aptitude Test has declined steeply in the past 10 years, the College Board reports.

The federal government transfers responsibility for administering the National Assessment of Educational Progress from the Education Commission of the States to the Educational Testing Service, which has proposed a wide range of improvements in the project.

At a meeting in Dallas, Ernest L. Boyer and Theodore R. Sizer disclose findings from their independent analyses of American high schools. Their general conclusion: Most students are not challenged academically.

At Yale University, 38 state school chiefs meet with the presidents of more than 40 leading colleges and universities to discuss ways to improve the teaching profession.

South Carolina's state schools chief issues a 41-point school-reform plan, the state board of education raises high school graduation requirements, and Gov. Richard W. Riley calls for a sales-tax increase for education.

April

"The educational foundations of our society are presently being eroded by a rising tide of mediocrity that threatens our very future as a nation and a people." —From *A Nation at Risk*, the report of the National Commission on Excellence in Education.

Although students' "routine" math skills are on the upswing, their higher-order skills have remained steady or are falling, the National Assessment of Educational Progress reports. A study conducted for the National Science Foundation concludes that high school students' interest and achievement in science continue to decline.

High school students are taking less demanding courses than they did in the 1960's, the National Institute of Education reports.

The Public Education Fund Network is formed. Its aim is to create grassroots education groups in 40 to 50 communities nationwide.

May

"We have expected too little of our schools over the past two decades—and we have gotten too little. The result is that our schools are not doing an adequate job of educating for today's requirements in the workplace, much less tomorrow's." —From the report of the Education Commission of the States' National Task Force on Education for Economic Growth.

"The task force believes that the schools must make a concerted effort to improve their performance and that there is a clear national interest in helping schools everywhere to do so. That interest can be asserted and dramatized most effectively by the federal government." —From the report of the Twentieth Century Fund's Task Force on Federal Elementary and Secondary Education Policy.

The state of Florida can legally withhold diplomas from students who fail to pass a minimum-competency test, a federal district court judge rules in a decision that has national repercussions.

More than half of all school districts over the past three years have increased the number of required credits in core subjects, and another 38 percent plan to do so, the National Center for Education Statistics reports.

The College Board recommends that all college-bound students demonstrate "basic learning" in six fields of study before they advance to college. It publishes a detailed list of skills in those fields.

A group of 16 college presidents and business executives delivers a 51-page letter to President Reagan calling for a coordinated national effort to "rebuild the nation's economy and strengthen our educational system."

A task force of the Southern Regional Education Board issues a 20-point school-reform plan.

Thirty-two states are considering measures to deal with an existing or expected shortage of mathematics and science teachers, an *Education Week* survey finds.

June

The Arkansas Supreme Court strikes down the state's school-finance system, contending that the reliance on property-taxes discriminates against children who live in property-poor areas.

July

Illinois lawmakers raise taxes by almost $1 billion; much of the money will go to education. They also raise high school graduation requirements.

California lawmakers pass a bill that re-establishes statewide graduation requirements, raises teacher pay, and creates a master-teacher program.

Florida lawmakers pass a major education bill that includes a master-teacher program.

North Carolina lawmakers approve a pilot project in two districts that will lengthen the school year to 200 days.

The National Governors' Association passes a resolution endorsing performance-based pay for teachers.

Education Week publishes a 64-page special report on the state of math and science instruction in the United States.

August

The presidents of six leading universities meet with the deans of four prominent schools of education to discuss the role of higher education in the nascent school-reform movement.

The annual Gallup Poll on education shows that the general public strongly agrees with the recommendations of the National Commission on Excellence in Education.

Secretary of Education Terrel H. Bell announces a two-day national "forum" on education reform; Congressional Democrats had earlier called for a national "summit." Mr. Bell also releases a survey of reforms in the 50 largest districts: 31 are increasing coursework requirements in math, science, and English; 44 have adopted competency testing; 20 will implement tougher graduation requirements this fall.

The National School Boards Association says two-thirds of a nationally representative sample of teachers it polled support performance-based pay.

Teachers' purchasing power declined by 12 percent between 1972-73 and 1982-83, a sign that the profession "is in crisis," the Carnegie Foundation for the Advancement of Teaching reports.

The Southern Regional Education Board resolves "to sustain and increase" reform efforts. It backs tougher high school curricula and graduation requirements, tougher college-admissions standards, performance-based teacher pay, and a teacher-certification test common to all states.

West Virginia adopts a rule requiring students to maintain a C average to participate in extracurricular activities.

September

Warning that American schoolchildren are in danger of becoming "stragglers in a world of technology," the National Science Board's Commission on Precollege Education in Mathematics, Science, and Technology issues a 12-year reform plan that would cost the federal government $6.5 billion.

The Carnegie Foundation for the Advancement of Teaching issues *High School*, Ernest L. Boyer's 355-page, three-year study. It recommends a new core curriculum, a requirement that teachers major in an academic subject rather than education, the abandonment of the Scholastic Aptitude Test in favor of a more effective assessment and guidance program, a new service requirement for high school students that would involve volunteer work in the community or at school, and the reorganization of large schools into smaller units.

Nearly three-fourths of the nation's schools of education have stiffened their admissions standards during the past five years, the National Center for Education Statistics reports.

The National Association of State Boards of Education creates a Task Force on Education Quality to influence the reform movement.

Average scores on the Scholastic Aptitude Test in 1983: verbal 425, down 1 point; mathematics 468, up 1 point.

An Arkansas commission chaired by Gov. Bill Clinton's wife, Hillary, calls for mandatory kindergarten, lower pupil-teacher ratios in the early grades, competency testing, tougher graduation standards, a longer school year, and raising teacher pay to the regional average.

Gov. Thomas H. Kean of New Jersey proposes an option that college graduates with no education school training be allowed to teach, higher pay for beginning teachers, a master-teacher program, a professional-development institute, and higher graduation and accreditation standards.

October

Eleven leading education groups issue a consensus reform agenda. It focuses on making the teaching profession more attractive and improving the quality of the teaching force.

The Carnegie Foundation for the Advancement of Teaching, the Atlantic Richfield Foundation, and the National Association of Secondary School Principals invite high schools to compete for $1.7 million in grants to implement reforms based on Ernest L. Boyer's study *High School*.

November

"Significant educational improvement of schooling, not mere tinkering, requires that we focus on entire schools, not just teachers or principals or curricula or organization or school-community relations but all these and more. ... If we are to improve schooling, we must improve individual schools." —From *A Place Called School* by John I. Goodlad.

Findings from a 50-state survey by *Education Week:* Since the release of *A Nation at Risk,* 54 state-level reform commissions have been formed; two states have approved differentiated pay for teachers, and 33 others have begun considering the issue; seven states have lengthened the school day; one state has lengthened the school year, and 16 others are considering doing so; 26 states have stiffened high school graduation requirements; seven states have approved teacher-competency tests.

In a major expansion of the Boston Compact, 25 area colleges and universities pledge to help reduce the dropout rate, increase the college-going rate, and strengthen the curricula of the city's public schools.

The Senate defeats legislation to provide tax credits to parents for private school expenses.

Arkansas lawmakers approve legislation making it the first state to require teachers and administrators to pass tests to keep their jobs. Gregory R. Anrig, the president of the Educational Testing Service, which produces the National Teachers' Examination, responds by saying the firm will not ship its tests to states that require practicing teachers to pass them.

December

A total of 2,500 educators and politicians attend Secretary of Education Terrel H. Bell's National Forum on Excellence in Education in Indianapolis.

Preoccupied with math and science education, few states are promoting instruction in the humanities, a survey by the Council of Chief State School Officers finds.

1984

January

Secretary of Education Terrel H. Bell issues the Education Department's first "wall chart" comparing the states on a wide array of education indicators.

Utah lawmakers adopt a career ladder for teachers.

February

Horace's Compromise by Theodore R. Sizer is released. Mr. Sizer also announces the formation of the Coalition of Essential Schools, which will attempt to implement the reform ideas outlined in his book.

Businesses are reassessing their giving programs to schools in the wake of *A Nation at Risk*, the Council on Financial Aid to Education says.

Some 30 states have approved competency testing for teachers, and 12 others are considering the idea, according to a study by the dean of the college of education at Western Kentucky University.

The largest association of teacher educators, the American Association of Colleges for Teacher Education, endorses shifting teacher training from the undergraduate to the graduate level.

Acting in special session, Tennessee lawmakers approve a career ladder for teachers.

The Florida state board of education approves a merit-pay plan that will provide $3,000 bonuses to 5,000 teachers in the fall.

March

Officials from 22 states meet in Florida to form a "cartel" to pressure publishers to improve textbooks. The move was applauded by Secretary of Education Terrel H. Bell, who warned that the reform movement could "fall flat and fail" if textbooks are not improved.

A national panel appointed by Secretary of Education Terrel H. Bell warns that the nation's "indifference" to foreign-language instruction "should be a source of national embarrassment," but recommends that reforms be undertaken in local schools, rather than at the federal level.

At a three-day national forum in San Francisco, educators discuss the need to redirect the school-reform movement from issues of "quantity" to issues of "quality."

The recent tightening of college-admissions standards will have little effect on academic standards in high schools, experts agree at a national conference at the Wingspread Center in Racine, Wis.

In perhaps the first effort of its kind, Gov. Thomas H. Kean of New Jersey outlines a comprehensive plan to improve urban schools.

April

Fifteen states have recently adopted "no pass, no play" rules for participation in extracurricular activities, an informal survey by *Education Week* finds.

Alaska, New York, Texas, and Missouri raise their state high school-graduation requirements. Wisconsin adopts such requirements for the first time. Vermont toughens its school-approval standards. Washington State, Kentucky, Nebraska, and Indiana lawmakers pass omnibus school-reform bills.

The director of the National Assessment of Educational Progress tells a Congressional committee that the testing program is prepared to provide states with the means to measure student achievement on an interstate basis.

California unveils a merit-schools program.

A study group in Texas headed by the industrialist Ross Perot unveils a far-ranging, $987 million school-reform plan.

May

Mississippi prepares to pilot-test what is described as the nation's first outcome-based school-accreditation system.

The average performance of American students in mathematics has remained stable relative to that of students in 24 other nations over the past 20 years, the Second International Mathematics Study finds.

Arizona, Connecticut, and Maine lawmakers pass school-reform bills.

High schools must prepare future workers who possess "the ability to learn and to adapt to changes in the workplace," a panel convened by the National Academy of Sciences concludes.

In Boston, several child-welfare groups sponsor what they say is the first national meeting on "latchkey" children.

U.S. students know more about biology and physical science than they did in 1970, researchers analyzing an international study conclude.

California's superintendent of public instruction urges the state board of education to approve

"radical" proposals for adopting reading textbooks that would yield books that emphasize "critical thinking" and that are "worthy of being read."

July

The Education Commission of the States' Task Force on Education for Economic Growth issues an overview of the past year's school-reform efforts. Among its highlights: more than 240 state-level reform groups were formed; and Arkansas, Florida, Massachusetts, North Carolina, Ohio, and Tennessee were cited for "significant initiatives."

Congress passes a two-year, $965 million bill to improve math and science instruction.

August

A shortage of qualified teachers will soon undermine the reform movement, the RAND Corporation warns in a report.

Only three of the Southern Regional Education Board's 14 member states have agreed to participate in a pilot project to report National Assessment of Educational Progress scores on a state-by-state basis.

Teachers must take control of their profession, including taking responsibility for removing incompetents, Albert Shanker, the president of the American Federation of Teachers, says in a speech at the union's annual meeting.

Atlanta's public schools say they will require high school students to perform community service as a requirement for graduation.

The University of California at Berkeley and the California state department of education create the Clio Project, an effort to define the history curriculum.

September

The High/Scope Educational Foundation releases a study that it says documents the value of high-quality preschool programs for poor children. It will be cited repeatedly in coming years by those favoring expansion of Head Start and other early-years programs.

Average scores on the Scholastic Aptitude Test in 1984: verbal 426, up 1 point; math 471, up 3 points. The average composite score on the American College Testing Program assessment rose slightly to 18.3.

Many states took advantage of their stronger financial positions in 1984 to raise education funding, the National Conference of State Legislatures reports.

Education Week publishes a 72-page special report on literacy in America.

October

Writing in *The Public Interest*, Chester E. Finn Jr. and Denis P. Doyle note a fundamental change in educational policymaking: Governors and legislatures are replacing local boards as the key players.

Education emerged as a vital issue in most of the year's gubernatorial elections.

November

Secretary of Education Terrel H. Bell announces he will resign at the end of the year. In one of his last acts, he creates a task force on educational technology and charges it with preparing a report comparable to *A Nation At Risk*. But the report, released in May 1986, receives little attention.

In a reversal of longstanding policy, the nation's state school chiefs vote to back the idea of state-by-state comparisons of student achievement. They also act to insure that they will have a hand in the development of new assessments on which such comparisons will be made.

State reforms emphasizing academic subjects "ignore the needs of those high school students who do not plan to go to college and who purposefully choose a vocational program," a study of vocational education concludes.

December

The decline in test scores between 1972 and 1980 was caused by decreased rigor in high schools and by a drop in the amount of time spent on homework, the Educational Testing Service reports.

The U.S. Education Department issues its second annual "wall chart" of state education indicators. Outgoing Secretary of Education Terrel H. Bell says it presages an "academic turnaround."

Two associations of geographers unveil a plan to revitalize the teaching of geography in grades K-12.

1985

January

Poor, nonwhite, handicapped, and female children have been ignored by the school-reform movement, concludes a study by the National Coalition of Advocates for Students. The study will prompt policymakers nationwide to focus on the problems of children "at risk."

Findings from an *Education Week* 50-state survey of reform activity during the past two years: all states are either studying or have enacted performance-based pay plans for teachers; nearly all have raised graduation requirements and instituted statewide student assessments; more than half have toughened teacher-licensing requirements, and a third have raised teacher pay.

The "school choice" debate reaches critical mass.

Gov. Rudy Perpich of Minnesota proposes an "open enrollment" program for 11th and 12th graders. Gov. Richard D. Lamm of Colorado proposes a "second chance" voucher program for dropouts. In April, Albert Shanker, the president of the American Federation of Teachers, will endorse choice in public education.

President Reagan chooses William J. Bennett to be the next Secretary of Education. The leitmotif of Mr. Bennett's term will be what he calls the "three C's"— content, character, and choice.

The Carnegie Corporation of New York announces the creation of the Carnegie Forum on Education and the Economy, a multi-million-dollar effort "to keep the nation's attention focused on educational improvement."

Albert Shanker, the president of the American Federation of Teachers, calls for a national professional exam for teachers. The National Science Teachers Association, meanwhile, announces it will issue its own national teacher-certification credential.

California launches a program to measure and publicize the performance of each of its 7,300 public schools. Other states will adopt similar "school report card" programs.

February

The National Commission for Excellence in Teacher Education recommends ways to improve teacher recruitment, training, and retention. It advocates that admission to and graduation from teacher-education programs be based on "rigorous" academic and performance standards; that special programs be developed to attract minority candidates; and that all new teachers complete an internship of at least one year's duration, for which they would be paid. The report also opposes alternative preparation programs.

The Michigan state board of education, in a move several states are considering, approves the development of a test of students' higher-order thinking skills.

Education Week publishes the first installment in a three-part, 52-page special report on schooling in Japan.

April

The National Education Association launches a $600,000 project, called "Mastery in Learning," to upgrade curricula and increase teachers' involvement in school decisionmaking.

Schools should develop comprehensive curricula for arts instruction in grades K-12, a report by the Getty Center for Education in the Arts argues.

Researchers at the University of Chicago, with funding from the Amoco Foundation, begin a $12.5 million project to improve math instruction.

May

A study panel sponsored by the National Institute of Education releases "Becoming a Nation of Readers," a compendium of research on effective instruction in the subject.

The Carnegie Forum on Education and the Economy forms the Task Force on Teaching as a Profession and charges it with developing a plan for improving the field.

Colorado lawmakers approve legislation providing dropouts with vouchers to attend the public school of their choice.

The Holmes Group, made up of the education deans of 23 leading research universities, tentatively adopts a plan that would require teacher candidates to earn a standard academic degree as undergraduates, pass an exam before graduation, and enter a post-baccalaureate program for professional training.

June

The National Council for the Accreditation of Teacher Education requires colleges of education to set strict admissions and exit standards.

The improvement of teacher-preparation programs must become an "urgent" item on the agenda of policymakers and college presidents in the South, the Southern Regional Education Board argues in a report.

The National Science Foundation launches a five-year program to improve precollegiate science and math instruction.

July

In a reversal of longstanding policy, the National Education Association endorses the testing of new teachers and the dismissal of teachers deemed incompetent.

August

The National Governors' Association says it will develop recommendations on seven of the "toughest issues" facing public schools in an effort to set the agenda for American education through the end of the decade.

September

States should set standards for schools, monitor them, and intervene when they fail to perform, concludes a panel of business executives and university presidents convened by the Committee for Economic Development. States should also let schools decide how to meet the goals, it says. The influential report, *Investing in Our Children,* also urges more help for "at risk" youths, as will a subsequent report, "Reconnecting Youth," by the Education Commission of the States.

Thousands of public school teachers are assigned to subject areas for which they are not trained or certified, according to a 50-state survey by the Council for Basic Education.

Minnesota lawmakers reject Gov. Rudy Perpich's proposed "open enrollment" program for 11th and 12th graders, but approve another that allows students in those grades to take college courses at state expense.

Children were reading better in 1984 than they were in 1971, but the upward trend for older children is leveling off, the National Assessment of Educational Progress reports.

Average scores on the Scholastic Aptitude Test in 1985: math 475, up 4 points; verbal 431, up 5 points. Average composite score on the American College Testing Program test: 18.6, up 0.1 point.

California, one of the biggest educational-materials markets, rejects 24 science textbooks because of their "watered down" treatment of evolution and sexual reproduction.

October

Secretary of Education William J. Bennett proclaims 1985-86 the "year of the elementary school" and announces the appointment of a study group on the field. Meanwhile, two other groups—the Carnegie Foundation for the Advancement of Teaching and a consortium from the Bank Street College of Education and the Wellesley College Center for Research on Women—also announce plans to study preschool and early-childhood education.

At least 28 states have recently enacted early-childhood-education initiatives, and a growing number of others are considering such moves, an informal survey by *Education Week* indicates.

The Educational Testing Service announces a $30 million, 15-year project to develop a new generation of high-tech tests that will instruct as well as assess.

Reflecting the changing priorities of the reform movement, the National Governors' Association adds two topics to its effort to set an agenda for American education: school readiness and parental choice.

The American Association for the Advancement of Science launches Project 2061, a long-term effort to redesign precollegiate science and math instruction.

November

Secretary of Education William J. Bennett unveils proposed legislation to distribute Chapter 1 remedial-education aid through vouchers that could be used at public or private schools. A month later, 18 national education groups issue a statement blasting him for what they call his "constant flow of negative and inflammatory statements about public schools."

The Rockefeller Foundation lends its support to a

national program to improve the teaching of the arts and humanities. Created in six cities, the program now known as Collaboratives for Humanities and Arts Teaching spreads to 14 sites.

The head of the Association for Supervision and Curriculum Development proposes a "world core curriculum" to insure "peaceful and cooperative existence among the human species on this planet."

Expanding its vision for what all students need to know and be able to do to prepare for college, the College Board introduces a series of curriculum guides outlining academic preparation in six high school subjects.

1986

January

The flood of costly, comprehensive school-reform bills that characterized state legislative sessions in recent years appears to have ebbed. Only a few states—Connecticut, for example—will consider such legislation this year.

Among the findings from a survey of state policies on teaching by the American Association of Colleges for Teacher Education: Two-thirds of the states have raised training and formal certification standards; half have "irregular" routes to certification; more than half have raised teacher pay; 15 have some form of merit pay or a career ladder.

Pioneering career-ladder plans in Tennessee and Alabama and a merit-pay plan in Florida founder in the face of criticism.

A schism emerges in the Holmes Group as eight of its 39 members criticize its "wholesale adoption of a single approach" to teacher education reform.

Education Week publishes a 12-page special report on the "effective schools" movement.

February

Secretary of Education William J. Bennett issues the third annual education "wall chart." He says it illustrates a "dramatic turnaround" in school performance.

March

President Reagan and Secretary of Education William J. Bennett release *What Works*, a compilation of education-research findings. To illustrate the importance of memorization, they take turns reciting lines from the poem "The Cremation of Sam McGee."

John I. Goodlad, the author of *A Place Called School*, announces he will undertake a similar examination of teacher education.

The vast majority of former teachers polled in a national survey say they have found higher pay and more satisfaction in their new careers and are unlikely to return to teaching.

U.S. 8th graders rank 12th among 14 industrialized nations, and 12th graders at the bottom among 12 nations, in mathematics achievement, the U.S. Education Department reports.

April

The Holmes Group issues *Tomorrow's Teachers*. The report recommends abolishing the undergraduate education major and recasting the profession into three tiers, with "career professionals" at the top and a pool of "instructors," with only liberal-arts degrees, at the bottom.

Most American students cannot write prose that successfully informs, persuades, or entertains, the National Assessment of Educational Progress reports.

Schools and universities in 10 states join forces to work on the reform agenda laid out by the University of Washington researcher John I. Goodlad.

Some 200 educators meet in Salt Lake City to mark the third anniversary of the release of *A Nation at Risk*.

Education Week publishes a 24-page special report on the state of elementary education in the United States.

May

The Carnegie Task Force on Teaching as a Profession releases its report, *A Nation Prepared: Teachers for the 21st Century*. Its recommendations include creating a "national board for professional teaching standards," giving teachers more control over schools in exchange for greater accountability, and eliminating the undergraduate education major. The Carnegie Corporation of New York simultaneously awards $817,000 to Stanford University for the development of prototype assessments for national teacher certification.

Almost all Texas teachers and administrators pass a literacy test that lawmakers mandated as a condition for keeping their certificates. Meanwhile, hearings begin in federal court in Alabama in a civil-rights suit challenging that state's teacher-testing program.

Education Week publishes a 25-page special report on the demographic forces shaping the nation's schools.

June

The Reagan Administration withdraws its proposed legislation to convert the Chapter 1 program into a voucher scheme.

Florida lawmakers replace the state's embattled master-teacher program with a career ladder.

August

The National Governors' Association issues *Time for Results*. Its recommendations include a national teacher-certification board, linking teacher pay to performance, greater choice among public schools, opening school buildings year-round, and "academic bankruptcy" for failing schools and districts.

September

Curricular reform and greater parental involvement are needed to strengthen elementary schools, Secretary of Education William J. Bennett concludes in *First Lessons: A Report on Elementary Education in America*.

The Carnegie Forum on Education and the Economy forms a planning group to set the groundwork for a national board for professional teaching standards.

Boston business leaders promise to provide all of the city's high school graduates with the financial resources for college and a job after college graduation.

Although basic illiteracy is not widespread among young adults, many lack the degree of literacy needed to function well in a technological society, the National Assessment of Educational Progress reports.

Average scores on the Scholastic Aptitude Test in 1986: 431 verbal, no change; 475 math, no change. Average composite score on the American College Testing Program test: 18.8, up 0.2.

October

The Carnegie Corporation of New York gives $890,000 to the National Governors' Association to help states implement the reforms outlined in the report of the Carnegie Task Force on Teaching as a Profession.

November

The U.S. Education Department and eight governors select 16 school districts in which to pilot test recommendations from the National Governors' Association report *Time for Results*.

Teachers are far more skeptical than most education leaders and policymakers about the impact of recent reforms on the profession, a survey conducted for the Metropolitan Life Insurance Company reveals.

Local school boards—the traditional bastion of lay governance in American education—have fallen in prestige and power, but are far from obsolete, according to a national study by the Institute for Educational Leadership.

December

The poor writing ability of students reflects a "pervasive lack" of emphasis on higher-order skills throughout the curriculum, the National Assessment of Educational Progress reports.

School administrators in Rochester, N.Y., sue their school district and local teachers union to force the dismantling of a "mentor teacher" plan that they say encroaches on their jobs as supervisors.

1987

January

Responding to new international studies showing that U.S. students lag far behind those of many other nations in math achievement, math educators call for a wide array of reforms.

February

Concerned that they have been left out of the development of recent school-improvement proposals, leaders of five major subject-matter organizations meet to discuss ways to influence the direction of reforms.

In a new book, *Public and Private High Schools: The Impact of Communities,* the education researchers James S. Coleman and Thomas Hoffer reassert the claim that Catholic schools do a better job than public schools of educating students. Advocates of private school vouchers will cite the book repeatedly over the coming years.

After four years of improvements in test scores and reductions in dropout rates, the reform movement has reached a plateau, Secretary of Education William J. Bennett says in releasing the annual "wall chart."

The Holmes Group meets to celebrate its inauguration as a membership organization representing 94 leading research universities.

March

The National Commission on Excellence in Educational Administration calls for an overhaul of the training and licensing of school administrators.

A blue-ribbon panel appointed by Secretary of Education William J. Bennett recommends a major expansion of the National Assessment of Educational Progress.

April

In *Cultural Literacy*, a controversial book that launches a heated debate over the content of school curricula, E.D. Hirsch, a University of Virginia English professor, argues that students' lack of knowledge of the common culture is at the root of literacy problems.

Without more progress in professionalizing teaching and improving instruction in the early grades, the gains of the reform movement may fall victim to "benign neglect," concludes a report, "... *the best of educations": Reforming America's Public Schools in the 1980's.*

U.S. students' science achievement has improved little over the past three years and still lags far behind that of students in other countries, an international study finds.

Education Week publishes a 32-page special report on bilingual education.

"The education-reform movement is being hijacked and held for ransom" by education bureaucrats and special-interest groups, Secretary of Education William J. Bennett asserts in a sharply disputed speech.

May

The Carnegie Forum on Education and the Economy establishes the National Board for Professional Teaching Standards.

Indiana lawmakers pass one of the few comprehensive school-reform measures considered by a state legislature this year. Among its provisions: linking accreditation with student performance, rewarding high-performing schools and threatening failing schools with takeovers, and expanding a student-testing program.

A document endorsed by a group of national leaders with wide-ranging political views calls on schools to do a better job of teaching democratic values.

June

Education Week publishes a 24-page special report on the parental-choice movement in education.

July

A national "summit meeting" of English educators calls for restructuring the way the subject is taught by focusing on students' writing, reading, and thinking, rather than on the content of instruction.

Continuing its effort to redesign instruction through statewide curriculum frameworks, the California state board of education adopts a history-social science framework that calls for boosting the teaching of history in all grades.

September

"Now we call on the nation to embark upon a third wave of reform that gives the highest priority to early and sustained intervention in the lives of disadvantaged children." From *Children in Need: Investment Strategies for the Educationally Disadvantaged*, the report of the research and policy committee of the Committee for Economic Development.

The Rochester, N.Y., school district and the Rochester Teachers Association announce a landmark contract that dramatically raises teachers' pay and

incorporates many of the recommendations of the Carnegie Task Force on Teaching as a Profession.

The recent rise in student-test scores predated the decade's wave of school reforms and "might well have continued in their absence," a report by the Congressional Budget Office concludes.

American 17-year-olds display a "shameful" knowledge of U.S. history and literature, concludes a book analyzing the results on the first assessment of student knowledge in those subjects. The book, written by the researchers Diane S. Ravitch and Chester E. Finn Jr., comes on the heels of a controversial report on humanities instruction by Lynne V. Cheney, the chairwoman of the National Endowment for the Humanities, both of which help fuel a debate over curricular content.

Average scores on the Scholastic Aptitude Test in 1987: verbal 430, down 1 point; math 476, up 1 point. Average composite score on the American College Testing Program assessment falls slightly to 18.7.

Henry M. Levin, a Stanford University economist, begins the first two pilot "accelerated schools" to test his theory that disadvantaged students demand acceleration, not remediation. His network will grow to more than 300 schools and be cited as a national model for school improvement.

A first—nine Presidential aspirants meet in Chapel Hill, N.C., to debate education issues.

November

At an education forum in Chicago, Secretary of Education William J. Bennett blasts the Chicago public school system as the "worst in the nation."

Setting forth the profession's "vision" for precollegiate instruction in the subject, the National Council of Teachers of Mathematics unveils a draft of its curriculum standards. The precedent-setting document will help lead to a movement to create standards in other subjects as well.

The Connecticut legislature unveils a plan to tie state aid to districts to student-test scores, the first such plan in the nation.

A panel created by the National Council for the Social Studies convenes to begin defining a "new and coherent vision" for the field.

December

In a report that casts a heavy shadow of doubt on schools' reliance on standardized tests, a West Virginia physician finds in a survey that the overwhelming majority of elementary school pupils score "above the national average."

Saying that there is a "common ground" of knowledge all schools should "reach and inhabit," Secretary of Education William J. Bennett releases

James Madison High School, a proposed core curriculum.

1988

January

"Educators have become so preoccupied with those who go on to college that they have lost sight of those who do not. And more and more of the non-college-bound now fall between the cracks when they are in school, drop out, or graduate inadequately prepared for the requirements of the society and the workplace." —From *The Forgotten Half: Pathways to Success for America's Youth and Young Families,* the report of the William T. Grant Foundation's Commission on Work, Family, and Citizenship.

February

Georgia becomes the first state to mandate consideration of standardized test scores in the promotion of kindergartners.

March

Arguing that "the reform movement has largely bypassed our most deeply troubled schools," the board of trustees of the Carnegie Foundation for the Advancement of Teaching lays out a comprehensive plan for rescuing urban schools and an "imperiled generation" of children.

The Annie E. Casey Foundation selects five cities to receive a total of $50 million over the next five years to help lower their dropout, teenage-pregnancy, and youth-unemployment rates. The participants involved in the "New Futures" initiative have pledged to reshape the way agencies serve disadvantaged children to promote more collaborative efforts.

America's top high school science students ranked below those of nearly every other country, a 24-nation study shows.

April

Minnesota becomes the first state to enact a plan giving parents broad discretion in their choice of schools.

Marking the fifth anniversary of *A Nation at Risk,* Secretary of Education William J. Bennett charges that student achievement remains unacceptably low despite reform efforts.

The first national assessment of the use of computers by students finds that few are knowledgeable about computer applications or programming.

Black students' achievement in math and science improved substantially in the 1980's, the National Science Board reports.

The Coalition for Essential Schools and the Education Commission of the States form a joint project to connect school-based reforms with state policies. The project, known as "Re:Learning," spreads to 10 states.

May

Most schools fail to provide students with effective instruction in the arts, the National Endowment for the Arts reports.

The state of New Jersey moves to take control of the Jersey City school district, making it the first in the nation to face takeover for "academic bankruptcy." Although interest in state takeovers heightens momentarily, few policymakers actually tread down this mine-filled path.

Secretary of Education William J. Bennett announces he will end his stormy tenure in September, four months before the end of the Reagan Administration. As his successor, President Reagan chooses Lauro F. Cavazos, the president of Texas Tech University, who becomes the first Hispanic Cabinet member.

June

U.S. students' proficiency in math is "dismal," a National Assessment of Educational Progress report finds.

Baton Rouge, La., begins what is called the nation's first school-improvement plan based on parental choice and school-based management.

The Washington State Board of Education selects 21 "schools for the 21st century" to take part in a pioneering statewide effort to allow individual schools to experiment with reforms of their own design.

West Virginia becomes the first state to deny driver's licenses to school dropouts. The idea quickly spreads through state legislatures.

July

The school committee in Chelsea, Mass., votes 5 to 1 to invite Boston University to take over the management of their troubled public schools over the next 10 years, setting off a nationwide debate about the wisdom of asking a privately run institution to operate a public school system.

Mississippi ends standardized testing of kindergartners.

August

In his last major report before leaving office, Secretary of Education William J. Bennett proposes *James Madison Elementary School: A Curriculum for American Students,* a model curriculum for elementary schools.

September

The Bradley Commission on History in Schools, a group of leading historians and history educators, urges schools to substantially boost the quantity and quality of instruction in the subject.

"We would not give the states a passing grade for what has been done for youth at risk up to now. We would have to hand out an F." —From *America's Shame, America's Hope*, a 50-state study underwritten by the Charles Stewart Mott Foundation.

Average scores on the Scholastic Aptitude Test in 1988: verbal 428, down 2 points; math 476, same as in 1987. Minority members, however, make sizable one-year gains, with blacks up 2 points on verbal to 353, and up 7 points on math to 384. The average composite score on the American College Testing Program assessment is up slightly to 18.8.

A National Assessment of Educational Progress report finds a "distressingly low" level of student achievement in science.

New Jersey becomes the first state to allow persons with no prior experience in education to become certified as principals.

Many urban teachers struggle with inadequate resources, substandard facilities, and a lack of support that would "not be tolerated in other professions," according to a study released by the Institute for Educational Leadership.

October

Vermont announces plans to assess student performance on the basis of work portfolios as well as test scores.

Continuing in its effort to use curriculum frameworks to influence instruction, the California state board of education selects a set of textbooks that focus on "real literature," rather than drill.

A panel of the National Association of State Boards of Education calls for scrapping graduation requirements based on Carnegie units and instead requiring students to meet defined performance standards.

The Educational Testing Service announces plans to replace the paper-and-pencil National Teacher Examinations with "radically different" forms of assessment.

The Pew Charitable Trusts awards $447,000 to the Philadelphia school district to help restructure its 21 comprehensive high schools. The foundation will provide more than $16 million to the reform effort over the next several years.

November

Business leaders in Boston refuse to renew their six-year-old "compact" with the city's schools until they speed up the pace of reform.

December

The Illinois legislature approves a bill to revamp the Chicago schools by giving power over individual schools to panels of teachers, parents, and principals.

1989

January

American students have a weak grasp of basic economic concepts, a survey sponsored by the Joint Council on Economic Education finds.

President-elect Bush signals that public school choice will be a high priority in his Administration, but is mum on the subject of any private school choice option.

The National Academy of Sciences issues an urgent call for improving the mathematical abilities of U.S. students. It recommends that emphasis on problem-solving ability rather than computational skills be increased and that teachers begin using hand-held calculators in classrooms.

February

The American Association for the Advancement of Science unveils a "revolutionary" blueprint of student-learning goals in science as part of Project 2061, a long-term effort to redesign science instruction nationwide.

The Montana Supreme Court unanimously overturns that state's school-finance system.

U.S. 13-year-olds perform at or near the bottom on a six-nation international assessment of science and math achievement.

March

The National Council of Teachers of Mathematics releases a final version of its influential curriculum standards for math, calling for a shift from paper-and-pencil drill to the development of students' "mathematical power."

Lawmakers in Iowa and Arkansas approve measures allowing children to be enrolled in virtually any school district in the state.

Georgia's state board of education eliminates the use of written tests of kindergartners' readiness for the 1st grade.

Education Week publishes a 10-page special report on the growing move to coordinate social, health, and education services for children.

A coalition of leading English-education groups argues in a report for a "fresh view" of teaching the subject to make students active learners.

April

President Bush calls for the "partial deregulation" of public schools by granting certain districts relief from restrictions on federal aid if they agree to be held accountable for their results.

A group of Chicago principals files suit against the new state law giving parents increased control over local schools. An Illinois judge later rules against them.

The U.S. Supreme Court upholds the Kansas City, Mo., desegregation plan that requires huge expenditures for capital improvements and the creation of the nation's most extensive magnet-schools program.

The National Science Teachers Association unveils a project to overhaul the "layer cake" curriculum that has characterized secondary school science instruction for nearly a century.

May

In releasing the Education Department's annual "wall chart" of state indicators, Secretary of Education Lauro F. Cavazos says the nation's educational performance is "stagnant."

A coalition of school administrators' groups calls for an overhaul of how members of their profession are recruited, trained, and certified.

June

The Kentucky Supreme Court strikes down the state's entire structure of school governance and finance and orders the legislature to re-create the precollege system.

School officials in Dade County, Fla., open an unprecedented competition for proposals to design and operate 49 new schools in the district. In a related development, officials in St. Paul are planning to open the "Saturn School of Tomorrow," a technology-based magnet school.

The Carnegie Council on Adolescent Development calls for major changes in the way the middle school grades are managed, taught, and supported.

July

Delegates to the National Education Association's annual convention vote to oppose all state or federally mandated parental-choice programs.

August

The annual Gallup Poll on education finds Americans are ready for a national curriculum and national achievement standards.

Teacher Magazine, the sister publication to *Education Week,* is launched by Editorial Projects in Education.

Education Week publishes a 16-page report on the education plight faced by Native Americans.

September

At an "education summit" in Charlottesville, Va., President Bush and the nation's governors agree to set performance goals for the nation's schools.

Average scores on Scholastic Aptitude Test in 1989: verbal 427, down 1 point; math 476, same as in past two years. The average composite score on the American College Testing Program assessment is down slightly to 18.6.

The American Association of Colleges for Teacher Education votes not to support the efforts of the National Board for Professional Teaching Standards.

October

The Texas Supreme Court declares the state's method of funding public education unconstitutional—a decision that will throw the state legislature into turmoil for years.

States have made only "modest" progress in meeting the goals set in *A Nation at Risk,* a federally supported education-research center concludes.

The Ford Foundation creates a $10 million project to improve math education for at-risk middle school students.

More than two-thirds of college faculty members surveyed think their students are underprepared in basic skills, a survey by the Carnegie Foundation for the Advancement of Teaching shows.

Gov. Ray Mabus of Mississippi unveils a $500 million education-reform package to be funded in part by a state lottery.

November

Two major business groups announce plans to support the development of a national system to assess high school graduates' skills and make the results available to potential employers.

The Council of Chief State School Officers releases a document that aims to define and guide school "restructuring."

The South Carolina state board of education gives an unprecedented degree of regulatory relief to about one-tenth of the state's public schools.

The Council of Chief State School Officers releases the first state-by-state comparisons of data on math and science education.

The National Commission on Social Studies in the Schools, taking a separate stand from that of other reform panels, argues that radical changes in the subject are not needed.

December

President Bush forms a task force on the educational attainment of Hispanics.

The governing board of the National Assessment of Educational Progress considers a plan to set national goals for student performance in the subject areas it tests.

Wendy Kopp, a 1989 graduate of Princeton University, starts "Teach for America," a program to bring recent college graduates into teaching jobs in districts facing shortages.

1990

January

Student achievement in reading and writing has shown few gains since the early 1970's, the National Assessment of Educational Progress reports.

The United States spends proportionately less on precollegiate education than 13 other major industrialized nations, the Economic Policy Institute charges. The Education Department strongly dissents.

Education and civil-rights groups urge President Bush and the nation's governors to use alternative assessments to measure progress toward national goals.

The Rockefeller Foundation launches an initiative to encourage adoption of the reform ideas and practices of the Yale University child psychiatrist James P. Comer.

Wyoming's state board of education tentatively approves a plan to tie school accreditation to performance.

President Bush uses his State of the Union Message to announce six national education goals. The nation's governors say the list is not final.

February

President Bush and the nation's governors formally adopt six national education goals for 2000. They are: All children will start school ready to learn; the high school graduation rate will increase to at least 90 percent; students will leave grades 4, 8, and 12 having demonstrated competency in challenging subject matter including English, mathematics, science, history, and geography; U.S. students will be first in the world in mathematics and science achievement; every adult will be literate and exercise the rights and responsibilities of citizenship; every school will be free of drugs and violence and will offer a disciplined environment conducive to learning.

The first national assessment of geography reveals "critical shortcomings" in high school seniors' knowledge of the subject, the National Assessment of Educational Progress announces.

Mississippi becomes the first state to mandate ungraded primary classrooms.

The New York State schools chief asks the state board of regents to endorse a plan to revise the public school curriculum to focus more attention on minorities and their cultures.

The Senate approves a $460 million education bill, including $25 million for the National Board for Professional Teaching Standards opposed by the Bush Administration.

The Carnegie Corporation of New York establishes a $7.2 million grant program to reform middle schools.

Some 150 participants at a conference on school restructuring sponsored by the Education Commission of the States agree on one thing: There is no single definition of the term.

The National Education Association forms the National Center for Innovation in Education to promote school-renewal efforts.

Few school districts take advantage of efforts in five states to deregulate schools in return for more accountability, the National Governors' Association reports.

March

Kentucky lawmakers approve a landmark school-reform bill in response to the state supreme court's sweeping order that the legislature create a new school system. It is the most far-reaching makeover of a state's education system to date.

The Wisconsin legislature approves a bill giving some 1,000 low-income Milwaukee public school students the option of attending nonsectarian private schools at state expense.

Forty-nine of Chicago's newly elected local school councils fire their principals.

The governing board of the National Assessment of Educational Progress adopts a 1992 reading-assessment strategy that will guide the first state-by-state comparisons in the subject. The plan includes assessments of oral reading and student portfolios.

The Council of the Great City Schools adopts six goals similar to those developed by President Bush and the nation's governors.

The nation's second-largest district moves toward school-based management as the Los Angeles school board issues guidelines under which schools may seek increased autonomy.

The National Science Foundation creates an $80 million grant program to help states make "systemic" school reforms in science and mathematics.

April

U.S. students show a "limited" understanding of fundamental concepts of U.S. history and civics, two reports from the National Assessment of Educational Progress reveal.

RJR Nabisco makes the first grants in its projected $30 million "Next Century Schools" program aimed at encouraging schools to take risks to improve student performance.

In enacting Gov. Booth Gardner's school-choice proposal, Washington becomes the second state to mandate that all districts adopt policies allowing intradistrict transfers by students.

Oklahoma lawmakers approve a long-delayed education-reform package that calls for $230 million in new taxes.

Few state education reforms to date have focused on the job of principal, even though principals are being given much more oversight responsibility for state mandates, a study by the Policy Center Network finds.

Education Week publishes the first installment in a four-part, 36-page special report on "parents as partners" in education.

May

The governing board of the National Assessment of Educational Progress approves a plan to set the first national standards for student achievement; "basic," "proficient," and "advanced" standards levels are to be set for each grade level.

Student achievement has reached a plateau after four years of little or no improvement, Secretary of Education Lauro F. Cavazos says in releasing the annual "wall chart" of education-performance indicators.

Schools and businesses should shift away from standardized tests toward multiple sources of information, including alternative forms of assessment to measure performance in school and on the job, states a report, *From Gatekeeper To Gateway*, issued by a panel funded by the Ford Foundation.

June

The education researchers John E. Chubb and Terry M. Moe call for a new system of school governance in which schools compete for students in an open market. Their book, *Politics, Markets, and America's Schools*, fuels a nationwide debate over school choice.

The National Commission on the Skills of the American Work Force releases a report, *America's Choice: High Skills or Low Wages*, containing a comprehensive strategy for upgrading the skills of American workers. It would require every teenager to earn a national certificate at about age 16 to qualify for employment or further education and training. The report also calls for the creation of a national examination board to set new world-class standards for educational performance, new "youth centers" that teenagers

through age 18 could attend to receive alternative education and training, and changes in the tax structure and other laws to encourage employers to invest in the educational attainment and productivity of their workers and to reorganize their workplaces for "high performance."

A for-profit firm, Education Alternatives Inc., wins a five-year contract to develop the educational program for and to train the principal and teachers at a new Dade County, Fla., public school—the first such agreement in the nation.

The New Jersey Supreme Court orders the legislature to bring spending in its poorest city schools up to the level of its wealthiest districts.

Gov. William P. Clements Jr. of Texas signs a landmark school-finance bill, thus avoiding a court-imposed plan.

Students spend little time reading or writing in school, a National Assessment of Educational Progress report finds. Moreover, those who spend more time at those tasks do better at them.

Eleven cities and states with a record of radical plans for reorganizing schools form a new National Alliance for Restructuring Education.

More than 80 percent of teachers surveyed in a Gallup Poll say that public schools need considerable improvement, and nearly all say they want a leading role in state and local restructuring efforts.

July

At their annual meeting in Mobile, Ala., the nation's governors approve the creation of a National Education Goals Panel to monitor progress toward meeting the six national education goals adopted by the governors and the President in February. In what will later become a sticking point, Congressional participants on the panel are limited to a nonvoting, ex officio status.

A task force of the National Governors' Association, chaired by Gov. Bill Clinton of Arkansas, calls for a fundamental restructuring of American education from preschool through adult education to meet the national education goals. Recommendations include eliminating student tracking and grouping, seeking new providers to create and run public schools, and developing an outcome-based system for preparing and licensing teachers.

One-fifth of all 8th graders, and two-fifths of blacks and Hispanics at that grade level, are at high risk of school failure, results from the National Education Longitudinal Study of 1988 show.

A federal advisory panel calls for an "Indian education bill of rights" to help improve the schooling of Native Americans.

The Education Department releases its first K-12 lesson plan in any area—a model drug-education curriculum.

August

Educators, business leaders, and public officials meet to begin planning what could become the first national standards for student achievement: a set of recommendations to the governing panel of the National Assessment of Educational Progress that would, for the first time, compare student performance on the national assessment to agreed-upon definitions of what students should know in mathematics.

The average verbal score on the Scholastic Aptitude Test falls to its lowest level since 1980-81, 424 out of a possible 800, while the average math score of 476 remains stable.

Leaders of 20 subject-area groups meet for the first time to begin a process to try to reach consensus on what to teach in the nation's schools and how to teach it.

Fewer teachers are satisfied with the degree of control they exert over their jobs, a study by the Carnegie Foundation for the Advancement of Teaching finds.

The annual Gallup Poll on education finds that, while Americans support the six national education goals, few believe they can be achieved by 2000.

An *Education Week* survey finds that at least five states have enacted some sort of school-choice plan, with other states considering such bills.

September

A National Assessment of Educational Progress report finds that student performance levels on tests given in various subjects since 1985 are "far below those that might indicate competence," and that performance has improved little in the past 20 years.

Average scores on the revamped American College Testing Program test remain stable, continuing a decade-long pattern of "modest" year-to-year changes. The average 1990 composite is 20.6 out of a possible 36.

The National Center on Education and the Economy and President Bush's Educational Policy Advisory Committee begin laying plans for a national examination system for all students.

A Texas judge strikes down a finance-reform measure approved by the legislature in response to a state supreme court order.

President Bush signs an executive order creating a new advisory panel on Hispanic education.

October

In *Teachers for Our Nation's Schools,* the education researcher John I. Goodlad recommends that colleges and universities create "centers of pedagogy," dedicated to teacher education and having the same amount of autonomy and authority now reserved for medical and law schools.

The College Board approves the most far-reaching changes in the Scholastic Aptitude Test in decades. The new test, to be taken by high school juniors and seniors for the first time in the spring of 1994, will place a greater emphasis on critical reading skills, require student-generated answers to math questions, and permit the use of calculators for the first time.

The National Board for Professional Teaching Standards awards its first contract to develop an assessment of accomplished teaching practice.

Lynne V. Cheney, the chairwoman of the National Endowment for the Humanities, charges in a report that school reform has been impeded by such practices as teacher education courses and the use of the Scholastic Aptitude Test.

Studying Africa and African-American history and culture can lead to improved overall academic performance among black students, a study by a North Carolina State University researcher suggests.

The Council of Chief State School Officers urges that research supporting "higher-order thinking" strategies be put to use in every one of the nation's schools.

The John D. and Catherine T. MacArthur Foundation commits $40 million in grants to support school reform in Chicago.

November

A state appellate court in Wisconsin strikes down Milwaukee's controversial program to enroll low-income students in nonsectarian private schools at state expense. The decision, a narrowly focused one, hinges on the method the legislature used to enact the legislation. The law will later be upheld by the Wisconsin Supreme Court.

The National Assessment Governing Board unveils what could become the nation's first set of national student-achievement standards for math in grades 4, 8, and 12. The standards outline what students at the "basic," "proficient," and "advanced" levels should know and be able to do at each grade level.

Nearly half of American workers need more training, a four-year federally funded study by the American Society for Training and Development finds.

The Illinois Supreme Court strikes down the 1988 law that brought sweeping reforms to the Chicago public schools, ruling that the way in which local school councils are elected violates the constitutional principle of "one person, one vote." The election procedures will later be revised, so that the law remains intact.

December

A report by the National Commission for the

Principalship recommends a complete overhaul of the way in which educators are trained to become administrators.

An "outreach office" is created within the Education Department to promote school choice.

President Bush fires Secretary of Education Lauro F. Cavazos and nominates former Gov. Lamar Alexander of Tennessee to succeed him.

An extraordinary number of vacancies in urban superintendencies—24 large districts are searching for chiefs in the wake of resignations and firings—prompts calls for reform in school governance.

Gov. Booth Gardner of Washington introduces a plan to overhaul the state's education system to make grades, grade levels, and high school diplomas irrelevant. The plan, which calls for the setting of statewide performance standards and gives local educators great leeway in achieving those standards, is modeled on recommendations made by the National Commission on the Skills of the American Work Force.

Education Week publishes the first installment in a four-part, 36-page special report on teacher education.

1991

January

The National Governors' Association releases *Results in Education: 1990*, a candid report that concedes that progress toward carrying out the sweeping agenda for education that the governors set four years earlier in the landmark report *Time for Results* has been slower and more uneven than they predicted.

The Pew Charitable Trusts of Philadelphia and the John D. and Catherine T. MacArthur Foundation of Chicago award a total of more than $2 million to the National Center for Education and the Economy and the Learning Research and Development Center at the University of Pittsburgh to help launch the development of a new national examination system for students. A majority of President Bush's advisory panel on education policy, meanwhile, endorses a proposal to create national standards in school subjects and tests to measure student performance against them.

New York City joins Detroit in backing alternative public schools aimed at the specific needs of black and minority males as a method of improving their academic performance.

The Detroit school board weighs a landmark proposal that would allow some private schools in the city to become public schools paid for out of public funds.

Educate America, a new private group headed by Saul Cooperman, the former schools chief in New Jersey, unveils a plan to develop a national achievement test for all high school seniors and asks Congress to fund it and make it mandatory nationwide. Nothing ever comes of this proposal.

February

Unless more is done to meet the early health, social, and developmental needs of children, school reform is doomed to failure, the Committee for Economic Development concludes in its report *The Unfinished Agenda: A New Vision for Child Development and Education*. The report calls for coordinating child and youth services to better prepare young Americans for school and to help them achieve there.

President Bush introduces a $200 million plan to reward school districts that implement choice plans that include private schools.

A group of prominent American-history scholars publishes a document highlighting the importance of including non-Western and feminist perspectives in the school curriculum, but decrying some extreme efforts based on "bad history."

March

The National Commission on Music Education, a 60-member panel of prominent educators and artists, warns that music and arts education are being pushed out of the public school curriculum.

The National Education Goals Panel unveils a plan to create a national assessment system to measure progress toward the national education goals for the year 2000, including both existing indicators and new measures of school readiness and a student-identification system for tracking students across districts.

Intervening in Denver teacher negotiations, Gov. Roy Romer of Colorado writes a contract that would abolish many traditional protections in exchange for giving teachers unusually wide decisionmaking latitude in each school.

April

President Bush unveils America 2000, initially termed by observers the most far-reaching education plan of any President since Lyndon B. Johnson. Among its elements: creation of "New American Schools"; involvement of reform-minded communities as "America 2000 communities"; national examinations; and parental choice including private schools. The private New American Schools Development Corporation is chartered to encourage efforts to design new types of public schools.

The National Science Teachers Association launches a project to reform elementary school science teaching to complement its ongoing initiative to revamp the secondary school curriculum.

President Bush joins some 500 mathematics educators, business leaders, and policymakers at a national "summit" on assessment.

May

Chris Whittle, the chairman of Whittle Communications, announces a plan to develop a nationwide chain of private, for-profit schools that will be redesigned from the ground up. The firm plans to invest some $60 million in the "Edison Project" over three years to design the schools.

The National Science Foundation awards $75 million to 10 states as part of its effort to foster systemic reform to improve science education.

Minnesota lawmakers authorize the creation of "charter" schools—independently run public schools, created by groups of licensed teachers, and free from most state rules and regulations—a national first.

Gov. Guy Hunt of Alabama introduces a sweeping school-reform plan that includes intradistrict school choice, alternative teacher certification, a core curriculum, greater school-based decisionmaking, and a longer school year.

The U.S. Education Department finds that 74 percent of colleges and universities offer remedial-education courses.

Even though the nation's top-performing students appear to do well in college, the Educational Testing Service reports that there are few high achievers in elementary or secondary schools and that their level of performance is "unremarkable."

The first comprehensive state-by-state analysis of enrollment patterns in math and science courses reveals that the percentage of high school students taking such courses increased dramatically during the 1980's, the Council of Chief State School Officers reports.

Education Week publishes a 20-page special report to mark the 25th anniversary of the federal Chapter 1 remedial-education program.

June

The first-ever state-by-state assessment of student achievement finds that student performance in math varies widely among states, but that performance in all states remains low. Highlights: more than one-quarter of 4th graders cannot perform simple arithmetic reasoning with whole numbers, and only 5 percent of high school seniors have the skills needed for high-technology or college-level work.

The Oregon legislature approves a controversial plan to end traditional schooling in the 10th grade, after which students can choose between two years of technical-professional or college preparation.

Congress, in cooperation with the nation's governors, passes a bill to create a National Council on Education Standards and Testing to study the "feasibility and desirability" of creating national standards and a national examination system for students.

July

In *What Work Requires of Schools,* the Secretary's Commission on Achieving Necessary Skills of the U.S. Department of Labor lays out a set of core competencies and foundations that all students should achieve to succeed in the modern-day workplace. This workforce "know-how," the panel argues, should become part of any attempt to set world-class standards for achievement. Schools must teach them. Students must learn them. And they should be assessed. The new entry-level competencies include such generic skills as understanding systems, teamwork, creative thinking and problem-solving, and the ability to use and apply technology. The "SCANS report," as it is soon called, will become a major landmark in the effort to develop a conversation between educators and employers and a smoother school-to-work transition.

The New York State board of regents approves guidelines to bring multicultural perspectives into the teaching of social studies in the state's public schools.

A Tennessee judge finds the state's school-finance system unconstitutional.

Despite "signs of progress" on school restructuring, states have not made the comprehensive changes needed to improve the educational system, the National Governors' Association charges.

An informal survey by *Education Week* finds that many urban districts have put major reform efforts on hold, citing budgetary restraints.

August

Golden Rule Insurance Company announces plans to provide $1.2 million to poor parents in Indianapolis who wish to send their children to private schools. The decision will spur a number of copycat, privately funded voucher initiatives in other states.

In an unprecedented joint venture, three interfaith private schools open in inner-city Detroit—the first such interdenominational system to win the backing of both Protestant and Catholic religious leaders.

Average verbal scores on the Scholastic Aptitude Test hit an all-time low of 422 out of a possible 800, while math scores are down—for the first time since 1980—to 474, according to the College Board.

September

The first "report card" on the national education goals by the National Education Goals Panel finds only a few passing grades, several failures, and many incompletes.

The Carnegie Commission on Science, Technology, and Government urges the National Science Foundation and the Education Department to be "lead agencies" in reforming math and science education.

The New Jersey education department decides to implement the reform ideas of the Yale University child psychiatrist James P. Comer in dozens of urban districts in the state.

For the first time, more than half of the college-bound seniors taking the American College Testing Program test had taken a "core" academic curriculum, the firm says. Average scores remain stable at 20.6 out of a possible 36.

Two national groups release "Civitas," a comprehensive blueprint for reintroducing civics teaching in grades K through 12.

Science-education groups ask the National Academy of Sciences to oversee the development of national standards in science. The academy will be awarded a federal grant to undertake the effort.

Student performance levels have regained much of the ground lost in the 1970's and 1980's, and students are achieving much as they did in 1970, a National Assessment of Educational Progress study finds. Fewer than 20 percent of students, however, demonstrate competence over challenging subject matter in math.

The Bush Administration launches a massive public-relations campaign to promote its America 2000 education-reform program.

October

The author Jonathan Kozol publishes *Savage Inequalities: Children in America's Schools,* in which he concludes that schools are more racially and economically segregated than ever. "The dual society, at least in public education," he charges, "seems in general to be unquestioned."

Researchers at a federally funded laboratory in New Mexico conclude that those who contend that American education is in a systemwide crisis are overstating the case. Their report is never published.

The Florida education department signs an agreement with the National Council on the Accreditation of Teacher Education to conduct joint reviews of teachers' colleges using a similar set of standards.

The National Coalition of Advocates for Students publishes *The Good Common School,* a portrait of the ideal urban elementary school as one with a racially and ethnically mixed student body, run by a parent-dominated school council, and with teachers empowered to make decisions about curriculum and student grouping.

In a record turnout for the state, Oklahoma voters decide to keep a five-year, $2 billion school-improvement and revenue bill passed by the legislature.

Education Week publishes a 16-page special report on cognitive research and its implications for education.

An informal *Education Week* survey finds that foreign-language instruction is making a cautious comeback in the nation's schools.

November

A number of observers charge that school-reform advocates have overstated the magnitude of the problems in U.S. schools. "The evidence overwhelmingly shows that *American schools have never achieved more than they currently achieve.* And some indicators show them performing better than ever." —Gerald W. Bracey, writing in the October 1991 *Phi Delta Kappan.*

The four former secretaries of education hold an unprecedented panel discussion in San Francisco. They disagree on what ails the U.S. educational system, but agree that the nation must focus more of its attention on education.

More than 700 educators and policymakers from 43 states convene in Des Moines for what is billed a "strategy session" to help achieve the national education goals, but many leave without a clear sense of what the meeting was for.

The New Standards Project, a joint effort of the National Center on Education and the Economy and the Learning Research and Development Center at the University of Pittsburgh, begins planning for a national examination system by 1993.

More than three-quarters of Americans are totally unaware of the six national education goals adopted by President Bush and the nation's governors, a survey by the National PTA finds.

Kansas officials propose a bold new school-finance plan that would shift all school-funding responsibility and property-taxing authority to the state.

December

Nearly a decade after writing one of the most influential of the school-reform books, Theodore R. Sizer completes *Horace's School: Redesigning the American High School.* The book, based on Mr. Sizer's eight years overseeing the Coalition of Essential Schools, concludes that the reform movement of the 1980's barely touched the lives of his fictional English teacher, Horace Smith, or his students. On a more positive note, Mr. Sizer argues that there is a "growing army of Horace Smiths" ready to reinvent the schools, if given the opportunity.

The Carnegie Foundation for the Advancement of Teaching issues *Ready to Learn,* a seven-point plan to insure children's readiness for school, the first of the national education goals. The proposal includes improved community health care, parent-education programs, expansion of Head Start for all eligible children, promotion of "family friendly" workplace policies, and improved educational offerings on cable television for preschoolers.

The National Endowment for the Humanities and the Education Department launch a joint effort to develop national standards for history teaching.

1992

January

Asserting that the current education system has produced expectations for student performance that are "simply too low," the National Council on Education Standards and Testing calls for high national standards for student achievement and a national system of assessments to gauge their attainment.

A report from the National Center for Improving Science Education calls for restructuring the high school curriculum around a core of learning that would provide good science training for all, not just the college-bound.

Few schools have adopted a majority of the instructional strategies recommended by reformers, the National Assessment of Educational Progress reports.

The National Education Goals Panel is reconfigured so that Congressional representatives have voting power and its membership is evenly split between Democrats and Republicans.

Education Week publishes a 24-page special report highlighting "profiles in technology."

February

Girls face pervasive barriers to achievement in their precollegiate schooling, the American Association of University Women finds.

Students in the United States lag far behind most of their peers abroad in mathematics and science achievement, a 20-nation study by the Educational Testing Service finds.

Congress's Office of Technology Assessment, citing potential abuses and misuses of tests, expresses concern over the effort to create a new national system of student assessments.

The Fairfax County, Va., school board suspends its nationally watched merit-pay program for teachers as part of a budget-cutting move.

March

Nearly 700 teams from across the nation meet the deadline and submit ideas for creating "break the mold" schools to the New American Schools Development Corporation in hopes of receiving funding.

Few Chicago schools have put into place the bulk of the changes called for in the city's landmark reform act, a new study charges.

Few students are able to perform at high levels of proficiency in science, a National Assessment of Educational Progress report finds.

A California task force calls for an overhaul of the state's high schools aimed at upgrading courses and strengthening the connection between school and work. In the spring, a similar panel calls for overhauling the state's elementary schools "so that thinking pervades students' lives from kindergarten onward."

The Pennsylvania state board of education votes to make it one of the first states to require students to demonstrate that they have achieved a set of learner outcomes, rather than complete a series of courses, in order to graduate from high school. After considerable controversy, the board nearly a year later adopts the outcomes students must attain.

A national survey of mathematics teachers indicates that there are wide gaps between their practices and the vision outlined in the standards for math instruction produced by the National Council of Teachers of Mathematics.

April

The College Board announces the development of a new set of courses and examinations, known as "Pacesetter." Modeled after its successful Advanced Placement program, Pacesetter will create capstone courses and assessments for all high school students that will complement other efforts to create national standards and exams.

Local school boards should focus more on setting policy than on "micromanagement" of their districts, a report sponsored by the Twentieth Century Fund and the Danforth Foundation argues.

The National Center for History in Schools outlines in a massive document its view of what students should know about the subject and why they should know it.

Education Week publishes a 28-page special report on school boards.

May

The National Assessment Governing Board approves a "rigorous" framework for the first national student-achievement testing program in geography.

School-reform efforts in Alabama and Arizona die in their respective legislatures, largely as a result of budgetary problems.

U.S. students do very little reading in or out of

school, the National Assessment of Educational Progress reports.

Some 500 4th graders in 17 states and six school districts pilot-test the prototype for a national examination system.

A Minnesota appeals court upholds the use of public funds to allow high school students to take classes at public or private institutions of higher learning.

June

The nation's children are poorer, more diverse, and more likely to have fallen behind in school than 10 years earlier, new data from the 1990 Census indicate.

A conservative advocacy group files suits in Illinois and California state courts demanding that low-income families receive vouchers for private school tuition.

A Florida panel outlines a set of standards for what students should know and be able to do. The standards are part of a plan, mandated by the legislature, to set statewide goals for student performance and provide schools flexibility in how to attain them.

Three federal agencies award a grant to create a project to set national standards for student achievement in the arts.

Education Week publishes its first-ever special Commentary report—on the debate over the move to develop national standards and assessments.

July

Eleven out of 686 competitors win grants from the New American Schools Development Corporation to pursue their visions of radically different and more productive schools.

The high school graduation rate is rising, particularly among minorities, new data from the 1990 Census show.

U.S. students score only slightly below average on a small-scale geography test of 13-year-olds in nine nations, the Educational Testing Service says.

A survey by the Council of Chief State School Officers finds that most states have focused their mathematics and science reforms on curriculum and alternative assessments.

A task force of the National Governors' Association releases "benchmarks" that states can use to measure progress toward insuring that all children start school ready to learn.

Maryland becomes the first state to require community service by students as a condition of high school graduation.

Federal officials award more than $855,000 in grants for efforts to set national standards for student achievement in geography and civics.

August

Average verbal scores on the Scholastic Aptitude Test rose in 1991 for the first time since 1985, and average mathematics scores also increased, the College Board reports.

The Council of Chief State School Officers finds "uneven progress" among states in improving education in middle schools.

September

The annual Gallup Poll on education shows that, while the public supports efforts to improve schools, few Americans believe that elected officials can do the job.

Under a five-year contract with the Baltimore City school district, Education Alternatives Inc., a private management firm, takes over the day-to-day operation of nine public schools, launching one of the boldest experiments yet in public school privatization.

A report by the American College Testing Program finds few high school seniors who took the test this year are prepared for college-level calculus; 25 percent will need remedial mathematics in college. The average composite score remained 20.6, the same as in the past four years.

California becomes the second state after Minnesota to authorize teachers and others to create independently operated public schools under a contract, or "charter," with a school district.

Students from the United States outperformed those from nearly every other country in a 32-nation study of reading literacy, the International Association for the Evaluation of Educational Achievement reports.

An international comparison of education spending and attainment shows that the United States, though the world's richest nation, is not the biggest spender on education.

The New Hampshire state board of education eliminates most statewide minimum standards for schools. After criticism from a legislative panel, the board later modifies its changes.

The second annual report on the national education goals for 2000 shows that the nation has made "modest progress" toward achieving the targets.

Teachers in Detroit go on strike, contending that a series of proposals by the board of education to "empower" individual schools would destroy teachers' contractual protections.

Ernest L. Boyer, the president of the Carnegie Foundation for the Advancement of Teaching, and former U.S. Surgeon General Dr. C. Everett Koop announce the formation of the National Ready to Learn Council to promote school readiness.

A Gallup Poll finds wide support among the public for tuition vouchers for public, private, or parochial schools.

More than half of all public school teachers think at least 25 percent of their students are unprepared for grade-level work, according to a survey by the Metropolitan Life Insurance Company.

October

In their first joint effort in the area, the National Science Foundation and the Education Department issue an "action agenda" for reforming science and mathematics education.

Legislation to support state and local school-reform efforts and to authorize national education standards dies in Congress, but aides to President Clinton later vow to revive it in the 103rd Congress.

The Carnegie Foundation for the Advancement of Teaching creates a furor by charging that claims about the benefits of school choice "greatly outdistance the evidence."

School board members give themselves failing or barely passing grades in such core governance areas as leadership, policy oversight, and long-range planning, a study by the Institute for Educational Leadership reports, confirming the views of their critics.

A three-year study funded by the National Science Foundation finds evidence to confirm the view that standardized tests and textbook tests emphasize low-level thinking and knowledge and that they exert a profound, mostly negative, influence on instruction.

In a strong statement with far-ranging implications, the National Association of State Boards of Education endorses the "full inclusion" of students with disabilities in regular classrooms.

The Education Department awards a grant to a consortium of organizations to develop standards for student performance in English, completing its effort to spur standards-setting in core subjects. The department will later award another grant for a standards-setting project, in foreign languages. In all, national standards in eight subjects are expected to be developed by the middle of the decade.

A citywide coalition in Los Angeles releases a plan for restructuring the district's schools, including a large degree of site-based decisionmaking.

November

Colorado voters reject a voucher plan that includes private schools. A similar initiative in California fails to qualify for the November ballot, but backers pledge to revisit the issue in 1994.

A study by Claremont University Center and

Graduate School that looked at schools "from the inside" finds that strategies advocated by reformers bear little relation to the problems identified by students, parents, and teachers.

The results of a five-year pilot program by the Southern Regional Education Board suggest that an advanced curriculum that joins academic study and instruction about the workplace can dramatically improve performance of high school students in both vocational and general-education tracks.

The New Hampshire Supreme Court rules that local tax revenues cannot be used to finance tuition vouchers for students at private religious schools.

Would-be school reformers have paid scant attention to the need to give school personnel enough time to plan, implement, and refine improvement programs, a report by the RAND Corporation concludes.

In a glimpse of the future of mathematics assessment, the Mathematical Sciences Education Board releases a set of 13 "prototype" math-assessment tasks for 4th graders. The National Academy of Sciences releases prototype standards for what students should know and be able to do at various grade levels in several domains of science. The standards stress quality of knowledge rather than the amount learned through rote memorization.

The National Assessment Governing Board considers the first-ever standards for student performance in reading and writing.

A New York State panel recommends that the state adopt a unitary graduation system in which all students complete a portfolio of work to receive a diploma.

Nine moderately sized city districts join forces as the National Urban Reform Network to shape a national urban-education agenda.

December

An independent commission calls for a radical revision of the federal Chapter 1 program to transform it into a catalyst for schoolwide improvement, including efforts to force states to equalize services among school districts and to set tough new accountability standards based on new types of tests.

A report by the RAND Corporation finds that Vermont's pioneering assessment system has severe problems and raises questions about alternative forms of student assessment.

Education Week publishes a special eight-page Commentary report on the debate over parental choice in education.

CONDITIONS OF YOUTH

Following are 20 "snapshots" that show educational and related social conditions as they existed "then" (at or near the beginning of the school-reform movement) and as they are "now" (as close to the present as possible). We begin by updating 13 indicators of "risk" identified by the National Commission on Excellence in Education in *A Nation at Risk*.

College Board Achievement Test Scores

THEN:

Mean scores in selected subjects, 1982:

English Composition:	520	Math I:	545
Math II:	661	Biology:	541
Chemistry:	575	Physics:	592

NOW:

Mean scores in selected subjects, 1992:

English Composition:	521	Math I:	547
Math II:	663	Biology:	537
Chemistry:	544	Physics:	542

SOURCE: The College Board.

Teenage Functional Literacy

THEN:

Percentages of 17-year-olds performing at or above five levels of reading proficiency, 1980:

Level 150 (lowest):	100	Level 300:	38
Level 200:	97	Level 350 (highest):	5
Level 250:	81		

NOW:

Percentages of 17-year-olds performing at or above five levels of reading proficiency, 1990:

Level 150 (lowest):	100	Level 300:	41
Level 200:	98	Level 350 (highest):	7
Level 250:	84		

SOURCE: *Trends in Academic Progress*, U.S. Education Department, 1991.

NAEP Science Scores

Average score of 17-year-olds on National Assessment
of Educational Progress science assessment*

In 1969: 305
In 1982: 283
In 1990: 290   * Out of possible score of 500.

SOURCE: *Trends In Academic Progress*, National Center for Education Statistics, 1992.

Remediation in Colleges and Universities

THEN:

Percentage of U.S. colleges offering remedial instruction or tutoring, 1980-81

Four-Year Colleges: 78.9
Two-Year Colleges: 83.8

NOW:

Percentage of U.S. colleges offering remedial instruction or tutoring, 1991-92

Four-Year Colleges: 88.6
Two-Year Colleges: 90.9

SOURCE: *Digest of Education Statistics 1992.*

International Achievement Tests

THEN:

U.S. 14-year-olds' rank in mathematics among six selected nations, 1964: 5th
U.S. 14-year-olds' rank in science among seven selected nations, 1970: 4th

NOW:

U.S. 13-year-olds' rank in mathematics among 15 selected nations, 1991: 14th
U.S. 13-year-olds' rank in science among 15 selected nations, 1991: 4th

SOURCES: *The Condition of Education 1992, Digest of Education Statistics 1981,
Statistical Abstract of the United States 1992.*

S.A.T. Scores

Average Scholastic Aptitude

Test scores in:	Verbal	Math
1975-76	431	472
1980-81	424	466
1990-91	422	474

SOURCE: *Digest of Education Statistics 1992.*

■

Achievement Test Scores of College Graduates

Average score on the Graduate Record Examination
on combined verbal and quantitative sections

In 1965: 1,063
In 1982: 1,002
In 1991: 1,047

SOURCE: *Condition Of Education 1992.*

■

Underachievement Among the Gifted

THEN:

Percentage of gifted students who are underachievers, early 1970's: 54

NOW:

Percentage of 8th graders classified in the highest quartile on a standardized test who are also
in the lowest two quartiles based on grades of 6th through 8th graders, 1988: 14.5

SOURCE: Lenore H. Worcester, "Myths and Realities of the Gifted and Talented," *G/C/T*, Sept./Oct. 1981;
"National Education Longitudinal Study of 1988: Base Year Student Survey," U.S. Education Department.

■

High School Standardized Achievement Tests

Change in average scores on the California Test of Basic Skills: 1981-1989

Reading:	Grade 9 -2%	Grade 10 -8%	Grade 11 -5%	Grade 12 -11%
Language:	Grade 9 7%	Grade 10 2%	Grade 11 7%	Grade 12 0%
Mathematics:	Grade 9 8%	Grade 10 4%	Grade 11 8%	Grade 12 4%

SOURCE: "Achievement Trends Through the 1980's," CTB/Macmillan/McGraw-Hill, 1990.

Higher-Order Thinking Skills

THEN:

Percentage of 17-year-olds able to draw inferences from written material, 1980: 81

Percentage of 11th graders able to write an adequate persuasive essay, 1984: 25

Percentage of 17-year-olds able to solve multi-step mathematics problems, 1982: 7

NOW:

Percentage of 17-year-olds able to draw inferences from written material, 1990: 84

Percentage of 11th graders able to write an adequate persuasive essay, 1990: 28

Percentage of 17-year-olds able to solve multi-step mathematics problems, 1990: 7

SOURCE: *Trends In Academic Progress*, U.S. Education Department, 1991.

Remediation in Business

THEN:

Amount spent annually by U.S. businesses on basic literacy skills training for employees, early 1980's: "Millions of Dollars"

NOW:

Amount spent annually by U.S. businesses on basic literacy skills training for employees, late 1980's: $240 Million to $260 Million

SOURCES: Testimony in public hearings, National Commission on Excellence in Education, Denver, Sept. 16, 1982; *Workplace Basics: The Skills Employers Want*, American Society for Training and Development, 1988.

Adult Functional Illiteracy

THEN (1975):

23 million Americans are functionally illiterate as measured by tests of everyday reading, writing, and comprehension.

NOW (1985):

Fewer than one-quarter of young Americans ages 21-25 could summarize a long newspaper article, use a bus schedule successfully, or calculate a tip in a restaurant.

SOURCES: "Adult Illiteracy in the U.S.," by C. Hunter, and D. Harmon, APL Project, University of Texas, Austin, 1975; "Adult Literacy and Schooling," National Center for Education Statistics, 1985.

Number and Proportion of Those Scoring
At or Above 650 on the S.A.T.

THEN: (1980-81)

Verbal: 29,895   3%
Math: 70,307   7%

NOW: (1992)

Verbal: 32,883   3%
Math: 104,401 10%

SOURCES: *Digest of Education Statistics 1992; 1992 Profile of S.A.T. and Achievement Test Takers*, Educational Testing Service.

Graduate Record Examination Scores

THEN:

Mean score on education subject-matter test, 1982: 456

NOW:

Mean score on education subject-matter test, 1991: 457

SOURCE: *Digest of Education Statistics 1992.*

Death Rates From Accidents and Violence

THEN:

Rates per 100,000, ages 15-24, 1980:

White Males: 138.6	White Females: 37.3
Black Males: 162.0	Black Females: 35.0

NOW:

Rates per 100,000, ages 15-24, 1989:

White Males: 107.1	White Females: 32.7
Black Males: 188.0	Black Females: 33.9

SOURCE: *Statistical Abstract of the United States 1992.*

Divorces

THEN:

Rate per 1,000 population, 1981: 5.3

NOW:

Rate per 1,000 population, 1990: 4.7

SOURCE: *Statistical Abstract of the United States 1992.*

Mothers in the Workforce

THEN:

Percentage of women in the civilian labor force with children, 1980:

Single: 52.0
Married, Husband Present: 54.1
Widowed, Divorced, or Separated: 69.4

NOW:

Percentage of women in the civilian labor force with children, 1991:

Single: 53.6
Married, Husband Present: 66.8
Widowed, Divorced, or Separated: 72.7

SOURCE: *Statistical Abstract of the United States 1992.*

Television-Watching Habits

THEN:

Percentage of 8th graders who watch three to
five hours of television daily, 1983-84: 50

NOW:

Percentage of 13-year-olds who watch three to
four hours of television daily, 1988: 42

SOURCE: *Youth Indicators 1988; Youth Indicators 1991,* U.S. Education Department.

Child Poverty

THEN:

Percentage of children below the poverty level, 1981: 19.5

NOW:

Percentage of children below the poverty level, 1990: 19.9

SOURCE: *Statistical Abstract of the United States 1992.*

Employment Rate of 25- to 34-Year-Olds, By Sex and Years of Schooling Completed

THEN:

Percent employed, 12 years of school, 1982: Male: 83.3   Female: 59.6

Percent employed, four or more years of college, 1982: Male: 91.9   Female: 77.7

NOW:

Percent employed, 12 years of school, 1991: Male: 84.9   Female: 67.0

Percent employed, four or more years of college, 1991: Male: 91.8   Female: 82.6

SOURCE: *The Condition of Education 1992.*